YANKEE Magazine's
Make It Last

Over 1,000 Ingenious Ways to Extend the Life of Everything You Own

By Earl Proulx
and the editors of YANKEE Magazine

YANKEE BOOKS

Printed in the United States of America on acid-free ∞, recycled ♻ paper

Library of Congress Cataloging-in-Publication Data
Proulx, Earl.
    Yankee magazine's make it last : over 1,000 ingenious ways to extend the life of everything you own / by Earl Proulx and the editors of Yankee magazine.
        p.   cm.
    Includes index.
    ISBN 0–87596–296–3 hardcover
    1. Home economics. 2. Dwellings—Maintenance and repair.
    I. Yankee (Dublin, N.H.) II. Title.
TX158.P76 1996
643'.7—dc20   96–14717

Distributed in the book trade by St. Martin's Press

    6   8   10   9   7   hardcover

To my son, Earl Merritt Proulx,
who shares my zeal for making things last,
and to the faithful readers of *Yankee* Magazine,
who have kept me young and busy
with their questions.

❖

MAKE IT LAST

YANKEE BOOKS STAFF
Senior Editors: Jeff Bredenberg, Sid Kirchheimer
Cover Designer: Kristen Morgan Downey

YANKEE PUBLISHING STAFF
Director of Books and New Media: Jamie Trowbridge
Book Editor: Sharon Smith
Contributing Writers: Linda Buchanan Allen, Lori Baird, Gordon Bock,
     Jim Collins, John Kitchener, Will Lange, Dougald MacDonald, Marylee
     MacDonald, Georgia Orcutt, Bill Scheller, Kay Scheller, Michelle
     Seaton, Jon Vara, Jay Wyant
Editorial Consultants: Nancy Bardes, Scott Bovy, John Brown,
     Russell C. Buchanan, Tom Cavalieri, Susan Crawford, Bill Drake,
     Richard Edmunds, Lisa Gold, Stanley Jay, Mad River Canoe Co.,
     Dave Mitchell, Joel Mortensen, Anne Nestelberger, Wilma Sagurton,
     Charles J. Sherrard, Mary Ellen Wright
Book Designer: Jill Shaffer
Illustrators: Susan Dunholter, Maryann Mattson, Jill Shaffer
Cover Illustrator: Brian Jenson
Fact Checkers: Lori Baird, Gordon Bock, Isabel Clukay, Linda Clukay,
     Dougald MacDonald, Marylee MacDonald
Copy Editor: Barbara Jatkola
Proofreader: Faith Hanson
Computer Keyboarder: Jacinta Monniere
Editorial Assistant: Nancy Trafford

Contents

Introduction

I STOPPED BY EARL PROULX'S HOUSE in Surry, New Hampshire, the other day. It sits atop a wooded hill overlooking the city of Keene and surrounding hills and mountains. Earl has lived in the Keene area since he was born in 1913, and he, his wife, Thelma, and their son built this Surry house brand-new in 1951. He told me he spent the better part of a day up in an oak tree on the site where the house was to be placed, to observe the light and shadows and to make certain planes from the Keene airport didn't fly over. He had no desire to spend the rest of his life listening to roaring engines. When Earl goes about something, he makes sure everything is right.

Before going to his office to discuss how to handle his ever-growing avalanche of mail from *Yankee* magazine readers responding to his question-and-answer column, "Plain Talk," we stood for a moment at the living room windows admiring the view. The massive expanse of November sky before us was dark over Mount Monadnock to the southeast, but the sun was shining through swirls of low, misty clouds everywhere else. It looked just like the sky in the large oil painting by Earl that hangs over his sofa. Earl and Thelma both enjoyed painting, and their framed pictures hang on various walls throughout the house. But Earl hasn't touched a canvas since Thelma died in 1980. "I've been too busy answering *Yankee* readers' questions," he says. That may be true, but, as the quintessential New Englander, Earl isn't likely to discuss much of anything smacking of emotion.

On the stone patio Earl built directly below the living room windows, the circular fountain was already covered for the winter. During the summer months, it provides a lovely water display, powered by an old engine that once pumped draft beer from the cellar at the Hinsdale (N.H.) Greyhound Park up to the bars in the clubhouse. Earl and his crew had been doing some renovating work there when the owner told him he could junk the old beer pump. "Well, I'll junk it at my place," Earl had replied. That was almost 50 years ago.

Above us were additional examples of Earl's Yankee ingenuity. They support the ceiling and roof—huge beams, one 36 feet long, he salvaged from a condemned grade school building in nearby Peterborough. The beams had developed serious sag from too much weight. No problem for Earl. He brought them home, cut them into shorter lengths and eliminated the sag by sawing the tops and bottoms along "a snap line," as he puts it. They are still pretty huge . . . and, of course, as good as new.

A crackling fire was burning in the living room fireplace—supplied by wood brought up from the cellar in a dumbwaiter powered by a "coal stoker" engine Earl acquired from a local dentist some 60 years ago. The granite stones in the fireplace? "Those are cull stones the mason rejected when he was building a granite altar in the Episcopal church in Keene," Earl explained.

It was getting dark, but Earl snapped off all the living room lights before we headed downstairs. He never leaves lights on in an empty room. On the ground floor, Earl has a recreation room with an old player piano, his office with a window overlooking the view and a large, fully equipped workshop. Along all four walls of the workshop is a valuable collection of old tools he started to put together as a teenager and expanded when his father, just before he died, gave him a few of *his* old tools. "Were you close to your father?" I asked. Of course, Earl, as I should have known, would sidestep that sort of question.

"He never thought I would amount to anything because of my foot," he replied after some thought. Earl has a slight limp, not always noticeable, due to a clubfoot for which he underwent several operations during his youth. "One time when my leg was in a cast," he went on, "I overheard my father telling my two brothers they would have to support me in later life because I wouldn't be able to make a living. I'll never forget that."

I knew that years later it was Earl, by then a successful building contractor, who ended up hiring both his brothers and his father when they could not find work.

I've known Earl ever since he built an addition onto our Yankee offices in 1965, and his reputation has never changed. He has always been known as someone who'll go that extra mile on any job he takes on. Maybe it has something to do with what he overheard his father say to his brothers that day years ago. For instance, I recall the daughter of a Dublin "summer person" from New York telling me how Earl had once built a cottage for her mother next to a stream at the base of Mount Monadnock. She said that when it was finished, her mother's only complaint was that the stream didn't "gurgle." She wanted to be next to the proverbial "gurgling brook." So, for the next week, Earl lugged stones off the mountain and piled them across the stream next to her cottage. When the mother returned from New York the following weekend, her stream "gurgled."

Although retired as a contractor now, Earl still leads an active life. In his shed and cellar are almost ten cords of neatly stacked wood—all recently cut and split by him on his own land. He still plows his own and his neighbors' driveways every winter. And, *except* during the winter, he still plays golf several times a week—as he has been doing ever since he was in high school.

"All that activity—is that what keeps you healthy?" I asked as we walked into his recreation room to hear his player piano. (I always want to hear his player piano when I visit.) "Well, maybe," he replied, and then, with a tiny twinkle in his eye, he added, "but I also restrict my diet to the four basic food groups." Naturally, I obliged by asking what those might be. "Bottled, bagged, frozen and canned," he said, the twinkle turning into a hint of a smile.

We were both still chuckling when he started one of the 800 player piano rolls he's collected. Suddenly, the room was alive with rollicking honky-tonk music. Earl had to raise his voice to explain that this was really *two* player pianos. He had acquired one with the basic instrumentation parts intact but with a hopelessly damaged wooden housing. Then, several years later, he found another with most of the musical parts missing but with a decent wooden frame. Presto! Earl had himself one an-tique player piano that will last forever—powered, inci-dentally, by a vacuum cleaner. "Works on suction, you know," he said, as if I really *should* know.

In Earl's office are half a dozen files crammed full of ideas on how to fix things, do things and make things last longer. "I've been collecting hints for sixty-eight years," Earl said. "One day when I was in the hospital, after one of my foot operations, I came across a copy of *Popular Science* in a rubbish pile. Just for something to do, I copied out a bunch of good, practical hints. That was 1928. Guess that's when I got the bug, because I have been taking hints out of magazines and books ever since. Tried 'em all out, too."

On his desk was a pile of *Yankee* readers' letters he had been working on before I arrived. I glanced at the one on top. It was from Minnesota. "Is there any practical use for a china egg?" it asked. Earl had already scribbled his answer along the margin: "Two uses: One, makes a hen feel broody. Two, cures her of pecking and breaking her own eggs. So a china egg makes eggs last." Then I no-ticed that at the bottom of the letter, Earl had asked him-self a question: "For the book?"

Obviously, this book has been on Earl's mind for a long time. Come to think of it, since 1928! To be sure, not every single item has come from his files. Some orig-inated with various *Yankee* editors and readers. But rest assured that Earl has checked out, okayed and improved upon everything. Right there at his desk, in the sturdy house he and Thelma built among the trees atop a hill, overlooking a large chunk of southern New Hampshire. You can picture him there now. Today. And as your chil-dren, grandchildren and, yes, great-grandchildren even-tually peruse these pages, they can picture him there, too. Always and forever.

Judson D. Hale, Sr.
Editor, *Yankee* Magazine and
The Old Farmer's Almanac

Kitchen and Household

MAKING HOUSEHOLD APPLIANCES and housewares last is a whole lot easier when the manufacturer has the same idea. A friend was lucky enough to get one of the very first refrigerators to have a separate freezer compartment on top. She never remembers to vacuum the coils and empties the drip pan only when it starts to smell like low tide at Cape Cod. But her refrigerator predates the concept of planned obsolescence and is cooling TV dinners and frozen yogurts that hadn't even come on the market when the appliance was built.

Most of us, however, aren't that fortunate—or that old—and paying for a "name" brand isn't always a guarantee of quality and durability. In fact, some of the newer small, cordless appliances are actually designed to be disposed of rather than fixed. That's a concept that thoroughly rattles Yankee sensibilities.

So, after the warranty runs out, we're on our own when it comes to keeping the fridge cold, the oven hot, the batteries charged and the clocks ticking. Fortunately, there are a lot of tricks to this everyday trade that don't require a lot of specialized knowledge. The same applies to all the smaller, less complicated paraphernalia we keep around the kitchen and elsewhere in the house. In this chapter, we'll take a look at how you can extend the life of everything from crystal and cutlery to steam irons and vacuum cleaners—without first earning a degree in appliance repair. And we'll begin at the beginning, by telling you how you can keep your food fresher, too.

DAIRY PRODUCTS

Cheese Wiz

❖ To keep it from getting moldy, store your cheese in an airtight container with a couple of lumps of sugar.

❖ Another way to keep mold away from cheese is to moisten a paper towel lightly with vinegar and store that with the cheese. Don't be too generous with the vinegar, or it will affect the taste of the cheese.

❖ If you're not going to use it right away, store your cheese in the freezer. Soft cheeses like Brie and Camembert stay usable for up to one year if frozen. Hard cheeses like Parmesan and Romano will last twice that long if they're tightly wrapped before freezing.

Eggs under Cover

❖ Store your eggs in a covered bowl, not in the egg tray of your refrigerator. Because their shells are porous, eggs absorb odors and release moisture when left uncovered for too long.

BAKING SUPPLIES

Leaf It Alone

❖ Add a bay leaf to your flour or sugar tin to keep insects out.

Salt: Keep It Moving Ricely

❖ Add raw rice to your saltshakers to keep the salt from forming lumps.

Hard Facts about Brown Sugar

❖ To prevent brown sugar from absorbing moisture and caking into one solid mass, store it in a plastic bag in-

PUZZLER

THIS DEVICE WAS MADE FOR lifting a little cardboard disk from its tight glass fitting. The cat and the baby were happy to see it used.

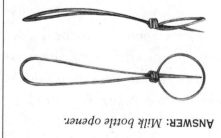

ANSWER: *Milk bottle opener.*

MAKE IT LAST

side an airtight container. If it still cakes up despite your best efforts, it's easier to loosen it up by manipulating the bag than by breaking off pieces of the solid sugar.

❖ If your brown sugar has already hardened, the simplest way to soften it is to add a few marshmallows or a slice of fresh bread to the bag, seal it and wait a couple of days. The moisture from the bread will soften the sugar.

❖ When you're in a hurry to soften brown sugar, a slice of apple will do the trick. Place the opened plastic bag of sugar in a microwave with the apple and heat for 15 seconds on High. The steam from the apple will soften the sugar.

Save Those Old Containers

Don't throw out those old coffee cans, soup cans or plastic containers from frozen orange juice. Cover them with contact paper or wallpaper scraps and use them to hold small tools, toys or pens and pencils.

Too Hot to Cook

❖ If you have baker's yeast on hand at the beginning of the summer and don't plan to use it till the weather cools, pop it in the freezer. Baker's yeast will keep well for several months if frozen.

FRUITS

Avoid Brownouts

❖ Squeeze a few drops of lemon juice over fruits like apples, peaches, pears or bananas once they've been cut. This will keep most of them from turning brown. (This works with avocados, too.)

Hot Lemon Aid

❖ If you warm your lemons in the oven at a low temperature (about 200°F) for several minutes before squeezing them, they will yield almost twice as much juice. Or you can stick them in the microwave on High for 30 seconds or submerge them in hot water for 10 to 15 minutes before squeezing.

Raisins: Fatten 'Em Up

❖ To plump stale raisins, first rinse them in cold water. Then, without drying them, put them in a covered dish and bake them at 350°F for about five minutes.

COMMON MISTAKES

Refreezing

YOU'VE ALWAYS BEEN told not to refreeze meats like chicken and beef, with the stern warning that it's dangerous. Actually, it's not. As long as the meat has not spoiled, it will refreeze easily for later use. But freezing foods again will rob them of taste and texture, so when you do prepare them, they will be rather bland and dry. Choose your recipes accordingly.

Bananas Don't Have to Drive You up a Tree

❖ If your bananas are on the verge of going by, you don't have to whip up a batch of banana bread. Just stick them in the freezer. The skins will turn brown, but you can still use the fruit when it's convenient.

An Apple Away . . .

❖ Store apples as close to 32°F as possible as soon as you bring them indoors. If you have too many to refrigerate (and want to keep them through fall and winter), pack them in a Styrofoam cooler and set it under your basement bulkhead. Or pack them in a crate with sand or sawdust. (The sawdust route also works with carrots.)

Apples: The Untouchables

❖ Each time you remove apples from storage, take out any that show signs of rotting. Remember, a rotten apple spoils the barrel . . . or cooler. And prevent stored apples from touching each other if you can. They'll keep longer that way.

VEGETABLES

Eliminate Limp Carrots

❖ Rinse fresh carrots and scrub them with a vegetable brush. Immediately pat them dry with a dish towel, seal them in plastic bags and store them in the refrigerator. Otherwise they will become limp in just a few hours.

Unwashed Cabbage Lives Longer

❖ Keep cabbage for several weeks by storing it un-wrapped and unwashed in the refrigerator.

A Sure Cure

❖ To make winter squash, pumpkins and sweet potatoes last through the winter, cure them at 75° to 85°F for about ten days. Put them on a sunny porch or in any warm place that's out of the way—perhaps on the attic floor. Then store them, along with eggplant, at 50° to 60°F.

One Potato, Two Potatoes

❖ If you plan to store potatoes for any length of time, you'll need to let the skins toughen first. (Thin-skinned immature potatoes shrivel and become soft shortly after picking.) Place them in the sun for four to five hours to dry. Then brush off excess soil (don't wash them) and store them in a dark, moist place such as an unheated cellar. Be sure to keep them in total darkness. Tubers exposed to light will develop an inedible green coloration.

❖ Store potatoes with an apple to keep them from sprouting.

Potato Revival

❖ When boiling old potatoes, add sugar to the water to revive some of the flavor.

❖ If your potatoes have gone soft, soak them in cold water for an hour to revive them.

Cozy Quarters for Crops

❖ For long-term storage, place your root vegetables in an unheated section of the basement that is dark, well ven-

Shelf Life: The Refrigerator

WHEN YOU RESTOCK the fridge, do what the re-stockers at the supermarket do: place the newest foods in the back and the oldest ones in the front, where you're likely to see them and use them more quickly. Be sure to use up or freeze all foods before they exceed the storage guidelines listed below.

FOOD	SHELF LIFE
Butter	1 month
Buttermilk	2 weeks
Chicken	1–2 days
Cooked meats or leftovers	2–5 days
Ground beef	1–2 days
Hard cheese	3–8 months
Milk	3–5 days
Pork chops and ribs	3 days
Roasts and steaks	2–5 days
Sour cream	10 days
Turkey	4–5 days
Yogurt	2 weeks

tilated, evenly cool and enclosed in screening or hardware cloth to keep out rodents. Keep humidity as high as possible (90 to 95 percent is ideal) by splashing water from a bucket on the walls each time you visit the area. Mount a humidity meter and a thermometer on the wall to monitor storage conditions.

Topless Veggies

❖ Before storing carrots and beets, cut the greens off to make them last longer. If you don't do this, the tops will continue to pull moisture and nutrients from the roots.

Onions: A Sure Root to Success

❖ If a recipe calls for only half an onion, use the top half. The root will help preserve the lower half for later use.

A Can of Nutrition

❖ Freeze the juice drained from canned vegetables such as carrots, sweet potatoes or mushrooms. It will make an excellent addition to stews and soups.

❖ An alternative is to pour the vegetable juice over dry dog or cat food to add extra nutrients to your pet's diet.

Boeuf Corné au Cabeau

IN THE WHITE HOUSE, President Grover Cleveland often lamented the fact that he was expected to eat the fancy French foods prepared by his chef. One night he noticed the familiar smell of corned beef coming from the servants' kitchen. He asked to trade his dinner for that of one of the maids. Cleveland ate heartily that evening and later told a friend that "it was the best meal I'd had in months—*boeuf corné au cabeau.*"

Spare the Asparagus

❖ Trim the bottoms of asparagus stalks and wrap the freshly cut stalks in wet paper towels to keep them fresh longer.

The Layered Look

❖ To keep your vegetables crisp, put a layer of newspaper and then a layer of paper towels in both refrigerator bins to soak up the moisture that will wilt or rot them prematurely.

Bathe Your Veggies

❖ Stuck with a bunch of wilted vegetables? Add 1 tablespoon of vinegar or the juice of 1 lemon to a bowl of cold water. Soak the greens in the mixture for an hour, and they'll revive.

Keep the Crunch

❖ Add a small piece of horseradish to the pickle jar. It will keep the vinegar active while preventing the pickles from becoming soft.

After the Pickles Are Gone

❖ Use the leftover juice from your pickle jar in place of plain vinegar when making coleslaw. It's not only economical; it tastes better, too.

❖ Slice extra cucumbers and onions and store them in pickle juice in the refrigerator. In 48 hours, they will have become a crunchy, tasty side dish.

A SECOND LIFE

Dress Up Your Ketchup

TO MAKE A QUICK salad dressing, pour oil and vinegar into the remains on the bottom of a container of ketchup, mustard or other sandwich spread and shake vigorously.

HERBS AND SPICES

A Touch of Glass

❖ Store dried spices in glass jars with tight lids. If such containers aren't available, use tins, which will keep them fresh nearly as long. Avoid storing spices in plastic bags, which will not retain their freshness.

Herbal Tease

❖ Hang your spice rack in a cool, dry place away from the microwave or oven. Otherwise the heat from cooking will parch the spices, and they will turn dull and stale quickly.

❖ Buy spices in small quantities, and be sure to date your favorites so that you can replace them as soon as they start to age. They will begin to lose flavor within three months, and their taste will decrease noticeably in six months.

Give Them a Rubdown

❖ To revive stale herbs, simply rub them vigorously before adding them to dishes.

BAKED GOODS

Cookies: The Hard Stuff

❖ To soften cookies that have become too hard to eat, place a crust of bread in the tin with the cookies. The cookies will absorb the moisture from the bread, making them edible again.

Shelf Life: The Home Freezer

MAKING FOODS LAST is a worthwhile endeavor, but there *is* such a thing as going too far. Label your purchases when you put them in the freezer, then throw them out if you haven't used them within the time guidelines suggested below.

FOOD	SHELF LIFE
Butter	1 year
Chicken	12 months
Ground beef	4 months
Hard cheese	2 years
Ice cream	8 months
Pork chops and ribs	2–3 months
Roasts and steaks	8–12 months
Turkey	6 months
TV dinners and precooked foods	3 months

Keep the Snap in Those Gingersnaps

❖ Store crisp cookies in a container with a tight lid to keep them from getting soft. If they do soften, simply heat them in a 200°F oven for a few minutes.

Apple Magic

❖ Store half an apple with your cake, cookies or bread to keep the baked goods fresh. The apple will release moisture and keep the baked goods from drying out.

A Mist-Dew Solution

❖ To revive hard rolls or crusty bread that's gone stale, sprinkle with water and reheat at 350°F for about ten minutes. A plant mister works well for this.

No Sog Stories

❖ To keep frozen loaves of bread from becoming soggy, put a cloth (not paper) towel in the bag with the bread as it freezes. The towel will draw out the moisture and keep the bread firm.

Crisp and Crunchy

❖ To crisp up crackers or cereals that have succumbed to humidity, try placing them in a 350°F oven for five to ten minutes.

The Ice Cube Tray, Reconsidered

❖ Use ice cube trays to freeze leftovers such as pesto, egg whites and honey in handy single-serving sizes.

Know Their Place

❖ If you want to make sure your popcorn kernels pop, keep them in the freezer. This also prolongs the life of other nonperishables such as coffee beans and nuts, because the freezer protects them from moisture.

Fast Food for Lunch

❖ Prepare cold-cut sandwiches ahead of time and store them in the freezer for up to two weeks. But skip the mayo, mustard and ketchup (as well as the jelly for the PB&J crowd) until you're ready to eat the sandwich. Condiments don't do so well at low temperatures and will tend to make your lunch soggy. Wrap the sandwiches in foil or waxed paper until you're ready to use them.

Ready for S'mores . . .

❖ To soften stale marshmallows, place a few slices of fresh bread in the bag with them and leave for a few days.

POTS AND PANS

Dealing with Kitchen Burnout

❖ Sometimes when food is badly burned onto aluminum pots and pans, the temptation is to throw the piece away. Resist the temptation. Instead, clean out burned-on food by heating some tomato juice or tomato sauce in the item, then rinsing. The acid in the tomato will loosen the food from the pan.

❖ Burned-on food also can be removed by scrubbing the affected area with a brush made for cleaning suede.

❖ Another way to clean burned-on food from aluminum is to fill the pot halfway with hot water, then add a solution of ½ cup of vinegar and 2 tablespoons of baking soda. Bring the mixture to a boil, cover, reduce the heat and let simmer for 30 minutes. This should loosen the food so that you can rinse it out.

Help Your Pans Maintain an Untarnished Reputation

❖ Clean slightly tarnished aluminum with a solution of hot soapy water and a little ammonia. After cleaning, wipe the piece dry and then rub it with salt. Follow up by polishing the item with a soft, dry cloth.

In High School, It Seemed Like Light Work

I USED TO WORK AT AUCTIONS when I was in high school. Every chance I got, I would buy old earthenware jugs for about 50 cents each. At the same time, I had an arrangement with the man who ran the local dump. He salvaged the sockets from discarded lamps and sold them to me for 5 cents each. I'd pour sand in the jug, wire up the socket, insert the socket in the jug with a cork and top it all off with a new lampshade. Then I'd take my lamps to a local gas station, where I could sell them for $5 or $6 each.

EARL
remembers...

Back then, I was putting those old jugs and sockets to good use. But now I wish I'd just saved the jugs. They sell for about $80 each!

Boil Those Stains Away

❖ Are your aluminum pieces so badly stained that you're ready to put them in the next tag sale? Boil them in a pot with some water and grapefruit or lemon rinds for about 30 minutes. The acid in the fruit will remove the stains.

❖ An alternative way to remove stains from aluminum utensils is to boil a large pot of water, add 2 heaping tablespoons of cream of tartar and boil the utensils in this mixture for about 30 minutes.

Degrease

❖ To clean grease out of an aluminum pan, fill the pan with water and add a tablespoon of cream of tartar. Boil the solution for a couple of minutes, dump out the water and then wipe out the grease. Wash and rinse as usual.

'Tis the Season for Cast Iron

❖ Before using a cast-iron skillet, pot or wok for the first time, season it by putting in some cooking oil, heating it and rubbing it into the surface. Seasoning the item will prevent any food cooked in it from tasting like cast iron. It also will make food less likely to stick to the pan.

Baked-In Protection

❖ To prevent new steel baking pans from rusting, cover them with a layer of lard and place them in a hot (350°F) oven until the grease melts and soaks in. Remove them from the oven and allow them to cool. Then wash them in warm soapy water and dry.

Who Burned the Bacon?

❖ If food burns onto a cast-iron pot or pan, fill the pan with water and dishwashing liquid and let it simmer on the stove until the food loosens. Reseason the piece before you use it again.

Don't Take the Plunge

❖ After using your cast-iron skillet, let it sit off the burner until it cools to at least lukewarm before washing it. Don't plunge a hot cast-iron skillet into cold water. The change in temperature will warp it.

Take the Metal from the Kettle

❖ To avoid the buildup of mineral deposits inside your teakettle, place a small piece of loofah inside the kettle. When the loofah is permeated with mineral deposits, remove it and rinse it, saving the sediment to clean enamel objects. Then place the rinsed loofah back in the kettle and start again.

WOODENWARE AND BUTCHER BLOCK

Odor There

❖ To remove lingering onion and garlic odors from a wooden cutting board or from butcher block, sprinkle the surface with baking soda, rub it in with a damp cloth and clean the board well with a clean, damp cloth.

A Sticky Situation

❖ When wooden bowls get sticky, sand them with the grain—using a fine-grit sandpaper—until the residue is gone. Then apply a light coat of vegetable oil.

If You Can't Stand the Heat . . .

❖ Don't put wooden bowls or utensils in the dishwasher. The heat will dry out the wood.

CRYSTAL AND FINE GLASSWARE

Etchings Don't Belong in the Kitchen

❖ The best way to clean glass is by hand. Wash the objects in a plastic bucket or basin or on top of a towel folded on the bottom of the sink. Never wash fine glassware in a dishwasher; it will etch the glass and cause milk glass to yellow. And don't subject glass to sudden changes of temperature. Dumping ice water out of a fine glass goblet and then plunging the glass into hot dishwater is likely to make it crack.

Streakers Need Not Apply

❖ For clean, streak-free glass, wash your fine glassware with 1 tablespoon of rubbing alcohol or vinegar mixed with a basin of water.

Don't Do the Twist

❖ When you clean stemware, hold on to the bowl of the piece, not the round base. Twisting the glass while holding on to the base is likely to break the stem.

> **A SECOND LIFE**
>
> # Soda Pop to the Rescue
>
> COLA GONE FLAT? No problem. You can use it as a highly effective toilet-bowl cleaner. Just pour it in and scrub lightly.

Soften 'Em Up

❖ To clean out a glass with food or drink dried inside it, fill the piece with water, dishwashing liquid and laundry water softener. Let it soak overnight, then go after the residue with a bottle brush or toothbrush.

Might As Well Throw Your Teeth In

❖ If glass gets a cloudy, hazy look, it's usually from hard-water lime deposits. Fill the item with water and add several teaspoons of ammonia or two denture-cleaning tablets. (Don't use the tablets in glass with ornamental gold or silver trim.) Let the piece soak overnight, then clean it with a bottle brush and soapy water.

Peel Off Those Deposits

❖ Another way to remove lime deposits from glass is to cover the affected area with wet potato peelings and let the whole thing sit for 24 hours. Then rinse the piece in cold water and dry.

Aye, There's the Rub

❖ To remove stains from crystal, rub them with a cloth dipped in turpentine, or use a cut lemon.

A Chip off the Old Glass

❖ To prevent chipping, cover the shelves on which you store crystal with felt or thick paper.

❖ If a fine glass gets a small chip on the edge, don't toss it. Take it to a repair shop (check under Glass Repairing in the Yellow Pages). The repairman will reheat the glass until it starts to melt, then smooth out the chip.

❖ If the chip in a glass rim isn't severe enough—or if the glass isn't expensive enough—to justify professional help, try smoothing the chip with sandpaper. Glue a piece of extra-fine-grit wet-or-dry sandpaper to a wooden board. Turn the glass over and rotate the rim on the sandpaper until the chip is gone. Then wrap a small piece of sandpaper around a pencil and rub it on the chip to finish the job.

CHINA

Don't Let Metal Leave Its Mark

❖ Never wash china in an aluminum pan or allow it to come in contact with aluminum in the dishwasher. Aluminum rubbing against china can create gray, pencil-thin lines that are often impossible to get out.

❖ If a metal utensil or another object does leave a dark mark on your china, gently rub the dish with a mild scouring powder such as Bon Ami or with a plastic scouring pad. Be careful to avoid scrubbing off any decorative trim.

Watch Out for the Latest Craze

❖ Wash china in water that's warm, not hot. Water that is too hot can lead to crazing—small lines and cracks in the glaze.

PUZZLER

FASTEN THIS LITTLE APPLIANCE to the side of a counter, and you're ready for a quick draw that will keep your best kitchen helpers on edge.

ANSWER: Knife sharpener.

❖ If your china is already crazed, don't use it to serve food. Butter, fruit, cheese and cream can cause staining along the crack lines.

A Staggering Thought

❖ When you load china in the dishwasher, stagger plates of differing sizes. That way, their edges won't touch, and you'll avoid chipping and scratches.

When the Inevitable Happens

❖ To mend broken china, apply a coating of epoxy—which forms a strong bond and is both waterproof and oil resistant. Available from hardware stores in regular and fast-setting strengths, it comes in two parts—a resin and a hardener—which are usually mixed in equal proportions according to package directions. Apply the epoxy with a brush, then clean the brush with acetone (available at pharmacies). Or, as much as the idea goes against the Yankee grain, apply the glue with an inexpensive brush and then throw away the brush.

Let the Chips Fall Where They May— But Find Them All

❖ Before you begin gluing a piece of broken china, make sure all the components are clean and dry. Then rebuild it without the adhesive to see how everything will fit together. When you start applying an epoxy (sold at hardware stores), glue the small pieces to the larger ones; allow each part to harden before going on to the next one. If there's a handle, save it for last and tape it in place until the epoxy has hardened.

❖ To fill a cavity left by a missing chip in china, coat the hole with epoxy and then fill it in with a thick epoxide filler (available from a hardware store). After everything has dried, use a single-edge razor blade to scrape off any excess adhesive.

A Safe Move

❖ When packing china for a move, wrap each piece individually. Use white paper towels, cloth towels or bubble wrap—not newspaper, which will leave black smudges. Don't wrap two pieces together. If any of the pieces have tops, remove them and wrap them separately.

❖ If you're stacking several pieces of china in one box for moving, place the heavier items on the bottom and the lighter ones on top.

Display Cases: Get in the Groove

❖ If you store plates in a display case with a little narrow groove in the shelf to hold the plates, add a small safety bar in front of the groove. This will keep the plates from sliding out of the groove and breaking if the case is accidentally nudged or the door is shut too vigorously.

How Does Your China Stack Up?

❖ The best way to store china plates is in a wooden rack that allows them to stand vertically, with a small piece of felt protecting the edge of each plate.

For All the Tea in China . . .

❖ Wash your china cups, saucers and teapots as soon after using them as you can. If there is a tiny crack in the glaze, coffee or tea left there will stain the china.

❖ You can sometimes get tea and coffee stains out of your china by applying baking soda on a wet dishrag.

❖ Another treatment for tea or coffee stains on china is to apply 20 percent hydrogen peroxide, wash and rinse. (Regular household hydrogen peroxide is 3 percent strength. The 20 percent solution—available at pharmacies—acts as a bleaching agent.)

Kill the Grease, Save the Dishes

❖ To clean a panful of very dirty dishes, add 1 tablespoon of vinegar to your dishwater and cut the grease.

❖ An alternative approach to hand-washing greasy dishes is to pour ½ cup of baking soda into your dishwater along with the soap. This will cut grease and give dishes an extra shine.

UNBREAKABLE DISHES

Beware the Power of Your Scour

❖ To clean plastic dishes, rub them with a damp cloth dipped in baking soda. Never clean plastic dishes with anything abrasive, such as steel wool or scouring powder, as it will leave scratches.

Plastic Is Persnickety

❖ Wash plastic utensils by hand, not in the dishwasher. The heat from the machine will warp them.

❖ Use a paste-type silver polish to remove stains from plastic. Don't try to bleach it; that will ruin the finish.

Kill the Smell, Not the Container

❖ You don't have to throw out a storage container when it picks up food smells. Wash it in hot soapy water, rinse and dry it, and then put a crumpled piece of newspaper in

All That Glitters Will Not Last

EARL
remembers...

S TAINLESS STEEL KNIVES may look better, but I think plain old carbon steel knives are more enduring. They are easier to sharpen and hold an edge longer.

Carbon steel knives can be expensive, though, if you buy them new. So try looking for used knives at yard sales or flea markets. You'll recognize carbon steel by the rust spots—a problem that would stop some people, but one that you can easily correct by scrubbing with a steel wool soap pad.

You can't keep carbon steel knives shiny, but you can keep them from rusting. Just be sure to dry them with a dish towel immediately after you wash them. The knives will last for years.

the container and seal it. Store the sealed container overnight. The ink will absorb the odors. (Don't use paper with colored ink, such as the Sunday comics or magazine sections. Those inks can be hazardous.) Wash the container again before using it.

❖ To get rid of the musty smell in a plastic container, fill it with warm water, add a few drops of vanilla extract, let it soak for two days and then rinse it well.

Knives: The Cutting Edge

YOU GET WHAT you pay for with knives. Price is determined by a number of factors, including the kind of metal in the blade, the length of the tang (the metal part embedded in the handle) and the composition of the handle. The better the metal, the longer the knife—with care—will last. A knife with a tang that extends the entire length—or at least half the length—of the handle is stronger, and thus more durable, than one with a shorter tang. And a handle made of a good-quality hardwood or plastic will stand up best to repeated use and cleaning.

A longer tang (as on the right) means a longer-lasting knife.

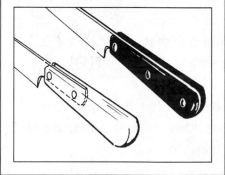

CUTLERY

Handle with Care

❖ Hand-wash knives with wooden handles. The heat of the dishwasher will dry out the wood.

❖ If food has dried on a knife with a wooden handle, soak the blade by standing the knife in a glass filled with water only to the base of the blade. Don't leave the knife to soak in a pan of water. This can swell and split the wood.

❖ If your wooden knife handle has already dried out, buy some water sealer—the kind used on porches and decks—at the hardware store. Pour some in a container that's deeper than the handle and dip the handle into the sealer. Let it soak for a few minutes, then remove the knife and allow it to drip-dry.

You'll Wonder Where the Yellow Went

❖ Have your bone-handled knives yellowed with age? Don't toss them out. Whiten them with a piece of flannel moistened with a little hydrogen peroxide and water.

It's the Pits

❖ Always wash chrome-plated knives immediately after use to prevent them from pitting.

SILVER

These May Be Hazardous to Your Silver

❖ Check the label to make sure the soap you use to clean your silver doesn't contain phosphorus or sulfur compounds, as these will cause staining.

❖ Be sure to wash silver immediately after it's come in contact with eggs, brussels sprouts, vinegar or salt. All of these foods contain sulfur compounds, which cause silver to tarnish.

❖ If you live in an area with hard water (water that contains a lot of minerals), use distilled water to clean your silver. Hard water may leave mineral deposits that can cause pitting.

Skip the Drying Cycle

❖ If your water is hard and you must clean your silver in the dishwasher, minimize spotting by removing silver pieces from the dishwasher before the drying cycle, which can "bake on" the spots. Drying them by hand will prevent this. This is also a good idea if any of the pieces have hollow handles, as the heat can loosen the blades.

Don't Take the Silver on a Picnic

❖ Avoid letting your silver come in contact with mustard, mayonnaise or plastic wrap. At best, they'll tarnish the silver; at worst, they'll pit it beyond repair.

Don't Let Your Silver Just Sit There

❖ The best way to keep silver clean is to use it regularly. After each use, simply wash it with a mild dishwashing liquid, rinse and wipe dry. Every time you polish silver, you wear off a fine layer of the metal, so polish only when you have to, and do it as gently as you can.

Steak Is Too Expensive for a Party Anyway

❖ Avoid using steak knives with your best silverware. You may scratch your forks while cutting food.

Polish It Off

❖ To clean silver, make a paste of baking soda and water. Rub it on with a soft cloth, rinse and buff till it shines. A soft toothbrush or cotton swab can help you get into crevices. Wash the silver well to get all the cleaner off.

❖ An alternative recipe for homemade silver polish starts with 2 tablespoons of powdered alum and ½ cup of talcum powder stirred into 1 cup of cold water. Add ¼ cup of ammonia and ¼ cup of turpentine, then shake well. This mixture can be bottled, corked and stored for future cleanings. Be sure to shake it before each use.

❖ Remove egg stains from silver by rubbing on salt with your fingertips, then washing in dishwashing liquid and rinsing well. Don't skip the washing and rinsing stages, or you'll get new stains from the salt.

It's Never Too Late

❖ To soften commercial polish that's hardened, just add hot water—a tablespoon or so at a time—and stir until it softens.

❖ So you're getting ready for a big dinner party and you're out of silver polish? Get out an old soft-bristled toothbrush and some toothpaste (not the gel type). Coat the silver with the toothpaste, run it under warm water and work up a foam. Then rinse it off. Use the toothbrush to clean out the grooves. Don't use the toothpaste straight, however, as it may cause scratches.

Rubber and Silver Don't Mix

❖ Always use *plastic* gloves—not rubber ones—when polishing silver. Rubber can make silver tarnish faster, and the gloves will leave fingerprints that are hard to remove.

❖ Never put a rubber band around a piece of silver. Over time, it will leave a brown stain that will be nearly impossible to remove.

❖ Drain your freshly washed silver on paper or cloth towels—never on rubber mats, which will make the pieces tarnish faster.

Ion Out the Dirt

❖ The easiest approach to cleaning silver is the electrolytic method, which works by means of ion exchange. Put silver items on a sheet of aluminum foil in a glass or other nonaluminum dish and cover them with 1 quart of hot water mixed with 1 tablespoon of baking soda. The chemical reaction between the foil and the silver will remove tarnish. Don't try this method on pieces with raised designs, however, or you'll lose the dark accents that have built up over time. And don't try it on cemented pieces. The soaking process may loosen the cement.

❖ Here's an approach to ion exchange that's convenient enough to use every day: Put a good-size piece of aluminum foil in a large mason jar, add 2 tablespoons of kosher salt and fill the jar with cold water. Cover the jar and place it near your kitchen sink. When you have a piece of stained cutlery, dip it into the jar and leave it there for two minutes, then rinse.

Soak, Don't Stack

❖ When you clear the table after using silver utensils at a meal, fill a bowl with hot soapy water and immediately place all the dirty silverware into the bowl to soak before washing. Don't stack used silver with the dirty china. The pressure can bend the silverware.

No Crowding, Please

❖ You can put solid sterling silver in the dishwasher, but don't crowd the pieces and be sure to keep them away

PUZZLER

PAMPERED VICTORIANS WOULD not be without one of these. Fill it with hot water, and your servers stay warm. (Hint: It isn't the butler's bathtub.)

ANSWER: *Spoon warmer.*

from stainless steel. If the two come in contact, the silver may pit.

Wrap It While It's Still Warm

❖ If you're going to store silver for quite a while, put it in a warm place for a few hours before wrapping it up. This will ensure that the silver is completely dry.

Pacific Protection for Sterling

❖ Store your silver in special bags made of a material that has been impregnated with a chemical that inhibits tarnish. The bags, called Pacific Cloth or Silver Keeper, can be ordered from jewelry stores. If you clean your silver carefully and wrap it securely in these bags, you shouldn't get tarnish for years. (Silver tarnish is caused by sulfur compounds in the air reacting with the metal. Eventually, this process will harm the silver.)

ORNAMENTAL SILVER
AND HOLLOWWARE

The Butler Did It

❖ Once you've polished your silver, handle it just as the butlers of old did: with white cotton gloves. The secret the butlers knew is that oils and acids on the skin can cause silver to tarnish.

Give Wax the Big Freeze . . .

❖ To remove wax from your silver candlesticks, put them in the freezer for a few hours and then peel off the wax.

. . . Or Put On the Heat

❖ An alternative way to get wax off silver is to heat the wax with a hand-held hair dryer and then wipe it off.

Silver under Glass

❖ When displaying silver in a glass case, place a small cake of refined camphor inside the case to keep the silver from tarnishing.

Shake the Salt Spots

❖ Are there salt spots on your plated saltshakers? Smear them with olive oil and let them sit for a few days, then wipe them off.

STAINLESS FLATWARE

Keep the Stains off the Stainless

❖ Stainless steel is dishwasher safe, but contrary to its name, it can stain. To remove the film some foods leave, apply silver polish or a paste made of three parts baking soda and one part water.

❖ To remove spots on stainless steel left by minerals in the water, just rinse the pieces and dry them with a cloth towel.

PEWTER

Give It the Light Touch

❖ Pewter has a low melting point and will tarnish easily in the dishwasher, so it should be washed by hand with dishwashing liquid and warm water.

Toward Perfect Pewter

❖ To polish pewter, rub it with silver or brass polish. Or wipe it with a cloth dipped in a solution of 2 tablespoons of ammonia and 1 quart of hot soapy water.

❖ To clean old pewter, rub it gently with a mild kitchen scouring powder moistened with olive oil. Be careful not to scrub too hard. Old pewter is generally somewhat soft and easily scratched.

❖ To remove a very stubborn stain from old pewter, rub it gently with extra-fine-grade steel wool. Test the steel wool in an inconspicuous spot first, to be sure it won't leave scratches.

> ### BUY IT TO LAST
>
> # Stainless Steel Flatware
>
> WHEN PURCHASING stainless steel flatware, look for pieces that have a high percentage of chromium and nickel. The more chromium, the more stain-resistant the utensils will be; the higher the nickel content, the better their luster and strength.

Don't Leave It Fuming

❖ If you display your pewter in a case, make sure the case is made of glass or metal and not wood. Paint and wood—especially oak—give off gases that can harm the pewter, so a painted oak storage case is a definite no-no for pewter.

❖ Don't put pewter back into a room that has been freshly painted. The fumes from the paint will attack the surface.

❖ Avoid storing pewter near cardboard, chipboard or vinegar. These, too, give off gases that are harmful to pewter.

A SECOND LIFE

A Little Ragtime

EVEN OLD RAGS can still work for you. Take a look—you might have some terrific kitchen aids squirreled away in the ragbag.

Any nylon netting? It makes great dishcloths and is particularly handy for scouring burnt-on food out of pots. It's also a great substitute for a drain basket in your sink. (You can even use it to remove dried-on bugs when washing the car's windshield.) Old cotton shirts make wonderful lint-free dish towels—just be sure to remove buttons to prevent scratching. And, of course, old cloth diapers have always made the best dust cloths.

BRASS

Kitchen Cleanups

❖ Since brass is not often used to serve food, a lot of brass pieces have been coated with lacquer or varnish to prevent tarnishing. To clean such pieces, apply a paste of lemon juice and cream of tartar. Leave the mixture on the brass for five minutes, then wash the piece in warm water and dry it. Never scour lacquered or varnished brass.

The Top Brass

❖ Clean unlacquered brass as you would any other serving piece—in warm water with dishwashing liquid.

❖ To clean very dirty brass, boil the piece in a pan of water with 1 tablespoon of salt and 1 cup of white vinegar for several hours. (This works for copper, too.)

Recipes for Homemade Brass Polish

❖ To polish unlacquered brass, apply Worcestershire sauce directly to the brass. Rub with extra-fine-grade steel wool, rinse and wipe dry.

❖ An alternative recipe for homemade brass polish is to stir together 1 tablespoon of salt, 1 tablespoon of flour and 1 tablespoon of white vinegar. Apply the mixture to the brass with a damp cloth or sponge, rub gently, rinse and wipe dry.

COPPER

Hold the Pickle, Hold the Lettuce

❖ Clean copper with ketchup or with half a lemon liberally dipped in salt. Rub either one on the copper, rinse thoroughly and dry.

❖ When using acidic cleaners such as ketchup or lemon, be sure to wash the piece thoroughly in warm soapy water after cleaning to remove all traces of the acid. Otherwise the acid could cause etching.

Stain Killers

❖ To remove stains from copper, scrub very gently with toothpaste (not the gel type) on damp extra-fine-grade steel wool.

❖ If copper is caked with grime and smoke or corroded in some areas, soak the item in a weak solution of ammonia and cold water and gently rub the affected area with extra-fine-grade steel wool. Dry the piece immediately, then polish it with a paste of wood ashes and denatured alcohol.

ELECTRIC FRYING PANS AND GRIDDLES

Terminal Conditions

❖ Those little pins on an electric frying pan that the detachable cord plugs into are called terminals. Wipe them after each use and be sure to clean them with metal polish whenever they look grimy. Like all electrical connections, they must be kept clean of dirt and grease to keep the electricity flowing.

❖ If your electric frying pan or griddle is made of a metal (stainless steel or aluminum) that can be cleaned with a scouring pad, be sure to clean away any pad particles that are left near the terminals after you finish scrubbing. They could interfere with a good electrical contact between the prongs and the receptacles.

Don't Get Burned

❖ Sooner or later, we all burn food onto the bottom of a pan so badly that we're tempted to chuck the whole thing into the trash. With an electric pan, this is an expensive temptation. Here's what to do: Soak a cloth in ammonia, lay it on top of the mess, put the pan in a plastic bag and seal it up tight. Let it sit overnight. In the morning, the residue should clean right off with dishwashing liquid and water.

ELECTRIC JUICE EXTRACTORS

Don't Push It

❖ To make your juicer last, remember—less is best. Use gentle pressure when feeding fruits and vegetables through the grating disk. Pushing too hard may harm the motor.

Pulp Is a Problem

❖ To prevent pulp buildup, clean the disk and strainer often—particularly when juicing fibrous vegetables such as celery or beets. If pulp builds up unevenly on the sides of the strainer, it may throw the parts out of balance and eventually cause the motor to overheat.

MIXERS AND BLENDERS

Don't Get Mixed Up

❖ Using the right machine for the right job is the best way to make your mixer and blender last. Use your blender only to blend liquids and your mixer only to mix dough. Mixers and blenders have different kinds of motors and are designed for separate functions. Your blender won't mix cake flour or cookie dough well, and your mixer won't make a decent daiquiri or chocolate frappe. Attempting to use a blender for kneading or cracking will put an undue strain on the motor, which may lead to its early demise.

Mixer Methodology

❖ To put as little stress as possible on the mixer motor, cook foods such as potatoes as much as possible before you whip them.

❖ If you hear the beaters on your mixer slowing down or working hard, stop the machine. Otherwise you may overheat and burn out the motor. Don't try to mix densely textured foods unless you're sure your mixer can handle it.

Keep It Safe

❖ It sounds obvious, but people forget: always remove beaters from the housing before cleaning them under the faucet. And never hold any part of the unit under a running faucet while the machine is still plugged in.

❖ After every few uses, check the mixer's air vents to make sure they're not clogged. If you find any dirt, clean it out with a pipe cleaner.

Blender Bonanzas

❖ Blend your blender clean after you use it. Fill the container half full of water, add a few drops of dishwashing liquid, put on the lid and let 'er rip for about ten seconds. Empty the jar, rinse, fill it halfway with clear water and run the machine for ten seconds. Then empty the jar and run the blender for ten seconds more to dry out the blade.

❖ After every few uses, be sure to clean the blade assembly well with warm soapy water and dry it thoroughly. Hardened sediment that collects on the bottom of the

PUZZLER

THIS WASN'T A TEACHER'S AID IN some early physics class, but something you used to get the old bean in shape for the daily grind.

ANSWER: *Coffee bean roaster.*

blender can prevent the blades from turning, putting a strain on the motor.

ELECTRIC CAN OPENERS

The Low-Tech Fix-It Kit

❖ An old toothbrush, a pipe cleaner, some soapy water and a few drops of oil are all you need to keep your electric can opener working. The parts that do the work are the feed gear and the cutter wheel, and both are easy to see. After unplugging the appliance, wash the feed gear with the soapy water, clean out any remaining food particles with the toothbrush and dry the gear well. Use the pipe cleaner to clean between the parts. After cleaning, put a drop of cooking oil on the parts to keep them lubricated and prevent them from rusting.

Another Can of Beans

ALTHOUGH THE tin can, invented by Peter Duran, was patented as early as 1810 and became the preeminent food storage container of its day, it would be almost another fifty years before someone came up with the can opener. That's not so surprising when you consider that those early tin cans were made by hand of such heavy sheets of metal that they usually far outweighed their contents. No modern can opener would have made a dent. Housewives used hammers and chisels to open the heavy-duty containers, but soldiers who lived on canned meals relied on field knives, rocks and bayonets to get at their food. Rumor has it that when the situation got desperate, some soldiers even resorted to gunfire. (It does give a whole new meaning to the idea of shooting your dinner.) Eventually, manufacturers began mass-producing cans from much thinner steel, and not too long after that, in 1858, Ezra Warner took out his patent on the first can opener.

It was no household boon. In fact, no one really noticed the gadget for a couple of decades. Those who did shrank away in fear. It looked more like a bayonet than a kitchen tool, and by this time most folks had grown pretty handy with a chisel. The hapless invention would have died out completely if it hadn't eventually caught on with the U.S. military—perhaps as a means to conserve ammunition.

COFFEE GRINDERS

Dull Is Dangerous

❖ A coffee grinder is a simple, inexpensive device designed to cut or grind coffee beans. The biggest threat to the longevity of both the cutting and the grinding models is a dull cutting blade or grinder. Replace the dull mechanism immediately rather than trying to compensate for the dullness by running the motor for an extra-long time. Excessive running may burn out the unit—and rather than replacing an inexpensive part, you could end up replacing the machine.

Don't Let Your Grinder Get Stoned

❖ If you have a cutting-type grinder, watch for those small gray or black coffee-bean-size stones that get swept up with the beans during harvest. If one gets tossed into the grinder with the beans, it will nick—or break—the blade.

A Little Pepper in Your Café au Lait?

❖ Cutting-type coffee grinders are handy for grinding and pulverizing other foods like spices and nuts. But be sure to clean the grinder well before using it again for beans— unless you like nutmeg- or pepper-flavored coffee.

COFFEEMAKERS

Oil Is Crude

❖ Keeping all parts of your coffeemaker scrupulously clean is the best way to make the appliance last. Coffee has oil in it, and some residual oil is inevitably left behind each time you brew a pot. If you don't get rid of this residue, your coffee will taste bitter, and you may start thinking it's time for a new unit.

A Cleaner That Works Again and Again

❖ If your model has a reservoir, at least once a month fill it with white vinegar or a commercial cleaning solution and run the machine through the brewing cycle. If your water is hard (contains a lot of minerals), do it twice a month. You can even recycle the cleaning vinegar. Save the vinegar that comes through the brewing cycle, pour it into a bottle and let the minerals collect at the bottom. Pour off the clear vinegar for use in the next cleaning.

Ingenuity Is the Key

❖ A baby-bottle brush, a square of nylon netting on the end of a stick or a pipe cleaner makes a great tool for cleaning the spouts and tubes of an electric percolator.

❖ Speaking of babies, a new cloth diaper makes a great rag for cleaning out the water compartment of a coffeemaker. The diaper is a much better alternative than a paper towel, which may leave particles that can get into the water circulation system and clog it.

To clean a drip-style coffeemaker, first unclog the holes at the base of the water tank (A). Then clear out the inside of the drip-control bar (B).

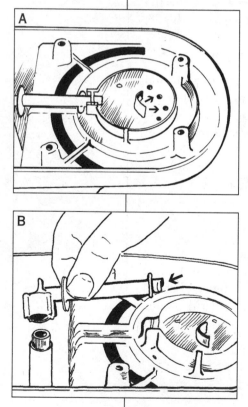

What Drips Can Clog

❖ For drip-style coffeemakers, use a thin wire or the end of a paper clip to clean the holes in the bottom of the water tank and on the drip-control bar. Clean the drip tube on pump-feeding models.

When the Light's On, So's the Coffee

❖ One of those little night-lights available in discount stores can serve as a useful reminder to turn off the coffeepot. Plug one into the socket with your coffeemaker, then unplug it when you turn off the pot.

Add Salt to Your Coffeepot's Diet

❖ You forgot the night-light, and now the bottom of your glass coffeepot is burnt? Sprinkle some salt on the bottom, let it sit for a few minutes and then rinse out the pot.

An Instant Filter

❖ Out of coffee filters? Improvise by cutting a heavy-duty paper towel or paper napkin to fit.

MICROWAVE OVENS

Clear the Way

❖ Microwave ovens generate heat when they operate. When setting up your microwave, be sure to allow several inches of clearance at the top and sides where the heat vents are. Without this space, the oven may overheat.

No-No's Arc

❖ Never put anything metal in the microwave. It will cause arcing (think of it as a mini lightning bolt), which can blow out the magnetron tube—the heart of your oven.

❖ Use dental floss, not metal twists, to seal your microwave cooking bags. But don't seal them completely, as the steam will need some means to escape. For this purpose, make a small slit in a part of the bag where liquid can't leak out.

Micro Management

❖ Before using a container in your microwave, make sure it's microwave safe. Most glass, paper, pottery, ceramic and special microwave plastic containers are okay. Most newer dishes have marks on the bottom indicating whether they're suitable for microwave use. If you have any question, perform the following test: Put the dish in the microwave next to a glass filled

COMMON MISTAKES

Microwave Madness

A MICROWAVE OVEN can be a great convenience—if it's used properly. Don't use your microwave to:

• Heat baby bottles. Microwaves cook from the inside out, so a bottle may feel cool to the touch even if the liquid inside is boiling hot.

• Pop popcorn, unless it's in a bag made specifically for the microwave. Scorched kernels may catch fire in a container (such as a paper bag) that's not microwave safe.

• Deep-fry anything. It may cause a fire.

• Cook an egg in its shell. Steam can build up inside the egg and cause it to explode, which at worst may damage the oven and at best will create a mess.

• Reheat spaghetti sauce—or any other tomato-based food—in a plastic container. Doing this won't hurt the microwave, but the acid in the tomato sauce will eat into the plastic and ruin the container.

with 1 cup of cold water. Turn the microwave on High for 1 minute. If the dish feels cool but the water is hot, it's okay to use. If the dish feels hot, don't use it in the microwave.

❖ Leave a microwave-safe bowl or cup of water in the microwave when you're not using it. If the unit is accidentally turned on when empty and your model doesn't have a safety shutoff, the water will keep the magnetron tube from burning out after 10 to 15 minutes.

Odor Eaters

❖ To remove odors in the microwave and thus keep it usable longer, make a solution of 1 cup of water and 2 to 3 tablespoons of lemon juice and boil it in the oven for five minutes.

Pull Out That Sponge

❖ Use a mild solution of dishwashing liquid and water to keep the oven, door and seals clean. Wipe up spatters immediately after using the microwave, when they're still relatively liquid and easy to remove.

CONVECTION OVENS

Let It Vent

❖ As with microwaves, be sure your convection oven has at least a few inches of space around it so that the unit can vent properly. A convection oven has a fan that circulates hot air, cooking food more quickly and economically than a conventional oven. The hot air is intended to escape through exhaust vents on the top and sides. If the vents are blocked, the trapped heat could damage the unit in no time.

A Current Affair

❖ Give your convection oven its own circuit. It requires a lot of current, and you might blow a fuse if you operate another appliance on the same circuit.

A Fan-Tastic Idea

❖ If your convection oven has a filter in front of the fan, remove the filter and wash the grease off in soapy water every few weeks to make sure the air can flow through unimpeded. To remove the screen, just unscrew the nuts that hold it in place.

Paint It (Almost) Perfect

ONCE I WAS REMODELING a woman's kitchen with a crew of helpers. One of the men accidentally banged the new white-enamel kitchen sink with his hammer and chipped off a piece of enamel about the size of a quarter.

The woman was standing right there when it happened, and she insisted that we replace the sink with a new one. Of course I agreed, but I asked her if she'd mind if I repaired the sink before I returned it to the store. I told her that the store would be able to sell the repaired sink. She was suspicious, but she let me proceed.

The next day, I came to her house with a small vial of white enamel paint. The woman watched with interest as I carefully brushed the

EARL remembers...

paint onto the chipped sink. Each of the next four nights, I applied a coat of paint to the chip, sanding the patch carefully between coats with fine-grit sandpaper. Gradually, the thickness of the patch built up to the thickness of the enamel.

When I was satisfied that the chip was patched as well as it could be, I said to the woman, "I guess we're ready to take the sink back now." She admitted that the chip was fully repaired and decided to keep the sink after all. She insisted, though, that I give her my "special" vial of paint—in case the sink ever got chipped again. She didn't realize that it was plain old enamel paint, and I decided not to tell her.

Cleaning Convections

❖ If your convection oven is self-cleaning, don't use abrasive cleaners to help it along—they can harm the special coating on the oven's walls. Use a cloth, warm water and dishwashing liquid for additional spot cleaning.

❖ To clean a convection oven that's not self-cleaning, boil 2 quarts of water and add ½ cup of ammonia (keep it away from your nose—the fumes are dangerous). Put the mixture in the oven and let it sit overnight. The ammonia will loosen the dirt, which you can wipe off with a damp cloth in the morning.

PASTA MAKERS

Avoid Stress

❖ Pasta dough tends to be stiff at first, so put less stress on the gears of your pasta maker—whether it's a manual or an electric model—by starting out with the widest roller setting and working your way down as the dough becomes thinner.

Pasta Perfect

❖ After each pasta-making session, use a small wooden object such as a toothpick or chopstick to clean out all the leftover dough. The job will be easier if you wait for the dough to dry and harden a bit.

❖ If your pasta maker is a manual model, dab a few drops of cooking oil on the exposed gears after each use to keep them lubricated.

TOASTERS AND
TOASTER OVENS

The Icing on the Cake

❖ Don't toast anything with icing or filling in a well-type toaster. The stuff will gum up the works and may catch fire.

Take a Shine to It

❖ Baby oil, club soda or lemon juice will bring back the shine on the chrome of a toaster oven. Just rub in whichever you choose, wipe with a damp cloth and then rub the unit with a soft, dry cloth.

Get Out the Plastic

❖ Concerned about melted plastic on the outside surface of your toaster oven? Unplug the oven and let it cool, then cover the plastic with a rag soaked in ammonia. After a few minutes, the plastic should scrape right off with a plastic scouring pad.

The Old Two-Step

❖ To clean a very dirty toaster oven window, first spray it with oven cleaner. Wipe it off, then spray on glass cleaner and wipe that off.

A Crumby Break

❖ Don't line the crumb tray of a toaster oven with aluminum foil. The tray sits very close to the heating element. Foil may obstruct the cooking process or even catch fire.

PUZZLER

CALLED A SLASHER IN England, this cutting-edge tool looks a bit like an ax and has a different name in America—and it's not intended to inflict bodily harm.

ANSWER: Bill hook, used to cut brush and young trees.

WAFFLE IRONS

Grid and Bare It

❖ After each use, clean the grids of a waffle iron with a toothbrush and a paste made of baking soda and water.

An Iron for All Seasons

❖ "Seasoning" a waffle iron before each use will prevent sticking. To season the iron, just brush both sides of a piece of bread with a light, salt-free cooking oil, turn on the iron, put the bread in the iron and close the lid. The fat will grease the surfaces as the bread browns.

❖ You can also season the iron with vegetable oil. Just brush it on with a clean pastry brush.

My Iron Runneth Over

❖ To prevent batter from running over and making a mess of the iron, let the batter cook for a while before you close the lid. (This also will produce lighter and fluffier waffles.)

TRASH COMPACTORS

Don't Ask It to Run with the Crowd

❖ A compactor uses a lot of electricity. Make sure to run it on its own circuit.

PUZZLER

THESE WEREN'T USED FOR ICE climbing. French country folks once wore them to stamp the hulls from a popular fall crop.

ANSWER: *Chestnut-hulling shoes.*

Give It Room to Throw a Punch

❖ Don't overload the sack. If you do, the ram won't be able to crush the trash, and it may jam.

Kill the Trash, Save the Family

❖ When crushing glass bottles, first wrap them in newspaper or paper towels or put them inside a cardboard container such as a milk carton. Lay the package flat inside the bin before crushing. This will contain otherwise dangerous bits of glass.

❖ Never put aerosol containers, or any container for flammable fluids, insecticides or other strong chemicals, in the compactor. They could explode and/or release dangerous fumes.

GARBAGE DISPOSALS

Keep Your Cool

❖ It's a good idea to run a hard stream of cold water before you turn on the unit, during grinding and for at least

20 to 30 seconds after grinding sounds stop. The cold water will congeal any grease in the unit, which will help flush it down the drain, and the hard stream of water will help ensure that all the garbage is thoroughly ground up and flushed. Never use hot water, as it will melt any grease that is in the disposal, and that may clog the drain.

Don't Shy Away from the Hard Stuff

❖ For the most efficient grinding, mix hard and soft foods together when you fill the disposal.

Hit the Switch—Now!

❖ Once you put food in the disposal, grind it up immediately. Never store food in the disposal between grindings. At best, it will cause a stench; at worst, it could pack down and cause the unit to jam.

Oh, No, Not the Goldfish!

❖ Don't try to grind anything other than what is intended to go into the disposal. No-no's include bones, glass, rubber, paper, metal, plastic, dishcloths and fibrous materials—such as corn husks—which are extremely difficult to grind up and may jam the unit. Be especially careful with coins. They have a way of sneaking into the disposal and jamming up the works.

A Ready Retrieval

❖ If you hear something hard rattling around when you turn on the disposal, turn off the unit immediately. Put a piece of clay or putty on the end of a wooden chopstick or a spoon and fish out the offending material before using the unit again.

It May Never Smell Like Roses, But . . .

❖ Every few weeks—or whenever it smells bad—toss a tray of ice cubes and some lemon rinds into the disposal. Turn on the water and run the unit for a minute. This will flush the offending food particles down the drain and deodorize the area at the same time.

DISHWASHERS

Dishwasher, Clean Thyself

❖ To clean the inside of a dishwasher, put a cup of vinegar in the bottom of the empty dishwasher and run it through the wash and rinse cycles. Shut the machine off before it goes through the drying cycle.

❖ If odors linger after you run the dishwasher, sprinkle half a box of baking soda over the bottom and run the unit through the rinse cycle.

A Safety Net

❖ Place a piece of nylon netting at the bottom of your dishwasher's silverware basket to keep small objects from slipping through and possibly interfering with the rotating sprayer on the bottom of the machine. If the sprayer cannot rotate freely, the spray will not wash and rinse dishes evenly.

Let Your Dishwasher Be a Sponge Washer

❖ The dishwasher can help your kitchen sponge last longer. Just attach the sponge to the top shelf with a clothespin so that it doesn't fall and jam the rotating sprayer. Then wash it with your dishes.

On the Rack

❖ If the plastic covering on your dishwasher racks is wearing thin, apply a light coating of silicone caulk on the worn spots to inhibit rust. Let it set for the time recommended on the package before you run the dishwasher again.

❖ To cover rust on dishwasher racks—and to prevent it from spreading—pick up a product called Plasti-Dip at the hardware store and apply it to the rusted area with a brush.

Rack 'n' Roll

❖ If the dish racks don't slide in and out easily, the axles they glide on may be rusty. Remove the racks, scour the

A Tale of Two Dishwashers

I ONCE WAS GIVEN a dishwasher when I was working on a house. The people were converting a residence into an office, and they had no need for the appliance. I took it home and put it in the garage, just as I do with everything else I think might come in handy.

About three years later, I was remodeling another house. The owner complained that she couldn't find anyone who could fix her dishwasher, which happened to be the same model as the one I had been given earlier. So I took the parts she needed from my machine and installed them in hers.

A year later, she decided to get a new dishwasher and offered me her old one. I took it and installed it in my house, where we used it for years. When it needed repairs, I took the parts I needed from the one in the garage. Finally, my wife decided she wanted a new dishwasher. I sold the old one, since there was nothing wrong with it.

If you have the space, it pays to keep a spare machine for parts.

---

axles with a steel wool soap pad and then use a vinegar-soaked sponge or rag to clean off any rust and pad residue.

❖ If the racks stick even though the axles aren't rusty, apply some silicone spray, available at hardware stores, to the axles to loosen them.

Detergent Details

❖ Be sure to use only detergents that are specially formulated for your automatic dishwasher. Don't use ordinary dishwashing liquid. It will create excess foam and hamper the machine's washing and rinsing cycles.

❖ Store your dishwasher detergent on a cool, dry shelf, not under the sink, where it's moist. Moisture will cause it to get lumpy, and lumpy detergent won't dissolve properly in your machine.

❖ Wait to add dishwasher detergent until you're ready to turn on the machine. If you add it too early and leave it sitting in the machine, it will cake up and won't dissolve properly when you run the machine.

STOVES

An Ounce of Prevention

❖ Be sure to wipe up oven spills while they're still wet. If you wait until they've baked on, they'll be far more difficult to remove.

❖ Wipe the walls of your oven periodically with a cloth dampened in a mixture of equal parts vinegar and water. This will prevent grease buildup.

❖ To prevent pans from boiling over and making a mess on top of the stove, avoid filling them more than three-quarters full. This leaves room for the liquid to boil.

A Pound of Cure

❖ You don't have to start off with elbow grease to clean a grimy electric oven. Boil 2 quarts of water in a large pot and add ½ cup of ammonia. Place the pot in a cold oven overnight. The ammonia will loosen the grime, and the next morning you can wipe the oven clean.

❖ This method also works for gas ovens—but only if you first turn off the main gas valve that lets gas into the stove and make sure the pilot lights for the range-top burners and oven are

BUY IT TO LAST

Gas vs. Electric Stoves

SHOULD YOU CHOOSE gas or electric when purchasing a stove? Either will generally last about 15 to 20 years, so the choice depends on other factors. If efficiency is your major concern, go with the electric. About 75 percent of the energy from an electric stove reaches the food as heat, versus 40 percent of a gas burner's energy. If operating cost is your major determinant, go with gas. Although a gas stove often costs a bit more to purchase, over the years it will cost less to run.

out. You don't want the ammonia fumes coming into contact with a flame and igniting.

It Does Windows

❖ The plastic ice scraper you keep in your car is a handy tool for cleaning the inside window of your oven door. Wipe on some ammonia, let it sit for half an hour and then use the scraper to remove the grime.

❖ No ice scraper? Rub the window with a damp cloth dipped in baking soda.

❖ If you can't get the window clean, grime may be trapped between the panes of glass. Unscrew the panel, clean between the panes and then screw the panel back in place.

Clean Up Your Racks

❖ You can get rid of grease buildup on oven racks by giving them a bath. Put an old sheet or towel in your bathtub to protect it from scratches, then put in the racks and add enough hot water to cover them. Add a mixture of ¼ cup of dishwasher detergent and ¼ cup of white vinegar, stirred to dissolve the detergent. Let the racks sit for an hour, then rinse and dry them. The mixture is a sure grease cutter. (Be sure to drain and wipe the bathtub right away, however, or you'll end up with a messy tub.)

A Chip off the Old Block

❖ If the porcelain on your stove top chips, buy a porcelain enamel kit at an appliance store and touch up the rough spots.

Cooking with Gas

❖ To remove food that's spattered onto a heating element of a gas oven, scrape it off with a plastic—not a metal—tool. Metal could damage the element.

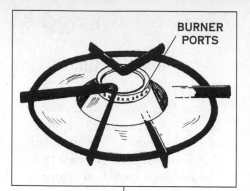

BURNER PORTS

Check for clogged burner ports if the burner flames on your gas stove are uneven. A wire brush will help to clean them out.

❖ If the burner flames are uneven on a gas stove, the problem may be that the burner ports are clogged. Use a small, stiff wire brush to clean them out.

Cleaning the Bibs and the Oven

❖ When burner bibs get spattered, clean them with a paste of baking soda and water.

❖ To remove particularly tough stains on burner bibs, scrub with acetone (available at pharmacies) on a rag. When using acetone, be sure to allow adequate ventilation. The fumes can be dangerous.

❖ If you have a continuous-cleaning oven, wipe it periodically with dishwashing liquid and a nylon pad to remove the residue left by the cleaning process.

REFRIGERATORS AND FREEZERS

Location, Location, Location

❖ When planning your kitchen layout, place the fridge out of direct sunlight and away from anything that generates heat—a stove, water heater, furnace or radiator. That way, the motor won't have to work as hard to do its job.

❖ The condenser coils, underneath or in back of the fridge, give off heat as refrigerant circulates through them. To be sure they have enough room to vent properly, leave a few inches of space between the fridge and the wall or other appliances. The coils will last longer.

Keep the Coils Clean

❖ Vacuum the condenser coils thoroughly at least twice a year, using the suction attachment of your vacuum cleaner. Keeping the coils clean will put less strain on the motor (and save electricity). If the coils get too dirty, the motor may even give up the ghost.

A Movable Feast

❖ Do you need to move your fridge to clean the condenser coils? Recruit a friend and locate a straw broom. Shove the bristles of the broom under the unit and have your friend help you tip the fridge onto the bristles. You can then easily slide the appliance away from the wall. To put it back, use the same method.

❖ If the condenser coils are in the back, you can get at them with a long-handled brush—the kind designed for washing the car.

Keep It Clean

❖ You'll give your fridge less of a chance to harbor food-spoiling bacteria if you keep the inside clean. Wipe up spills immediately. Once a month, dip a cloth in a solution of 1 tablespoon of baking soda and 1 quart of water. Use this to wipe the inside walls; sponge off the front, sides and top; and clean the shelves and bins. Wipe the floor of the refrigerator while the bins are out of it.

❖ To clean underneath the fridge, wrap a cloth around a yardstick or other flat stick and slide it under the unit. Or grab the dust with the long-handled brush you normally use to clear snow off your car's windshield.

If Something Smells Funny . . .

❖ If you notice an unpleasant smell coming from beneath your refrigerator, chances are you have one of the models that requires periodic cleaning of the drip pan. (In most units, melted frost from the freezer drips down through a hose and collects in this pan at the base of the refrigerator.) If left to sit, the water in the pan may smell. Snap off the grill at the bottom of the unit, remove the drip pan and wash it in warm soapy

PUZZLER

THIS GIZMO PROBABLY CAME INTO use after the United States annexed Hawaii. It was used for "blinding" a certain tropical fruit.

ANSWER: *Pineapple eye snippers.*

water. Remember to repeat the process periodically to avoid that odor.

Defrost, Defrost!

❖ If your refrigerator isn't a frost-free model, you'll help the unit maintain a proper temperature—and use less electricity—if you unplug the unit and defrost the freezer before the frost buildup gets to a ¼-inch thickness. Appliance stores sell a handy little electric defroster unit that makes the job easier. A model with a metal case is more durable, but be careful not to close the cord in the door when you use the defroster.

❖ If you're defrosting without a defroster unit, fill a spray bottle with hot water and give the box—and the coils—a good spritz. It'll speed up the melting process. Pans of boiling water also will do the trick, but be sure to keep them away from the coils and any plastic parts. Put them in, close the freezer door and keep replacing them with hot ones as they cool.

Let Them Shine

❖ To prevent your metal refrigerator racks from rusting, give them a light coat of floor wax several times a year.

❖ Apply a coat of creamy appliance polish to the exterior of your fridge twice a year to protect it and prevent it from rusting. You can get the polish from any store that sells appliances.

Stress-Free Living Means a Longer Life

❖ Your upright freezer will live longer if you place it in a cool, dry and well-ventilated room where the temperature

---

A SECOND LIFE

Use a Jug, Save a Landfill

THOSE PLASTIC JARS and bottles that are clogging up our landfills can help you make things last around the kitchen. Instead of tossing your used containers, try any of these ideas.

• Punch a few holes in the bottom of a big plastic jar, and you have a handy storage container for lettuce and other vegetables.

• Cut a hole near the top of a gallon milk jug and use it to store your plastic bags.

• Rinse out a small plastic squeeze bottle, buy dishwashing liquid in bulk and decant some of the liquid into the small bottle for everyday use. You'll save money by purchasing the larger quantity and find that you tend to use less when you're working from a smaller bottle and can measure more accurately.

doesn't drop below 40°F. That way, the motor won't have to work as hard.

Kitchen and
Household

❖

WASHING MACHINES AND DRYERS

Washtub Vinaigrette

❖ Every three months, run 1 quart of vinegar in an empty hot wash cycle of your washing machine to clean out any mold or bacteria and prolong the life of the washtub. After many uses, a washing machine can build up a layer of film in the tub, and this routine will eliminate it.

Wipe Out Potential Problems

❖ After running a load of laundry, make it a habit to wipe the tub with a sponge soaked in warm water. This will help prevent buildup.

A SECOND LIFE

Bury the Dead Body

THE BARREL OF a dead washing machine makes a dandy outdoor planter. Just build a wooden box around it to disguise the metal. Really.

Dryers Need to Blow Off Steam

❖ Make sure that your clothes dryer is vented to the outside of your house and the hole is well sealed around the vent. Don't let the dryer vent inside the house, as this can cause condensation on your windows in winter and add to humidity in summer.

BATTERIES

Freeze!

❖ Store unused batteries in a sealed plastic bag in your freezer. Package them so that the terminals don't touch each other. If they do, each will lose its charge. Allow batteries to thaw for 24 hours before using them, so that the chemicals inside will be fully active.

The Day Time Stood Still

I'VE HAD AN ELECTRIC CLOCK in my office for years. One day time stopped: I could hear the motor buzzing, but the hands weren't going around.

EARL remembers...

I figured that the gears that drove the hands must have worn down. So I turned the works one-quarter turn in the case of the clock. Now the gears are bearing differently, and my clock is keeping time.

When an old electric or mechanical item seems to have worn itself out, it pays to be creative. Sometimes a simple fix will give the piece a whole new life.

The Condition May Be Terminal

❖ Battery-operated appliance stopped working? Before you replace the batteries, lightly sand both terminals with a piece of fine-grit sandpaper or an emery board to remove dirt that may be impeding the flow of electricity between the battery and the appliance.

Some Mistakes Can Be Erased

❖ If the batteries in your small appliance appear just slightly corroded, try rubbing the corroded end with a pencil eraser. Often this is enough to clear up the problem.

CLOCKS

A Timely Idea

❖ If your electric clock stops running, turn it upside down for a few hours. The oil inside will seep into the gears, which may have dried out. Sometimes that's all it takes to get the clock going again.

Get It Moving like Clockwork

❖ If your clock isn't keeping the right time, the problem may be in the stem that holds the base of the hands in place. Unplug the clock and pry the plastic cover off with a knife blade. Tighten the stem by gently squeezing it with a pair of pliers. Then put the plastic cover back on.

ELECTRIC BLANKETS AND HEATING PADS

Don't Top It

❖ Avoid placing anything heavy on top of an electric blanket, and don't tuck in the wired portions. The wires that run through the blanket can be easily damaged, and that in turn will limit the blanket's heating power and shorten its life.

Restore Contact

❖ If your electric blanket doesn't heat up, the terminals on the blanket plug may be dirty. Try sanding them lightly with extra-fine-grit sandpaper. The same approach works on the switch contacts of a heating pad's temperature control unit when the heating pad is running too hot or too cold.

STEAM IRONS

Clean-Water Act

❖ Instead of tap water, which contains corrosive minerals, use distilled or demineralized water in your steam iron.

❖ You can also use rainwater in your steam iron, but you'll need to filter it first. Place a piece of cotton in a funnel to catch any debris, then pour the rain-

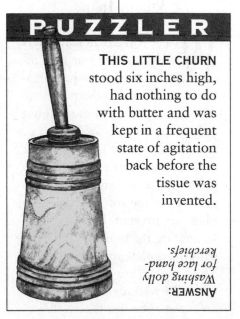

PUZZLER

THIS LITTLE CHURN stood six inches high, had nothing to do with butter and was kept in a frequent state of agitation back before the tissue was invented.

ANSWER: Washing dolly for lace handkerchiefs.

water through the cotton and funnel. The filtered water is okay to use in the iron.

Tacky but True

❖ Even if your iron doesn't have a nonstick finish, you don't have to toss it when starch gunks up the soleplate (bottom). Put a piece of brown paper bag on a board, sprinkle it with salt and slide the heated iron around in the salt until the bottom is clean. Then slide the iron over a double thickness of waxed paper to remove any residual tackiness.

❖ You can also remove starch from the bottom of an iron without a nonstick finish by wrapping a piece of white candle in a scrap of cloth and running it over the warm iron.

Steaming Along

❖ After using a steam iron, empty the water while the iron is still hot. The heat will evaporate any remaining moisture (and resulting mineral deposits, which can plug up the steam jets) from the reservoir.

❖ Store a steam iron upright on its heel, not flat. Otherwise residual moisture may cause the soleplate to discolor.

Don't Leave a Trail

❖ Is your iron leaving a trail of brown spots on your freshly laundered shirts? The steam vents are plugged—it's time to flush them out. Unplug the iron and use the end of a paper clip to clean as much residue as possible out of the vents. Then fill the iron with a mixture of equal parts water and vinegar. Put it on a rack over a broiling pan, plug it in, wait a minute for the water to drip into the steam chamber and then set it on Steam. After the iron stops steam-

---

BUY IT TO LAST

Steam Irons

WHEN YOU SHOP for a new iron, look for one that offers at least these basic features: an adjustable thermostat so that you can control the amount of heat and avoid scorching your favorite togs; a see-through water tank so that you can keep up a good head of steam; button grooves in the sides of the soleplate to prevent buttons from scratching the bottom; and controls to regulate spray and steam. Those who are absentminded would be well advised to look for an automatic shutoff as well.

ing, set the temperature to its maximum level and leave it on for another half hour. (For safety reasons, do not leave it unattended.) Before using the iron, run it over a damp cloth to wipe off any excess sediment.

Cover-Up

❖ A worn-out blanket makes great padding for your ironing board cover. It's absorbent and soaks up steam without leaving a watery mess.

HANDHELD
VACUUM CLEANERS

Avoid Temperature Extremes

❖ To prolong your mini vacuum's life, store its recharging base where the temperature is at least 40°F and not over 105°F.

Even a Cleaner Needs Cleaning

❖ You can also extend the life of a hand-held vacuum by cleaning it occasionally. After hand-washing the filter bag with a mild detergent, put a paper towel in the bag and squeeze it to remove moisture. Be sure the bag is completely dry before reattaching it to the unit.

CANISTER-TYPE
VACUUM CLEANERS

Time for a Refill

❖ Replace disposable dust bags when they're about three-quarters full. This will prevent them from overflowing and making a worse mess than the one you're trying to clean up.

Get Unplugged

❖ If the suction on your vacuum is poor, the hose may be blocked. Try dropping a quarter through it. If there's a slight blockage, the coin may push it through. If the coin doesn't come out, you have a more severe blockage. Try reaming it out with a broom handle, straightened coat hanger or drain auger.

❖ If the quarter falls right through your hose and the suction remains poor, check the hose for a hole or crack, which can be patched with electrical tape until you have time to replace the hose.

FLOOR POLISHERS

Avoid Clogged Arteries

❖ When using your polisher to wax or shampoo, empty the tank after each use to prevent the dispensing tubes from clogging.

❖ If the tubes do clog, fill the tank with hot water to loosen the buildup. Once the offending material has softened, empty the tank immediately.

A Detached Attitude Can Be Good

❖ To keep your floor polisher working longer, detach the brushes periodically and clean out the dirt that has collected around the shafts.

Clean the Old Pads

❖ Make old, dirty waxing pads last by placing them between white paper towels and pressing down firmly with a fairly warm iron. This should transfer the wax to the towels.

HUMIDIFIERS

No Return on Deposits

❖ White vinegar is great for getting rid of mineral deposits that form in your humidifier as hard water evaporates. Soak the humidifier bowl, screen, water pan, belts and drums in a mixture of ¼ cup of vinegar and 1 quart of water for a few hours (overnight if the buildup is heavy). If your humidifier has an impeller (a rod that sticks into the water), be sure to soak it in the solution, too. This is important because if the deposits are left unattended, they will quickly clog up the works and affect the efficiency of the unit.

❖ If you want to avoid mineral deposits completely, use distilled water.

SEWING MACHINES

Caution: Enemy Attack

❖ Dust is your machine's enemy. Make sure to cover the machine when it's not in use.

Sew Easy

❖ Use a small brush to clean the dust and loose threads from hard-to-reach places on your sewing machine.

Soft-Pedaling

❖ To keep the pedal of your sewing machine clean and prevent it from wearing out, cover it with a plastic bag tied closed with a piece of string.

The Case for Pinups

❖ One of the most frequent sources of damage to sewing machine cabinets is common pins left on the surface when the cabinet is closed, so that their heads dig into the wood. To prevent this, wrap a narrow strip of felt or other fairly heavy fabric around the neck of the machine at any point where it won't interfere with the controls. Fasten the ends of the fabric together. As you sew, stick any extra pins into the fabric instead of letting them lie loose on top of the cabinet.

Clothing, Accessories and Household Linens

MY WIFE HAD MANY handbags, but her favorite was an old leather one she'd had for many years. She carried it with her everywhere, and over time the oil from her fingers would stain the leather at the top where she opened it. When the stain got bad, she'd ask me to clean the bag. It was easy: I'd just wipe the leather with a simple mixture of alcohol and water on a rag. Then I'd take an old toothbrush, wet it with the same mixture, and use that to scrub the grime out of the embossed letters on the bag. It wasn't a lot of effort on my part, but this simple cleaning allowed her to hold on to that bag for years.

The same thing is true for all kinds of clothing, accessories and household linens. If you choose your purchases with an eye to more than just the latest fashion, treat them right and invest a few minutes in some simple preservation measures, your favorite pieces will last for years. In this chapter, we'll show you how to kill the smell in those old gym sneakers, remove "pilling" from sweaters, resole your bedroom slippers and cope with runs in panty hose. We'll offer ways to get rid of stains caused by everything from chocolate to ballpoint ink to mildew—so that you can treat a garment instead of throwing it out. We'll even fill you in on how you can use plain old blackboard chalk to cure ring-around-the-collar and how to stretch a woolen sweater that's shrunk from washing. Let's begin with some simple tricks you can use every day to prolong the life of your wardrobe.

EVERYDAY CARE

Clothing, Accessories and Household Linens

But Put Them On One Leg at a Time

❖ If you buy a suit with two pairs of pants, rotate your wearing of the pants right from the beginning rather than saving one pair until the other wears out. That way, you'll make sure that both pairs always look as if they go with the jacket, rather than have the second pair look a lot newer.

What's That Guy's Collar Say?

❖ Having a worn collar turned by a seamstress can nearly double the life of a favorite shirt. (Most commercial laundries offer this service, too.) But think ahead. If you patronize a commercial laundry, tell them, from day one, to put their indelible mark on the inside of the yoke, not the collar. Otherwise, when collar-turning time comes, you'll be sporting a number code or the first three letters of your name.

Know When to Fold 'Em

❖ If you want a woolen or cotton pullover sweater to keep its shape, never hang it by its neck from a clothes hook. Fold sweaters by placing them front side down, making sure the front and back are even at the bottom. Fold the arms crosswise across the back, then fold the sweater in half with the front on top. You can fold cardigans this way, too, or hang them on a wooden or heavy plastic (never wire) hanger.

To fold a sweater, first place it with the front side down (A). Fold the sleeves across the back (B), then fold the sweater in half horizontally (C).

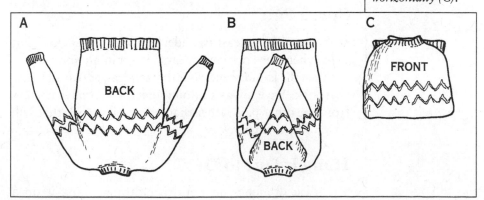

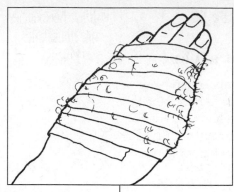

To remove pet hair and other lint, wrap masking tape around your hand with the sticky side out, then dab it against the garment.

If Your Jacket Looks Ready to Beg for Biscuits

❖ An ordinary roll of masking tape is your best ally in getting rid of pet hair on woolen clothing. Just wrap several widths of tape around your fingers, sticky side out, and blot up the hair with a series of patting motions. For big jobs, you may have to replace the tape a few times.

De-Pill-Atory

❖ Cotton and woolen sweaters—and especially synthetics—are prone to pilling, in which little balls of fiber appear on the surface. Although stores and catalogs sell little gizmos that look like rotary electric shavers for removing pills, one of the best ways to do the job is to stroke gently over the affected area with a pumice stone, the kind they sell at the drugstore for use on calluses.

Allow It Some Flextime

❖ Rotate the order in which you wear your underwear or any other clothing that has elastic in it. Don't save the new pieces until the old ones have worn out completely or allow your least favorite pieces to stay at the bottom of the drawer. Elastic that's left unused will dry out and lose its flexibility. Your only choice will be to throw it out. (The same principle applies to fitted bedsheets.)

Spare Pair

❖ Always buy at least two identical pairs of socks. That way, when one sock disappears into thin air somewhere between the laundry and your dresser drawer (we all know that socks have a way of doing that), you'll have a spare from the other pair rather than one useless sock that will have to be thrown away.

Hang It Out to Dry

❖ If rain drenches an item of clothing, hang it on a wooden hanger to dry completely before putting it away or stashing it in the laundry hamper. This will help prevent odors and mildew from forming.

Give Neckties a Rubdown

❖ When you take off a silk necktie, run it back and forth across your thigh to lift up the nap and remove wrinkles or creases. This will keep it in shape longer.

Let Your Tie Jump Off the Carousel

❖ Always hang up neckties when you're not wearing them. The best rack for this is a bathroom towel rack fastened to the wall of your closet or the back of your closet door. This type of rack allows ties to hang loosely without getting stretched or tangled the way they do on a tie "carousel."

BUY IT TO LAST

Room to Move

CERTAIN ITEMS in your wardrobe will last longer if you make sure they're a bit roomy in the first place. For example:

Coats and jackets. If you want the lining in a coat or jacket to last, make sure you assume as many typical positions as possible when you first try on the garment. Most important, sit in a chair and move your arms in front of you as you would when driving a car. Don't worry if the people in the store think you look like a kid playing race car driver. You can't tell if a garment has enough room in the chest, shoulders and arms by just standing there. And if it doesn't, the lining will be the first thing to go. (The outer stitching will be next.)

Men's all-cotton undershirts. If you want these to last, it's often wise to buy them a size larger than your regular shirt size. The reason? First, they're likely to shrink a bit if you machine-dry them. Second, a tight-fitting undershirt is going to be subjected to greater stress at the seams, which will cause it to rip and wear out prematurely.

Pajamas. These are another item that you're better off buying too large than too small. As you toss and turn in your sleep, pajamas that fit "just right" are going to bind and eventually give out along the seams. You can always have the legs taken up on a pair that's too long, and if the PJs look a little baggy—who's looking?

Wool Wins Out

RESEARCH HAS shown that an all-wool suit, subjected to normal frequency of wear, will last its owner more than six years. The average for a wool-synthetic blend suit is slightly more than four years, while all-synthetic suits are retired after three and a half years. Even when you take into account pure wool's premium cost, it still comes out on top in terms of value for the money.

Hook Your Belt

❖ Hang belts on a hook instead of winding them up and stashing them in a drawer. Winding them stretches the leather.

A Wrinkle Remover for Slacks

❖ Before putting away a pair of slacks, hang them upside down (by the cuffs or leg bottoms) from a closed bureau drawer overnight. Most wrinkles will disappear. This trick is especially helpful if you're going to store the slacks folded in a drawer, but it's useful if you're going to hang them in the closet, too, because it allows the wrinkles to disappear before the pants are pushed in among all your other garments.

Hang Up Down

❖ Hang down-filled jackets and vests loosely on a hanger in an uncrowded closet so that the down does not become compressed. This will maintain the loft—and thus the warmth—of the down.

Put On Your Galoshes

❖ Keep a pair of rubber-soled shoes to wear in the rain and leave your leather-soled shoes at home. Avoiding large puddles and downpours will help your good shoes last longer.

Let the Little Ones Go Sliding

❖ Toddlers' rubber boots are great for keeping feet dry, but prying them off the kids' feet can be a chore—and that can make you ditch the boots before their time. To avoid this problem, place a small plastic bag over each child's shoe and then insert foot, shoe, bag and all into the boot. They'll slide in easily, and when the child comes in from outside, taking the boots off will be a cinch.

Keep the Water Out

❖ Treat your leather boots to a waterproofing job before each season and now and then during the winter. Use a wax-based compound—wax shoe polish works very well—rather than an oil-based one. The wax will keep the boots supple but won't encourage stretching.

PREVENTIVE MAINTENANCE

Look like a Professor

❖ Since a lot of garments wear out first at the elbows, elbow patches are an inexpensive way to make shirts and jackets last. But make sure the patches you select have the same washing qualities as the article they're patching. You won't want to have suede or leather patches, for instance, on a garment you've been accustomed to throwing in the wash.

Call In the Reinforcements

❖ The best time to apply iron-on patches to a child's blue jeans may be before he wears holes in the knees. When the jeans are new, turn the legs inside out and iron the patches onto the inside. In addition to providing another layer for wear, the patches will help make the jeans last by improving the tensile strength of the fabric and keeping it from pulling apart under stress after it begins to weaken with repeated washings and use.

A Tip for Your Little Kittens

❖ Kids' mittens, it seems, seldom last long enough to wear out—they're always getting lost. To prevent this, tie or crochet a stout strand of yarn to connect the two mittens. Run the cord up one arm of the coat, around the back and down the other arm, then connect it the same way to the second

Use a simple chain stitch to crochet a string up one sleeve of a child's coat and down the other, connecting the two mittens. If you don't like to crochet, just tie each mitten to one end of a string of heavy yarn.

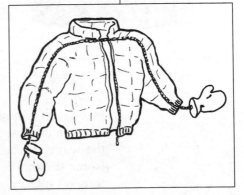

mitten. Make sure the cord is long enough for the child to move her arms freely. Now the coat and mittens can go on and off together. (The trouble with the little clips designed to hold mittens onto coat sleeves is that the clips get lost, too.)

It's a Snap

❖ A lot of young children's clothing has metal snaps rather than buttons. These are easy to fasten and keep toddlers from the hazard of swallowing buttons, but it's frustrating when a snap comes loose from the fabric and remains fastened to its mate on the other side. You can make kids' clothes (as well as grownups' items like pajamas) last longer by investing a couple of dollars in a snap fastener tool, available at any sewing supply store. Just load in a new snap, seat it on a sturdy part of the garment next to where the old snap was and press. Repeat the operation for the snap receptacle opposite, and you're all set.

Keep Shoulder Pads in Their Place

❖ The best way to keep shoulder pads in place (even when the thread attaching sewn-in pads has broken in the washing machine) is to use self-gripping fabric tape such as Velcro, available at sewing and fabric stores. Not only does it keep shoulder pads secure, but it also allows you to remove them easily to wash the garment.

Seal the Seams

❖ When you buy a new nylon or Gore-Tex rain jacket or pants, seal the seams with commercially prepared seam sealant (available at any outdoor-equipment store). Rub the sealant along the seams of the garment with your finger or a Q-Tip (some sealants come with a fabric applicator). Concentrate on stress points such as the elbows and shoulders.

PUZZLER

FEED THIS GIZMO A BIT of charcoal and it will run flat out.

ANSWER: *Charcoal-burning flatiron. The coals were inserted through the spout at the top of the iron.*

If You Don't Want to Get Your Feet Wet

THERE ARE A LOT of waterproofing treatments available for leather work boots, but I stand by neat's-foot oil as the best. Repeated applications of neat's-foot oil will keep your boots waterproof, but the oil doesn't close the pores of the leather as other treatments do. This allows the leather to breathe, and it makes your boots more comfortable to wear. (The one drawback is that you can't get a proper shine on a boot that's been treated with neat's-foot oil, so this treatment is best for work boots and other footwear for which durability is more important than polish.)

EARL remembers...

If you're going to use neat's-foot oil on your boots, it's important not to overdry them. When they get wet, stuff them with newspaper and let them dry at room temperature in a spot where the air circulates freely. Don't put them near a heat source, because you'll dry the oil as well as the water out of the boots. The worst thing you can do to an oiled boot is put it on a radiator.

If you keep the neat's-foot oil on the boots and the heat off them, you should be all set.

Do this in a well-ventilated area (sealants are usually flammable) before you use the garment.

A Fungus among Us

❖ Avoid leaving wet textiles where air can't circulate around them. This means you shouldn't put wet laundry in a hamper unless you're going to wash it right away, shouldn't leave damp towels or washcloths bunched up on the bathroom floor and shouldn't store clothing in damp basements. Any of these is an invitation to mildew—

which, after all, is actually a fungus that thrives in damp, dark, poorly ventilated places.

They're Not Just Little Fake Feet

❖ To make your leather shoes last longer, consider using shoe trees—those spring-loaded contraptions you snap inside your shoes after you take them off. Shoe trees serve two purposes. First, they keep shoes from eventually cracking along their natural crease lines. Second, they absorb the moisture and salts that build up during a day's wear and can corrode leather. The best shoe trees are made of unpolished cedar, a wood with fine absorptive qualities.

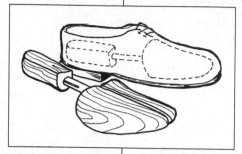

Shoe trees will help your footwear last longer.

Horning In

❖ Make sure your shoes—including athletic shoes—last by using a shoehorn when you put them on. The shoehorn will keep you from jamming down the backs, or counters, of the shoes, which destroys their structural strength and makes for a sloppy fit. (Incidentally, they're called shoehorns because that's the material they used to be made of—cattle horn.)

Sole Survival

❖ You can extend the life of a pair of leather house slippers—the kind that have a no-sole moccasin bottom—by reinforcing the bottoms with duct tape when you bring them home from the store. First, overlap as many strips of duct tape as you'll need to cover the bottom of each slipper. Lay the tape flat, sticky side up, on a piece of plywood or heavy cardboard that you won't mind cutting into. Press each slipper down onto the tape and trim away the excess tape with a hobby knife. Smooth the tape flat against the slipper bottoms, and you've got "soles." Replace the tape as it wears out, and you won't be replacing the slippers.

Place several overlapping layers of duct tape with the sticky side up. Press the slipper down onto the duct tape and then cut around the outline of the slipper.

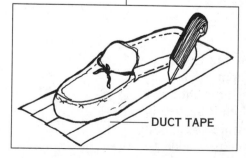

DUCT TAPE

Not Just Cosmetic

❖ Of course, your shoes look better when you keep them shined, but they also last longer. Polish them frequently. The wax contained in shoe polish keeps shoe surfaces smooth and prevents the leather from scuffing.

Save Your Sole

❖ When polishing leather-soled shoes, work the polish into the seam and around the edges of each shoe. This keeps damaging moisture out of the shoes.

And You Don't Have to Taste It

❖ Castor oil, which was once administered as a tonic to kids who dreaded the stuff, can bring dried-out shoes and other shiny leather goods back to life. Clean the articles to be treated with saddle soap and water, let dry and rub in the castor oil with a soft cloth. Apply to leather soles as well. Neat's-foot oil, a dressing made from cattle hooves, is a fine reconditioner for leather goods such as handbags, belts and briefcases, but it dulls the appearance of shoes and makes it difficult for them to take a shine afterward. This isn't a problem with castor oil.

Grease Your Boots

❖ To improve the water repellency of leather hiking or ski boots, rub them with boot grease (either wax or oil; both are available at outdoor-equipment stores). A wax-based grease coats the surface of the boot but does not penetrate. It loses its water repellency when it wears off the boot. An oil penetrates the leather. Apply either type of repellent to boots that are clean, warm and dry. You can rub wax over the entire boot, then hold it several inches above a stove burner, constantly rotating it, for better coverage. When you use oil, avoid saturating the boot.

BUY IT TO LAST

The Incredible Expanding Feet

NO MATTER HOW much care you lavish on a good pair of shoes, they aren't going to last as a part of your wardrobe if they never fit right in the first place. Always try to buy new shoes in the afternoon. By then, your feet have expanded to a slightly larger size than they were when you got up. Nobody wants to spend years walking around on afternoon feet stuffed into morning shoes.

CLEANING

You Never Know What You'll Find

❖ Before doing the wash, empty the pockets of everything going into the machine. Sharp objects, along with items that can melt or stain, are what you're after. Keep an especially close lookout if there are kids in the house. Anyone who's cleaned a dryer after a child's crayon has gone through the laundry knows how important this is.

The High Cost of Luxury

FEW FABRICS ARE more luxurious than genuine camel hair. But if you want an expensive overcoat or jacket to last, you might be wise to spend a little bit less and select a wool and camel hair blend. Garments made from 100 percent camel hair do not have the durability of blends and will likely show wear sooner.

Honey, About Those Navy Socks . . .

❖ When a stray tissue makes it through the pocket check, the shredded pieces can make a mess of your wash. If this is a frequent problem at your house, consider buying the new kind of tissue that's specially formulated not to disintegrate if it goes through the wash. (Look for it at your supermarket or discount store.) If you don't have to pick off the lint after every drying cycle, you may be able to hold on to your clothes—and your temper—longer.

Keep It Zipped

❖ To make zippers last, close them before putting garments in washers or dryers. Zipper teeth are more likely to go out of alignment and jam when the fasteners are left open during the rough tumbling of washing and drying.

You May Catch More Than You Bargained For

❖ Fasten hooks and eyes on garments—especially women's underwear—before running them through the wash. Loose ones are more likely to catch other articles of clothing and snag them.

Wrong to Wring

❖ Corduroy will look better longer if you let it drip- or spin-dry and avoid wringing it out. Wringing sets lines and wrinkles in corduroy, and ironing won't take them out.

Handle like Silk

❖ You can hand-wash simple, unlined silk articles such as blouses and scarves, but extra-gentle treatment is a must if you want the garments to last. Wash silk in cool to luke-warm water with a nonalkaline detergent such as Woo-lite, and squeeze rather than rub the fabric as you wash. Rinse in the same temperature water, then gently squeeze

Down but Not Out

ALTHOUGH LESS BULKY synthetics have taken over much of the market for sleeping bags and winter outerwear, a lot of folks still swear by articles stuffed with top-quality waterfowl down. The problem is, how do you clean a down garment or bag without sacrificing its warming abilities?

As with all insulators, down derives its heat-retaining qualities from its ability to trap air. The soft feathers from the underbellies of ducks and geese accommodate countless microscopic pockets of dead air, thanks to a quality called loft. Loft, put simply, is a state of extreme low density. The light, fluffy feathers pack so lightly that there's plenty of room for insulating air.

When you clean down, the trick is to avoid destroying its loft. Feathers that are packed or matted as a result of washing or careless dry cleaning will never hold as much air as they used to, and the garment will never be as warm. If you want to go the dry-cleaning route, choose a cleaner that specializes in down. Don't just take their word for it; ask around. A local outdoor club is a good place to start. If you want to wash a down garment at home, use a special product such as Nu-Down, following the instructions regarding washing and drying cycles. And be sure to throw an old sneaker or tennis ball into the dryer with your down-filled article. It'll help fluff the down and keep it from matting in one place.

Above all, don't wash or dry-clean down too often. Once every couple of years should be fine. (There's an argument for buying a dark-colored parka.) Once it's been cleaned, down never has quite the loft it had when it left the goose.

out moisture and pat the garment dry with a terry-cloth
towel. (Place the garment on top of the towel, roll the
whole thing up jelly-roll fashion and press gently to absorb as much water as possible.) To prevent water marks
from forming, dry in front of an electric fan—never in direct sunlight or near a heat source.

Keep Your Underwear in Shape

❖ When laundering women's underwear—or any other
garment that contains elastic—hang it on a clothesline or
rack to air dry after washing. Repeated drying at high temperatures, as in an electric clothes dryer, causes elastic to
stretch and give out before its time.

Block That Sweater!

❖ You hear people say that they don't like cotton sweaters
because they don't hold their shape. Actually, they'll hold
their shape just fine—if they're dried properly after washing. Never hang a wet cotton sweater on a line; its own

Stretch Your Sweater— and Your Dollars

EVERY WINTER, I GET letters from *Yankee*
readers asking how to stretch a woolen
sweater that has shrunk after washing. If
you didn't remember to block the sweater after
you washed it, here's what you can do.

Boil the sweater in one part vinegar and
two parts water for 25 minutes. You'll probably need a good-size pot for this. After 25 minutes, remove the sweater from the boiling water,
gently wring it out and reblock the garment to
its original size on a flat surface. Don't move the
sweater until it's dry.

This tip has saved many a sweater from the rummage sale.

EARL
remembers...

wet weight will pull it out of shape. Wet cotton sweaters should be "blocked," or laid out in their proper shape on a thick terry-cloth towel in a well-ventilated space. (Avoid direct sunlight, as some colors may fade.) Some of the gadget catalogs have been offering a device that looks like a miniature mesh trampoline. If you block a sweater on it, the sweater will dry quickly, as air will circulate above and below it.

Give It Another Dip

❖ It's best to hand-wash a swimsuit after wearing, especially if it's been used in a chlorinated pool or in salt water. If you don't have time for that, at least rinse the suit thoroughly in clean, cold water. Chlorine acts as a bleach on colors and can accelerate wear of cotton fabrics (more common in men's swimsuits than women's) and stitching.

Hold the Starch

❖ If you have your cotton dress shirts professionally laundered, skip the starch. Unstarched collars last longer.

Plus It Costs a Lot

❖ When you're traveling, avoid sending your clothing—especially 100 percent cottons—to the hotel laundry unless you're already satisfied that it's shrunk all it's going to shrink during previous washings and dryings. Hotels often use higher water temperature and dryer heat settings than you would at home, and it's maddening to get back a crisp, freshly laundered shirt only to discover that it would have fit perfectly . . . when you were in high school.

PUZZLER

THOSE INTERESTED IN KEEPING up with the latest fashions once used this adjustable wooden device to stay in shape.

ANSWER: *Beaver hat stretcher.*

Had Those Tweeds Dry-Cleaned for the Coronation in '53 . . .

❖ Save dry cleaning for prestorage or for stains you can't remove at home. One of the worst things you can do to a woolen garment is to dry-clean it too often. The process involves harsh chemicals that can wear down fibers and strip the natural oils from wool. Often all you really need

Don't Be Easily Suede

I F YOU'RE SHOPPING for running shoes or other athletic footwear, you're liable to assume that since leather makes the best shoes, suede makes the best sneakers. Think again. Actually, suede is quite a bit weaker than nylon mesh, an oxford weave or cotton canvas. It also tends to stretch, which means that the athletic shoes that fit in the store will feel sloppy on your feet after a few months of heavy service. If you do opt for suede, look for a shoe that is substantially reinforced with nylon or canvas.

to do is brush a garment gently and press as necessary. (Don't overdo it. Brushing too vigorously, too often, can remove the nap from soft-finished woolen goods and make them look threadbare before their time.)

A Repellent Idea

❖ A good-quality cloth raincoat should continue to repel water through several dry cleanings, although some resistance to water will be lost each time. If rain eventually begins to soak in too easily, ask your dry cleaner to retreat the garment with a chemical repellent. (It's much cheaper than buying a new raincoat.) Remember, even the best cloth raincoats are not designed to stand up to prolonged exposure to drenching rain; they're water repellent, not waterproof. (If you need something that will hold up in more of a downpour, consider a waxed cotton fabric—or, for the heaviest or longest rains, a plastic or rubberized slicker.)

Check the Stretch

❖ Before washing a new garment, try stretching it gently. If the fabric stretches more in one direction than another, it may shrink. (If you decide to go ahead and wash it, use cold water and avoid the dryer.)

Keep Nylon in the Dark

❖ When you wash a nylon windbreaker (or other outdoor garment made of nylon) or want to dry one that has been soaked by rain, don't leave it out in the sun. Nylon breaks down in the presence of ultraviolet light. Instead, allow it to dry in a shady spot or indoors.

Get More from Gore-Tex

❖ If your Gore-Tex jacket or pants seem to be leaking, try cleaning them in a washing machine on the gentle cycle with powder detergent. Rinse twice, then dry the garment in a clothes dryer turned to its lowest setting. The heat is necessary, but you must be careful not to harm the fabric. Gore-Tex never actually leaks—except through tears or holes. However, the outer layer of a Gore-Tex garment may become saturated when its water-repellent treatment gets old. This can lead to condensation inside the garment, making it seem as if it's leaking. Washing and heating restores the effectiveness of the treatment.

❖ Don't clean a Gore-Tex garment with liquid detergent, because its surfactants prevent water from beading up and rolling off the garment, as intended. And never dry-clean a Gore-Tex garment. The dry-cleaning chemicals will strip off the water-repellent treatment.

After the Honeymoon's Over

❖ When washing a large wedding veil or a lace tablecloth, fold it first. Turn the ends in toward the center and continue folding in this way. (The folding protects any lace, fine stitching, buttons and decorative trim.) Sew it up loosely with white cotton thread, then hand-wash it gently in cool water and a nonalkaline detergent such as Woolite. Carefully squeeze the soap solution through the fabric; do not wring or twist it. When you're done, remove the basting and unfold the piece as you folded it. Smooth it out on a clean white towel and allow it to air dry.

To *wash a large and delicate article, fold the sides in toward the center (A), then repeat the process for the top and bottom edges (B). Continue until the "package" is small enough to fit in a wash basin, then loosely stitch the folds in place (C) before immersing.*

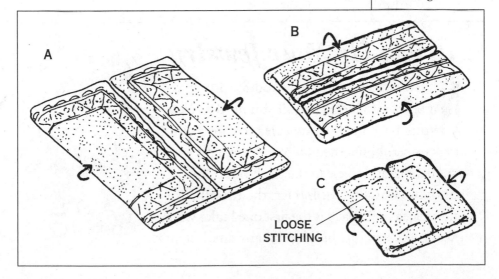

A

B

C

LOOSE STITCHING

Get Really Steamed

❖ Unless you live in a big city, it's getting harder and harder to find a place that cleans felt hats. You can bring a man's or woman's felt topper back to life by cleaning off surface dirt with a damp rubber sponge. Then hold the hat over a steaming teakettle to steam the crown. Using a clothes brush, brush gently in the direction of the nap, then repeat the process on the brim. Be careful not to scald your hands—and don't get the hat too wet, or the felt may shrink.

Put Those Wet
Leather Gloves Back On

❖ If your leather gloves get wet, put them on your hands while they're still damp, then work your fingers to stretch the leather back to the right size and shape. This will prevent the gloves from shrinking too much as they dry.

Work Hand in Glove

❖ You can bring tired-looking leather gloves back to life by putting them on, then working up a lather with saddle soap and wringing your hands and fingers together thoroughly. When the gloves are dry, repeat the process using neat's-foot oil or another leather conditioner, such as the cream used on leather furniture. (You can get the cream at any store that sells leather furniture.)

Brush Up Your Jewelry

NEVER THROW AWAY an old toothbrush. It and a bottle of vinegar are all you need to clean your jewelry. I always cleaned my wife's rings by scrubbing them with vinegar, and I still use this method to clean the gunk out of my expandable watchband. In fact, the toothbrush-and-vinegar approach is the first one I take when I want to clean dirt buildup on any small item.

EARL
remembers...

Sneaky Odors

❖ Sneaker odor can make your clothes closet smell like a gym locker and tempt you to throw out athletic shoes that may have a few good years left. To get rid of the smell, tie a few teaspoons of baking soda into a piece of cotton rag and put one of these "sneaker sachets" in each offending shoe. The sachets should work overnight and can be used several times.

Happy Trails

❖ If you want your hiking boots to last, let caked-on mud and trail dirt dry at room temperature after an outing, then brush it off with an old hairbrush or scrub brush (never use a brush with metal bristles). An old toothbrush comes in handy for cleaning out seams and the spaces between lugs on soles. When the boots are completely clean, apply leather conditioner and/or waterproofing according to the instructions on the container.

That Is, If the Kid Wants Them Clean

❖ A spray-on window cleaner such as Windex will do a creditable job on white leather sneakers. First spray on the cleaner, then clean with a damp cloth. This is a good quickie treatment, as cleaning products made for sneakers—though they do a good job—often involve a thorough soaking and a day or more of drying.

PUZZLER

DOING THE LAUNDRY BEFORE THE days of permanent press was no small task. This article could put a crimp in your style.

ANSWER: *Ruffle pleater.*

IRONING

Don't Leave Them Flat

❖ If you want washable corduroys to retain their plush, three-dimensional appearance, always iron them inside out. This will keep the ridges, called wales, from flatten-

Corduroy: To Wash or Not to Wash

CORDUROY SLACKS belong to that shadowy realm between home laundering and dry cleaning. How do you tell if a pair of corduroys belongs in the washer or should be sent to the cleaner? Don't go by label instructions alone, since some manufacturers want to emphasize washability at the expense of common sense. Instead, determine whether the garment is constructed or unconstructed.

A constructed, or tailored, garment is one that has linings, interfacings, a waistband and other elements of different materials than that used for its primary outer surfaces. These materials are used to enhance shape, appearance and draping quality, as in most suit jackets and dress slacks. In an unconstructed garment, the components of the outer shell are simply stitched together without any shaping enhancements. A prime example is a pair of jeans, whether made of denim, corduroy or other materials.

The reason you don't want to wash constructed garments is that the different materials used in their tailoring may shrink at different rates during washing and drying, leaving you with an article so out of shape that it is ready for the ragbag. Also, less expensive constructed apparel is often put together with glue and sizing, rather than stitching alone, and these components can be dissolved by washing. (They can sometimes be damaged by dry cleaning as well, which is why it's a good idea to spend more in the first place if you want clothing to last.)

So wash your unconstructed corduroys inside out on a cold-water setting, then air dry them or dry them at the lowest dryer setting. For dressier constructed cords, the dry cleaner is the answer.

ing. If you want to put a crease in a pair of corduroy slacks, place a handkerchief over the material before pressing.

❖ Whenever you're ironing a garment that has a raised pattern such as embroidery, appliqué or special weaving, turn it inside out before you start to press. Otherwise the pattern will be flattened and will lose its attractiveness.

Iron with Care

❖ Iron silks before they have dried completely, as later dampening may cause water marks. Also iron them inside out, using a warm setting. It's easy to scorch silk or turn white silks yellow by using too hot an iron.

Press the Point

❖ Iron woolen items when they're dry, but use a pressing cloth. Take a piece of old white cotton sheeting or a man's white handkerchief, wet it thoroughly and wring it out. Place it on top of the item to be pressed, then set the iron (heated to the wool setting) on top of it. This steams out the wrinkles. Do not rub the iron back and forth as you would on cotton. Instead, keep lifting it and setting it down on an adjacent spot until you have pressed the entire garment. (When you've used up all the wet areas of the pressing cloth, wet it again and repeat the process.)

❖ To press the pleats in a wool skirt, position a couple of the pleats on the ironing board and pin them to the board at the base of each pleat. Press, using a damp pressing cloth. Remove the pins, move to the next pair of pleats and repeat the process.

Iron Rule

❖ If a silk necktie takes a crease down near the point, it's easy enough to remove it by coming in from behind with a dry iron on a low setting. But never, ever iron a whole tie. The reason? If you iron knife edges into the sides of a tie, it won't give you a nice, full, soft knot.

Quit while You're Ahead

❖ If you want your synthetic-fabric shirts and blouses to last, stop ironing as soon as you feel the slightest resistance between the iron and the fabric. If the iron feels sticky and sluggish instead of gliding smoothly across the garment, it means that the heat setting

---

BUY IT TO LAST

Fit to Be Tied

IF YOU WANT a necktie that will last and always give you a full, shapely knot, turn the tie over and take a peek inside before you buy. A silk tie should have a strip of loosely woven wool serving as an inside lining. This will give it bulk and allow it to be knotted without looking skimpy or pulling out of shape. (This is not necessary for all-wool knitted ties or for very expensive "sevenfold" ties, in which extra layers of silk provide the heft.) Another thing to look for is loose handbasting, rather than tight machine stitching, where the tie is sewn together at the back. Ties that are hand-sewn in this fashion are less likely to pull out of shape with repeated tying and untying.

---

is too high and the fabric is actually beginning to melt. Follow the heat/fabric guidelines on your iron, but don't trust them blindly. The first time you iron a new synthetic, test-press a spot that won't show.

STORAGE

Don't Pack the Bugs a Lunch

❖ It's best to skip the starch altogether, but if you're not willing to do that, at least hold off on starching until you pull seasonal garments out of storage. Moth larvae, silverfish and other hungry insect pests are often more attracted by the condiments than the main dish. This means that you shouldn't store any item that's been starched. Starch, after all, is a food-based product (usually corn), and it's so tasty that the bugs will keep nibbling into the cotton or linen that accompanies it.

That Moth-Eaten Look

THERE ARE TWO common myths about moths and clothing. The first is that adult moths feed on textiles, and the second is that they eat only woolens. Actually, it is moth larvae that nibble holes in our clothes. And their tastes are diverse: the larvae of the culprit species will feast not only on wool but also on cotton, fur, feathers and even many synthetics that have been put into storage while still soiled.

And there's the key to saving your clothes from moths: nothing should go into storage that isn't spotlessly clean. (The moths feed on the dirt, then move on to the clothes.) Beyond simple cleanliness, it also makes sense to store clothes in a mothproof environment, such as a cedar chest or closet, or packed with mothballs or moth flakes. If storage space is at a premium, you don't have to go to such lengths or put up with the airing out that clothing stored with mothballs requires. Just hang your clean woolens in the closet where you keep your warm-weather clothes. The circulation of air and constant movement of garments that take place as you use the closet and its contents will likely discourage moths from setting up housekeeping and raising their families inside.

It's in the Bag

❖ To store a white dress, jacket or pair of trousers, place the item on a clothes hanger and protect it from dust and dirt with an opaque paper cover. Better laundries can provide these covers, but if yours can't, use rolls of brown package wrapping paper to create your own. Just roll out a piece a little bit wider than the garment and double its length. Fold it in the middle width-wise and make a hole for the hanger in the middle of the crease. Plastic dry cleaners' bags are suitable coverings if the item will not be exposed to light during storage, but if there's any question, go with the paper. The combination of a plastic cover and the sun's rays is a sure recipe for yellowing.

❖ Where high humidity is a problem, you're always better off with cloth storage bags for both white and colored clothing. They allow greater air circulation and reduce the risk of mold and mildew.

More Harm Than Good

❖ You may enjoy the scent that dried-flower sachets or potpourris give your linen drawers, but use the stuff only with items that you take out, wear and launder regularly— not with clothing or other textiles that will be stored for a long time. Oils from the dried flowers can eat away at adjacent fabrics.

Ah, the Fresh Scent of an Irish Spring

❖ As an alternative to expensive sachets and those all-too-fragrant mothballs, try leaving odds and ends of unwrapped bar soap in your dresser drawers. The soap will deter moths from getting at your fine woolens, and it will keep your clothing smelling fresh, too.

Save the Dress for Your Daughter's Wedding

❖ The best place to store valuable textiles is in a cool, dark, dry place such as the back of a closet. Keep them out of basements and attics. Heat and humidity will encourage mildew and eventually weaken the fabric, as will prolonged exposure to sunlight.

Look for More Than the Union Label

IF YOU WANT clothing that will last, it pays to shop with an eye toward more than price and style. Certain garment construction techniques can make the difference between long life and a quick trip to the ragbag. You'll fare better if you check out the following:

Fabric. The tighter the weave or knit, the longer the garment will wear.

Stitching. The stitches that hold a garment together should be even, with no puckers, gathering, broken stitches or "wandering" of the stitch off the true line that holds the goods together or creates a proper hem. As a general rule, the better the quality of a garment, the closer together the stitches will be. Ideally, any rough

A safety stitch along the raw edges of a garment is a sign of quality.

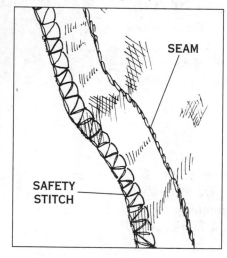

SEAM

SAFETY
STITCH

edges of fabric should be finished with a safety stitch to prevent unraveling.

Interlinings and interfacings. At places in a garment that require additional stiffening or support, such as collars or shoulders, the fabric used for this interlining or interfacing should be stitched, not glued or fused, to the primary fabric if the construction is going to hold up through repeated washings.

Buttons. Four holes for the thread that holds on buttons are better than two, unless it's a coat or sweater button with a single loop in back. There should be no loose threads hanging from buttons. If there are, you'll be sewing the buttons back on before long. Buttons should be sewn through at least two layers of fabric. And buttonholes should be finished smoothly and evenly, with no ragged edges.

Reinforcements. Make sure that stress points are properly reinforced. On shirts and blouses, look for double rows of stitching at armholes, cuffs and other stress points. Feel to make sure that the arm material extends at least half an inch inside the cuffs. Pocket openings—especially side pockets on slacks—should be reinforced at the top and bottom with bar stitches, heavy "bars" of stitching about one-quarter inch long.

If You Decide to Put Off Rehemming That Gown

❖ If there are any pins or brooches on a garment you're about to place in storage, take them off and store them separately. Similarly, do not place common pins in fine fabric and then store the piece with the pins in place. The pins are likely to rust and stain the material.

STAINS

But First, Get a Bandage

❖ Bloodstains can be difficult to remove if they aren't attended to promptly. The first line of defense is to soak the soiled fabric in a solution of ½ teaspoon of salt per 1 cup of cold water, rubbing as necessary until the stain has faded. Then wash as you normally would.

❖ Older bloodstains call for an initial soaking in a solution of 2 tablespoons of ammonia per 1 gallon of cold water. Wash in cold water and dishwashing liquid to remove any vestiges of the stain left after the ammonia treatment.

❖ If the bloodstain is on a large article, such as a blanket, that you don't want to soak completely, make a paste of cornstarch and water and slather it onto the stain. Let it dry, brush it off and keep repeating until the stain has disappeared.

A SECOND LIFE

Time to Reboot

YOU'LL GET longer life out of kids' winter boots if you buy the kind that have removable felt liners. When the child outgrows the boots, remove the liners. The boots will have a new lease on life for muddy-day wear in spring and fall, when the extra insulation isn't needed.

Your Own Hot Niagara

❖ Fresh coffee and tea stains call for the "hot waterfall" approach. First, stretch the stained part of the fabric over a bowl, as if you were putting a head on a drum, and secure it with a rubber band. Then pour boiling water over the stain from a height of two to three feet. Be careful not to burn yourself! Wash the article as you normally would, using a small amount of bleach if the fabric can tolerate it.

❖ The hot waterfall also works to loosen fruit and berry stains that haven't been allowed to set, and it works with red wine if you first sprinkle a little salt on the stain. (Never mind the old chestnut about pouring white wine on a red wine stain. Why waste good white wine?)

Then Turn to the Bigger Problem

❖ You can usually get lipstick stains out of fabric by rubbing the stained area with peanut butter. Before the peanut butter dries, wash the fabric with warm water and dishwashing liquid.

If You Wrote the Test Answers on Your Shirt Cuff

❖ Ballpoint ink stains on fabric will often yield to aerosol hair spray. Put a piece of scrap fabric beneath the stained spot to blot any ink that may come through. Then spray the stain evenly from four to six inches away. Blot the top surface of the stained article after spraying. You may have to repeat the process a couple of times. Finally, give the garment a regular laundering—if it's washable.

Oh, No! That Was Yaz's Autograph!

❖ Hair spray also will work to remove ballpoint ink stains from leather. Saturate the stain, let the spray dry and then brush lightly with a solution of equal parts white vinegar and water.

Your Jacket Looks Really Slick

❖ An alternative approach to removing ballpoint ink stains from leather is to coat them with petroleum jelly. You may need to leave the jelly on the stain for several days before wiping it off.

They Were Old Family Moths

A PROMINENT Massachusetts politician, the member of an old Boston Brahmin family, once carried the idea of "making it last" to what may be its most extreme degree. While donning a tuxedo that had served several generations of men in his family, he noticed a couple of moth holes in the upper part of the trousers. Undaunted—though he could have afforded to have Brooks Brothers rush him a new tux by messenger service—he took a black marker and colored in the area on his white underwear that would have been exposed by the holes. Now *that's* Yankee frugality.

After the Easter Bunny Visits

❖ Chocolate stains don't have to spell doom for fabrics that aren't already dyed brown. Just scrub the stained area immediately with ammonia, then wash as you normally would.

Grease Release

❖ Scrub grease stains on washable fabrics with a lather of laundry detergent and water. Distilled water works best for this, since "soft" water cuts grease better than water having a high mineral content.

The Stains That Made Milwaukee Famous

❖ If spilled beer has dried onto clothing or tablecloths, mix up a solution of equal parts vinegar and dishwashing liquid, then sponge it onto the stain. Rinse with warm water and launder as usual.

Wax Facts

❖ Small spots of hardened candle wax can be removed from tablecloths by rubbing with a generous dollop of vegetable oil. Wipe off any excess oil, then launder as usual.

❖ Another way to remove small amounts of wax hardened onto a tablecloth is to spread the affected area over a large bowl and secure it with rubber bands, then pour boiling water over the wax to melt it. Follow up by washing the tablecloth as usual.

❖ For larger wax deposits on tablecloths, first scrape off the excess with a dull knife, then place the stained area between two paper towels and press with an iron on a low setting. Replace the paper towels as the wax is absorbed into them, then launder when the paper no longer absorbs wax. (If the fabric is one that's especially sensitive to heat, avoid burning it by holding the iron a couple of inches

PUZZLER

WHEN WET WEATHER WAS AFOOT, this helped keep things warm and dry to boot.

ANSWER: Boot dryer. The person with the wet feet would place this on the stove with the boots mounted over the two spouts. The heat was thus directed to the insides of the footwear.

above the towels. You'll still get enough heat to melt the wax.)

An Idea You Can Sink Your (False) Teeth Into

❖ Yellow-stained fabric can often be revived with ordinary denture-cleaning tablets. Get a container large enough to hold the stained item—or at least the stained portion—and fill it with warm water. Add the denture tablets in the ratio recommended on the package, let them dissolve and immerse the fabric. Soak until the spots disappear.

Get the Lead Out

❖ It almost sounds too simple, but marks on fabric made by pencil lead—which is actually graphite—can usually be removed by gentle rubbing with a clean pencil eraser. Avoid ink erasers, which may be too abrasive for delicate fabrics.

This Will Do for Mildew

❖ To get rid of the black or gray stains caused by mildew, try moistening the stained area with lemon juice and salt, then drying the fabric in the sun. If this doesn't work, sponge the stain with hydrogen peroxide and sun-dry it.

❖ If you have a leather item stained with the powdery traces of surface mildew, wipe the affected area with a solution of equal parts rubbing alcohol and water. When the leather is dry, treat it with a conditioner such as neat's-foot oil or castor oil (use the latter if you want to be able to shine the item).

Good-Bye, Old Paint

❖ The first rule for treating paint stains—whether oil- or water-based—is to get to them before they have time to dry. For oil paints and varnishes, first scrape off any excess, then sponge the still-wet stain with whatever solvent

---

COMMON MISTAKES

Caution! Chlorine and Ammonia Don't Mix

I F YOU'RE puttering around trying to remove a troublesome stain, don't *ever* try a combination that mixes chlorine bleach with ammonia, lye, rust remover or vinegar. Such a mixture—or one involving chlorine bleach and oven or toilet-bowl cleaners—can create a deadly poisonous gas.

is recommended on the paint can, or with turpentine. Before the solvent dries, soak the stain in a concentrated solution of dishwashing liquid and water, then wash the item separately with laundry detergent. Repeat as many times as necessary.

❖ Water-based latex paints present less of a problem and will usually wash out with soap and water. But if you let any paint stains dry—well, now you've got clothing to paint in.

Eggs-ackly

❖ Egg stains aren't as awful as they're made out to be if you remember two things: first, attack them when they're fresh; second, don't use hot water—it will set the stain. Just scrape off the excess with a dull knife, then soak the stain in cold water. Launder as you usually would. If it's

To Restring Beads, Haul Out the Vacuum Cleaner

IT'S EASY TO RESTRING a broken string of beads. But first you have to pick up the beads, and the easiest way to do that is with your vacuum cleaner.

This is not as crazy as it sounds. You'll also need some old panty hose. First, remove the head from the end of your vacuum cleaner hose. Cut one leg off the panty hose and slip the "stocking" over the vacuum's hose. Now turn on the vacuum cleaner. The beads will be sucked toward the vacuum hose, but the panty hose will prevent them from being sucked into the vacuum cleaner. Simply gather the beads and put them in a container.

I've also used the vacuum cleaner in this way to pick up other small objects that are hard to handle or in places that are hard to reach.

EARL
remembers...

an article that requires dry cleaning, sponge the stain with cold water and take it to the dry cleaner without delay.

That Infamous Collar Ring

❖ Dark soil lines along the collar fold of a light-colored cotton dress shirt or blouse shouldn't mean that the garment has to be retired. Try drawing a heavy line over the stain with a piece of chalk, then let it set. The next day, launder as usual.

No Sweat

❖ If perspiration has stained a garment, you may be able to restore the color by sponging the spot with vinegar, then rinsing it in cold water.

Start from Scratch

❖ You can often get rid of small water marks on silk neckties by scratching gently with your fingernail. Working outward from the center of the stain toward its edges, scratch quickly and lightly back and forth in the same direction as the weave. Make sure your nail doesn't have any jagged edges, or you can pull a thread loose from the fabric.

Salt and Vinegar—
Not Just for French Fries

❖ The best way to get rid of white salt stains on leather boots or shoes is to sponge them off with a solution of three parts water and one part vinegar. As soon as the stains are gone, dry the leather with a clean cloth and polish as usual.

Works on Blue Suede Shoes, Too

❖ Stains on suede shoes will often yield to rubbing with an art gum eraser. For more persistent stains, try an emery board. Afterward, go over the entire shoe with a suede brush. If you don't have a brush, use a sheet of fine-grit sandpaper and a light touch.

A SECOND LIFE

For Old-Car Buffs

I T'S HARD TO FIND a better car-buffing cloth than a rag cut from an old sweatshirt or pair of sweatpants, turned inside out.

Clothing, Accessories
and Household
Linens

❖

Don't Let Them Go to Waist

❖ If the drawstring has broken on a pair of sweatpants or pajamas, or on a hooded shirt or jacket, don't toss out the garment. First, pull out the fragments of the old drawstring. Replace it with a woven bootlace of the proper length (make sure there's enough extra to tie a knot). To insert the lace, make a loop at one end of a straightened wire coat hanger. Tie one end of the lace to the loop and feed the hanger through one opening in the garment till it comes out the other. If the hard plastic ends of the bootlace are uncomfortable, just cut them off and tie tight overhand knots at the ends so that the lace won't unravel.

A Slippery Trick

❖ Before giving up on a stuck zipper, try rubbing a bar of soap, a wax candle or a bar of paraffin into the jammed components. With a little more manipulation, the zipper may yield once the coating begins to act as a lubricant.

Here's the Hook

❖ A crochet hook can be a sweater's best friend. When your sweater catches a snag and a loop of yarn is pulled out of place, carefully take off the garment and work the crochet hook through the knitting from behind, next to the pull. If it's a small pull, often all you'll have to do is draw it back to the inside of the sweater. For a big pull, snip the yarn at the center of the loop and use the hook to draw the two pieces to the inside, separated by a couple of strands of undisturbed yarn. Then carefully tie the two pieces together (don't pull the knot too tight), use a large needle to weave the ends back into the stitching and snip away any excess.

PUZZLER

IT LOOKS LIKE A CHRISTMAS DECoration, but it really was quite functional in the laundry room.

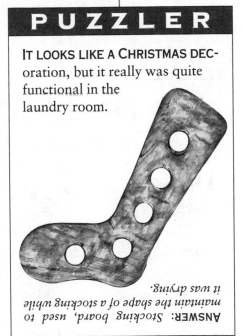

ANSWER: Stocking board, used to maintain the shape of a stocking while it was drying.

Stop That Run!

❖ When a run starts in a pair of panty hose, you can extend the nylon's life until you get home by dabbing a tiny drop of clear nail polish onto the top and bottom of the run. (It's especially important to cover the top, since that's the point at which most runs continue to grow.) The polish will harden and seal the run so that it can't expand. If the run is in an inconspicuous place, such as the sole of the foot, you may be able to get another day or two of wear out of the panty hose. Otherwise this is a short-term solution, because the polish will show as white after you remove the hose.

❖ Another short-term way to keep a run in panty hose from expanding is to give it a good dose of hair spray. Like the nail polish, the spray will dry clear but harden over the nylon.

I Can See Clearly Now

SUNLIGHT IS THE ENEMY of fabric, and I can prove it. I love the huge south-facing windows in my living room, but it didn't take long for the sun streaming through them to fade the fabric on my couch.

But not my drapes. I hung the drapes so that when they're pulled back, they're against the wall, free of the window, and the sun doesn't touch them. Beyond making my drapes last longer, this has another advantage: the full view of the window is revealed. I don't have any neighbors in sight of my house, so I don't need my drapes for privacy.

If I have a four-foot window, I want a four-foot view.

E A R L
remembers...

12 Uses for Dead Panty Hose

NO FRUGAL YANKEE would ever throw out old panty hose just because the hose had a run or two. Heaven forbid! If you have a drawerful of clean but damaged nylons, consider these possibilities:

1. Keep a pair in the trunk of your car. They don't take up much space and will serve you well as an emergency replacement for a broken engine belt.

2. Use panty hose to store Vidalia onions, which are not available year-round and are often bought in quantity. Cut the legs off the hose and knot one end. Then drop the onions in, one by one, tying a knot in the hose after each one. (The knots will separate the onions and allow air circulation, thus keeping them usable longer.) Hang the string of onions in the pantry for ready access.

3. Cut off a section, tie one end, fill it with freshly ground uncooked coffee and tie the other end. Place the filled section in a car ashtray, a dresser drawer or any other spot that you want to deodorize without spilling the loose grounds.

4. Cut strips that you can use to tie up plants. The nylon is much gentler than string on the plant stems.

5. Use them as part of a scarecrow. Stuff the panty part with hay, then glue on felt eyes, nose and mouth. Pass the legs of the hose through the belt loops on the scarecrow's pants, thus securing his head in place.

6. Turn them into Halloween masks. As bank robbers know, nylons will distort facial features so that a child is unrecognizable, but he will still be able to see the treats being offered.

7. Fill a section with soap scraps and use the whole thing as a sort of soap mitt. This allows you to use up the very last of the soap.

8. Remove the strings from an old tennis racquet. Stretch the end of one hose leg over the racquet and attach it to the frame to make a butterfly or minnow net.

9. Use old panty hose to buff freshly polished shoes. They'll leave a great shine.

10. Pack the leg with ice and tie it to an injured limb as an ice pack.

11. Use them to strain old paint, removing any lumps or debris that would otherwise mar your paint job.

12. Cut up scraps of old panty hose slightly larger than the tops of the jars in which your child stores his or her bug collection. Once the bugs are inside, cover the jars with the bits of nylon. Secure the material with rubber bands. The small mesh of the nylons will allow air, but not creepy crawlies, to pass through.

Off with Their Legs!

❖ When one leg of a pair of panty hose is damaged beyond repair, don't throw out the whole thing. Instead, cut off the unsalvageable leg. Do the same with another pair, then wear both panties—each with one leg attached—at the same time.

Down at the Heels

❖ If you wait too long to have the heels replaced on your shoes, the altered angle at which your foot strikes the ground will permanently distort the counter, or back, of the shoe. Have heels replaced as soon as their edges become sloped and rounded. It's cheap insurance for a major investment.

Adding a rubber insert to the heel is a good way to extend the life of a leather shoe.

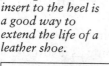

RUBBER
INSERT

Time Wounds All Heels

❖ If you like leather heels on your shoes, make them last longer by having your shoe repair person install heels that have a rubber bottom or a rubber insert along the outer rear edge of the heel. If you have these rubber components replaced before wear hits the leather part of the heel, your heels will last longer and repairs will be less expensive.

HOUSEHOLD LINENS

So They Don't Just Fade Away

❖ All curtains and drapes eventually fade, especially if they're on a side of the house exposed to strong sunlight. To keep the fading even and make the curtains last longer, swap them once in a while from one side of the window to the other. That way, the area that was against the wall will be exposed, and the area that was in the sun will get some rest.

❖ If your curtains are Cape Cod style or any other type that has decoration along one edge, you won't be able to swap the curtains from one side of the window to the other. But you can rotate them from one window to another. This is worth trying, especially in a room that has windows on more than one wall. Swapping the curtains occasionally means that the same fabric is not always hanging in the window that gets the most light, and this will extend its life.

Bedspread Grooming

❖ After washing and drying a tufted chenille bedspread, put it back on the bed and fluff up the tufts by going over them with a clean, dry whisk broom. There's no need for ironing, which will only flatten the tufts.

An Old-Time Secret

❖ If linen has yellowed, wash it with dishwashing liquid, Woolite or Ivory Snow, then rinse it well. While it's still wet, place it outside on a white cloth in bright sunlight for natural bleaching action. Years ago, New England weavers bleached their linen by setting it out when there was fresh snow on the ground. The white snow enhanced the brightness of the sun and its bleaching action. If you live out in the country where the snow is really white—and stays that way for more than a few minutes—go ahead and follow the old-timers' example.

Don't Throw In the Towel

❖ You can make your terrycloth bath towels last a lot longer by cutting down on the amount of time they spend in the washer and dryer. Instead of laundering them after every use, try switching to a once-a-week routine.

Get Down

JUST BECAUSE the cloth covering on a down quilt or comforter has gotten old and shabby, there's no reason to throw out the down. Put a new bag in your vacuum cleaner, open a seam on the comforter and vacuum out the down. It will probably take more than one vacuum bag to gather all the down, and you'll have to open several seams if the down was contained within separate baffled channels in the old comforter. Store the down in a big plastic bag—be careful not to compress it so tightly that the bag has no give when you poke it—and use it if you have a new comforter made.

When filling a garment or comforter with down, be careful not to overstuff it. When compressed too densely, it will lose rather than gain insulating ability, since it's the trapped air and not the tiny feathers themselves that keep you warm. You should be able to flatten the down-filled article with your open hand without too much pressure, but it should immediately fluff right back up to its original thickness when released.

Furniture

A YANKEE READER ONCE WROTE to me about a chair he'd seen with an imprint on the back saying "Made from Salvaged Pine, 1941." "What did they mean by 'salvaged'?" the reader wanted to know.

I responded that if the chair was built in 1941, the lumber was probably from trees salvaged after the Hurricane of 1938. The hurricane knocked down trees all over New England. For more than a year after it struck, logging crews worked full-time cutting the trees into logs and getting the logs into water to prevent them from rotting. I remember lakes and rivers choked with logs for years after that hurricane. Gradually, the demand for lumber depleted the floating reserves, but you could often find clues as to where the salvaged wood had been used. The water stained the pine unevenly, so most of the salvaged pine that ended up in furniture was stained dark or painted.

It was an enormous effort to harvest all the trees that blew down in that hurricane. But we frugal New Englanders couldn't stand the idea of all that valuable timber rotting on the ground. Similarly, it goes against the grain today for us to think of furniture being discarded before its time. So in the following pages, we'll tell you how to use items already in your cupboards and closets to extend the life of your tables, chairs and chests of drawers. Pull out the bar soap and the toothpaste, the instant coffee and the pastry skewers—and read on!

MAINTAINING WOODEN FURNITURE

Watch Out for Bleached Blonds

❖ Place your wooden chair, table, sideboard, entertainment center or the like away from direct sunlight so that the furniture will maintain an even color and not bleach out.

Positioning Is Everything

❖ Position your wooden furniture away from any hot-air registers, radiators or other heat sources. This will help keep it from cracking or warping. If you absolutely have to place that chair or bench next to a heat source, fasten blocks of wood or screw molding to the floor to keep the chair from sliding up too close to the heat.

❖ Place your wooden furniture away from a humidifier or vaporizer (either the warm-air or the cold-air type). Prolonged exposure to the jets of damp air will cause the wood to blacken with mildew.

An Open-and-Shut Case

❖ When you open a drawer, use both hands to keep the drawer straight. This will keep both the drawer and the cavity in good shape.

Carry with Care

❖ When moving a piece of wooden furniture, carry it by the frame, which is the strongest part of the piece. Tip a chair on its side (horizontal to the floor) and hold two legs just below the seat, with the bottom portion of the legs jutting out in front of you. That way, you won't bump into things and damage the piece.

If you lift your wooden furniture this way, you'll be able to hold onto it longer.

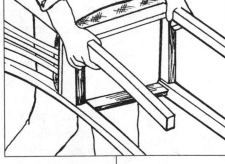

❖ If your bureau is too heavy to lift by the base, take out a few drawers and try again. If the piece is simply too bulky to maneuver by the base, remove all the drawers and grab onto the frame farther up. Don't try to lift the piece by the top board, which could separate from the frame.

Don't Twist and Turn

❖ When you set a piece of wooden furniture down, make sure all four legs touch the floor at once. This prevents the frame from twisting, which weakens wood and joints.

Do Slip and Slide

❖ If you're trying to move a heavy piece by yourself—or if the piece is too bulky even for two people to carry—lift one end of the furniture at a time and slip a drop cloth underneath the piece. Then slide the piece across the floor by pulling on the drop cloth. This not only helps you move the furniture properly but also protects the floor from dings or scratches. (This works on bare wood or linoleum floors or on tightly woven, dense carpet. Don't try it on shag carpet, and certainly not on an antique or braided rug.)

Move It Out

❖ When transporting a wooden cupboard by vehicle, fasten rope or webbing across the doors of the cupboard to keep them from flying open. To keep the rope or webbing from abrading the finish on the corners of your cupboard, slip cardboard between the rope and the wooden corners.

Maintain a Temperate Temperature

❖ Monitor the temperature and humidity in your house and use an air conditioner in summer if humidity is high. In winter, use a humidifier, set on low, to add a small amount of moisture to the air. Your home isn't a museum. But keeping the temperature and humidity constant will lengthen the life of all your furniture, particularly the wooden pieces. Dry winter air shrinks the wood, causing glued joints to loosen. In summer, humidity makes the wood expand. Drawers stick, and table leaves warp.

Through the Looking Glass

❖ To protect a fine table while still using it, have a piece of glass cut to fit the top. You can see the fine wood through the glass, and it's easy to keep the glass clean. Try this with desks, too. In this case, you can use the glass as a giant paperweight to anchor photos or essential notes where you can see them and they won't get lost.

BUY IT TO LAST

The Wooden Furniture Checklist

YOU'RE IN the market for wooden furniture. You have a budget, but you want to get the best—and longest-lasting—furniture your money will buy. How can you tell the good stuff from the bad?

Start with the wood. Good furniture is made of solid wood. Cherry, maple, oak, mahogany and pine are the most common. Cherry and maple are the hardest; pine is the softest, the most vulnerable to nicks and scratches. Much new furniture comprises several pieces of wood laminated together, which is sometimes more stable than a single, solid piece of wood.

Check the hardware. The way a piece of wooden furniture is held together tells you a lot about how long it will last. Antiques and finer furniture are usually joined by some combination of mortise and tenon, dovetailing (in drawers) and dowels (to hold chair rungs in place). Most new furniture is joined by— in descending order of quality— pegs, screws, nails or staples. These features help hold the furniture together when the wood expands and contracts due to climate changes. A good piece should be screwed and glued together. If a table has a metal brace holding the legs to the underside of the top, the brace should be anchored by nuts and bolts.

Inspect the drawer pulls. Make sure the metal is heavy enough not to bend. Details on the drawer pulls of better pieces are cast, not stamped.

Try moving the moving parts. A quality chest has a separate wooden cavity for each drawer, with "guides" on the bottom or side of each cavity. Drawers should glide easily in and out of their cavities. Open and close doors, lift and lower table leaves and pull out adjustable shelves to make sure they function properly. On pieces with paneled doors (such as armoires, entertainment centers and other cupboards), the panel should "float" in a mortise-and-tenoned frame instead of being glued. That way, expansion and contraction from temperature and humidity changes won't blow apart the door.

Finish with the finish. Beware of streaks, globs of finish or lack of uniformity in color. These tell you either that the finish is of poor quality or that it was applied poorly— or both.

CLEANING WOODEN FURNITURE

Take a Shine to It

❖ If your wooden furniture has a finish such as wax or varnish, clean it every few months with lemon oil (which is actually scented mineral oil). Slightly moisten a rag such as a soft T-shirt or an old cloth diaper with water, then add a little oil. Rub the rag over the furniture to pick up dust. Buff the surface well so that you leave a minimum of residue.

Brighter Is Better

❖ To clean wooden furniture with a dull or discolored shellac finish, use a solution of equal parts mineral oil, turpentine and white vinegar. Rub the solution in with a sponge, then wipe it off with a clean rag. As you work, continually stir or shake the solution to keep it well mixed.

Old Paint Can Live Again

❖ If you like the paint on an old piece of furniture but it appears a bit worn (and you don't want to repaint or refinish the piece), rub a little mineral oil into it. This will get rid of caked-on dust and brighten up the color.

❖ An alternative way to clean a painted piece is to wash it with mild dishwashing liquid.

Tear Down the Polish Buildup

❖ To clean oily buildup resulting from polishing, rub the piece twice with turpentine on a clean rag. Shift the rag periodically so that you are using a clean patch of it. If the whole rag becomes dirty, switch to a new one.

Don't Come Unhinged

❖ To remove wax buildup from the hinges of your furniture, use an artist's brush to paint turpentine onto the hinges (don't let the brush wander onto the wood). Then wipe the hinges with a damp cloth. Cleaning the hinges will keep them working properly.

❖ You can also remove wax buildup from hinges by scrubbing them with a small steel wool soap pad. (Be careful not to scrape the adjoining wood.) Again, wipe the hinges clean with a damp cloth.

Don't Let That Armchair Be a Drag

❖ If your wooden chairs are in a room with a waxed floor, wax the bottoms of the chairs' feet so that they slide eas-

The Knotty Spruce Mantel

ONE TIME MY BROTHER had a job as foreman on a team that was constructing a new house, and he asked me to take over for him while he went on vacation. When I arrived on the site, the mason was laying up a large natural-stone fireplace. The owner wanted to use an 8- by 8-inch timber as a mantelpiece. So I told the mason to cement two 6-inch bolts in the chimney when he reached the right height for the mantel.

EARL
remembers...

After the mason finished building the chimney, we mounted the spruce timber on the bolts, securing it with additional big bolts set beneath the surface of the wood. When the mantel was in place, the owner and I stepped back to review the work. He loved the mantel but didn't like the look of the bolt holes. I assured him that I wasn't done yet. I found two big knots in a pine board and carefully knocked them out. Then I chiseled away at the bolt holes until the pine knots plugged them perfectly. When the mantel was finished, there was no way to tell how it was supported.

That man has the only spruce mantel I know of that has pine knots in it!

ily along the floor. This protects both the chair and the floor.

When the Candle Drips on the Table

❖ To get candle wax off your wooden tabletop, gently scrape or peel up as much as you can get without gouging the wood. Then use a hand-held hair dryer to soften the wax that's left. Hold the dryer several inches away from the wax so that the wax doesn't heat up too much. (Otherwise it will actually adhere to the wood.) Once the wax is soft, blot it with a paper towel. Repeat if necessary.

❖ You can also use an iron to remove candle wax from wooden furniture. Again, gently scrape as much wax as you can from the wood. Then place three or four layers of paper towels or brown paper bags on top of the remaining wax. Hold a hot iron over the layers of paper, but don't touch the iron to the paper (the heat could burn right through the finish on the wood). As the wax melts, the paper will absorb it. Repeat if necessary.

When the Tablecloth Sticks

❖ Rub a liberal amount of mayonnaise over flannel that has come off the back of a tablecloth or table pad and stuck to your tabletop. Let the mayonnaise sink in for about an hour, then wipe up the muck with a clean paper or cloth towel.

White-Out

❖ White spots that appear on the surface of wooden furniture are caused by moisture. To remove such a spot, dip a piece of extra-fine-grade steel wool in mineral oil. Rub the steel wool back

---

Sleep Tight; Don't Let the Bedbugs Bite!

D URING THE eighteenth century, a typical bed was made of a wooden frame, across which ropes were stretched to support a mattress. Rope beds were more comfortable when the ropes were stretched taut. Thus instead of wishing loved ones "sweet dreams," people said "Sleep tight," an expression still used today.

Although wealthier classes filled their mattresses and pillows with feathers (a mattress could hold 70 pounds of down), average folks stuffed their bedding with straw and other dried grasses. Rodents and insects made nests inside the mattresses, which had to be emptied, aired out and refilled at least once a year. Hence the caution as someone shuffled off to bed, "Don't let the bedbugs bite!"

and forth over the stain—always rubbing with the grain of the wood—to distribute the oil liberally. By doing this, you will actually remove the finish in the area that has whitened. The soft abrasion of the steel wool will polish the revealed surface while removing the spot, concealing the fact that the area is now unfinished. You may want to follow up by applying a paste wax and buffing the spot.

❖ If a white stain is small and does not appear too deep, use your finger to gently rub a little toothpaste into it, then wipe the area clean. (Don't use the gel type; you need the abrasive effect of the toothpaste.)

❖ Another way to remove white stains from wooden furniture is to apply baking soda to them with a damp cloth, then wipe off the soda.

Oak Furniture: Kill the High-Water Mark

❖ Paint remover and a bleach solution can do a good job of taking out the dark, gray-black stains that appear on oak furniture as a result of either direct exposure to water or prolonged exposure to water vapor (such as from a humidifier). First apply paint remover to lift off the finish. Then mix up a solution of equal parts household (5 percent) bleach and water. Apply the solution to the stain with a brush (if the stain is large) or a clean rag (if the stain is small). Use the bleach solution on the stained area only, being careful not to let it bleed onto the good wood.

Erase Crayon Marks

❖ To remove crayon marks from your wooden furniture, rub mayonnaise into the affected area. Let it soak in for a few minutes, then rub the area clean with a damp cloth.

❖ You can also use dry laundry starch (available at supermarkets) to remove crayon marks. Mix the starch with water according to the package instructions. Apply the

PUZZLER

ITS NAME RHYMES WITH *gorp* and sounds a bit like a spider. When used correctly, this tool added another level of comfort to furniture.

ANSWER: *Scorp, or scorpen, which craftspeople used to hollow the seats on plank-bottomed chairs.*

mixture with a paintbrush and let it dry. Wipe the area clean with a dry cloth.

REPAIRING WOODEN FURNITURE

Get the Worms Out

❖ If you notice new punctures in a piece of wooden furniture and telltale wood powder around it, or if you actually hear a crunching sound, your furniture may be infested with woodworms. To solve the problem, place the affected piece outdoors or in a well-ventilated room. With a nail file, gently dig into and clean out the hole. If you hit

Get the Gist of Joints

FURNITURE IS held together by joints—the points at which the different pieces are attached with wood, glue or hardware (or a combination). There are many types of joints, some stronger than others. Since the strength—and ultimately the durability—of a piece of furniture often lies in the quality of its joints, it makes sense to learn what the most common types look like. All of the following wood joints are secured by glue, but some may be further reinforced by hardware.

Dowel *(A)*. Dowel joints are among the strongest. Dowels are cylindrical pieces of wood inserted into holes drilled in adjoining furniture pieces. Double-dowel joints (in which two dowels are placed side by side for extra strength) are common in high-quality upholstered furniture such as couches.

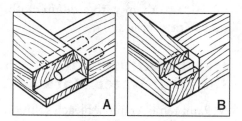

Mortise and tenon *(B)*. Also a very strong joint used in high-quality furniture. The tenon is a rectangular block inserted into the mortise, a hole of the same shape.

Spline *(C)*. A very strong joint usually found in finer old furniture. In a splined joint, a projection runs the entire length of a piece of wood and fits into a corresponding slot in the second piece of wood.

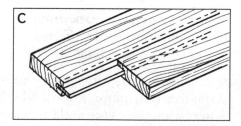

new wood powder, the worm may be nearby. If you find it, just extract it with tweezers. Then, using a medicine dropper, drip unleaded gasoline into the hole. The gasoline will kill any worms or insects and will evaporate quickly. It will not remove the finish. When the gasoline has evaporated, fill the hole with common crack filler or epoxy (the kind that takes stain or paint). Let the filling dry, then sand and stain or paint the area. Finish the job with an application of polyurethane, varnish or whatever finish is already on the rest of the piece.

Keep the Worms Out

❖ Concerned about a piece of wooden furniture that shows signs of possible past woodworm activity? If it

Dovetail *(D)*. There are many types of dovetails, but the basic idea consists of a fin-shaped projection that fits into a corresponding socket in another piece of wood for an especially strong joint. Often found in well-constructed drawers, dovetails usually require no extra support.

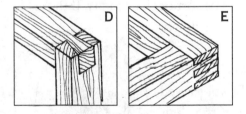

Slip or lock corner *(E)*. A squared-off modification of the dovetail, but not nearly as strong.

Blocked *(F)*. A joint in which a third block joins and supports the two pieces of wood to be attached.

Miter *(G)*. A diagonal cut at the ends of two pieces of wood to be joined (as at the corner of a picture frame).

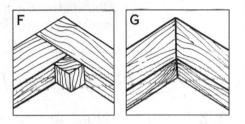

Butt—end to end *(H)*. Two boards fastened end to end with glue. If the boards are thick enough, this joint can be greatly strengthened with dowels.

Butt—end to side *(I)*. The end of one board fastened to the side of another with glue. Hardware such as a corner angle provides further support. Insertion of dowels gives this joint its optimum strength.

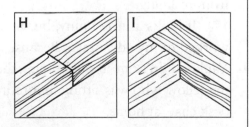

doesn't need refinishing or repair for any other reason, you can avoid further woodworm attacks with a mild preventive measure. Ask an antiques dealer, hardware store clerk or janitorial supply company for an insecticide that can be sprayed on furniture. Then use the product regularly, according to the instructions.

Sticky Drawers

❖ If a drawer sticks, rub the sides and bottom edge with a bar of soap. This should help it open and close more easily.

Sticky Doors

❖ If a cabinet door sticks, lift a corner of the piece and see if that allows the door to work more smoothly. If so, slide a shim (a thin piece of wood, cardboard or like material) under the corner of the piece to level it.

How I Kept My Seat

WHEN I RAN the maintenance department at Yankee, I had the worst desk chair. It had a pedestal base with four legs instead of the five that are common in this sort of chair today. If those legs were in the wrong position when I reclined, over I'd go.

The chair was comfortable enough when it was upright, so I decided to fix it. First I moved the pedestal base so that the weight of the chair was farther forward. Then I screwed a section of two-by-four into the back of the chair to keep it from reclining.

It looks a little funny, but in a way that's worked to my advantage. Because of its looks, Yankee didn't care about keeping the chair after

EARL
remembers...

the fellow who was sitting in it retired. It still serves me well as my desk chair at home.

❖ Sometimes a cabinet door will stick because moisture in the room has caused its wood to expand. To correct this problem, move the cabinet to a warm, dry spot in the house. The wood should contract again, improving the door's performance. When you return the piece to its original place, try to reduce the moisture and temperature changes in its environment.

Try This before You Refinish

❖ You can rub out surface scratches in your wooden furniture with a paste made of mineral oil and pumice (available in powder form at hardware and paint stores). Use extra-fine-grade steel wool to rub the mixture into the scratched area. Then wipe it off and buff with a dry cloth.

Scratch Cover-Ups

❖ Sometimes you can cover up a furniture scratch rather than actually removing it. Choose a wax crayon that matches the color of the finish on your scratched furniture. Color in the scratch, then rub the spot with your finger to blend the crayon with the finish.

❖ Another way to hide scratches is to cover them with an oil-based craft or artist's paint (from a tube). Choose a color that's darker than the finish on the furniture. Rub a little into the scratch, and the scratch will appear to blend in with the finish. (This will not work on furniture with a polyurethane finish.)

Paint It Perfect

❖ To hide scratches in varnished wooden furniture, apply watercolor paint to the affected area, using an artist's brush. Once a scratch is concealed, fill it in with varnish.

❖ Another solution for a scratch mark in wood is to "paint" the scratch with a brown felt-tipped marker. When the ink dries, cover the spot with wax or varnish.

Take a Coffee Break

❖ If your scratched wooden furniture has a dark stain, use instant coffee to cover the scratch. Make a thick paste of the coffee granules and water, then rub the paste into the scratch.

A Nutty Solution

❖ Use the oil from a walnut to conceal a surface scratch in wooden furniture. Crack the walnut and rub a piece of the walnut meat into the scratch. Polish the area with a soft rag, and the scratch should become invisible.

Polish Off Scuffs and Minor Scratches

❖ To freshen up wooden furniture that is scuffed or scratched, sand the damaged areas lightly with extra-fine-grade steel wool. Then apply one of the oil-based colored furniture polishes available at hardware stores. Allow the polish to dry completely (so that the oil can soak into the damaged area). If necessary, sand again lightly with the steel wool to feather in or soften the color.

Heat a Blister

❖ To flatten a blister that appears in a veneered surface, place a damp cloth over the spot and heat it with an iron turned to its lowest setting. When you feel the veneer and glue begin to soften, press down gently to move the blister back into place. Then remove the cloth and press the iron carefully on the blistered area itself. Allow the area to cool.

Metal attachments provide added support for sagging wooden shelves.

Tighten the Screws

❖ To tighten a loose screw in a piece of furniture, first re-move it. Insert wooden matchsticks or toothpicks into the hole, then replace the screw in the hole. The sticks should hold the screw tightly in place.

Shore Up Your Shelves

❖ To strengthen a shelf that is sagging (in a bookcase, for instance), screw metal supports to the underside of each end of the shelf and its corresponding upright. You can get the supports at a hardware or discount store.

Now, about That Old Playpen ...

YOU FEEL AS IF you've spent a fortune on furniture that your children will use for only a few years: changing table, toy box, child-size table and chairs, and so forth. Is there anything you can do with these pieces, short of relegating them to a yard sale? In many cases, the answer is yes, and you can approach the situation in two ways.

1. Use furniture that you already own (or buy with future uses in mind).

Instead of buying a changing table, try using a dry sink. Cut and cover a piece of foam to fit into the sink, where you will change the baby. Store diapers and other paraphernalia in drawers or on cupboard shelves below.

Instead of buying a child-size table, use a coffee table or a large container with a lid (one parent uses the empty metal bucket that once contained popcorn).

For a toy chest, use a large laundry basket or any other type of container that's safe for the child to use (the lid should not be able to fall shut on the youngster).

2. If you have children's furniture that the kids have outgrown, put it to good use in other ways.

A changing table becomes an efficient toy shelf, especially if you buy some brightly colored baskets that divide the shelves into bins and that children can handle easily.

Use an old toy box as a chest for sweaters, blankets, sheets and the like.

With big, soft pillows stacked against the wall, turn a toddler's bed into a couch in the child's room.

Turn a child-size table (if it's a nice wooden one) into a coffee table or a place to display houseplants.

Use child-size chairs to hold treasured dolls or stuffed animals in a decorative manner.

Before You Take It Apart ...

❖ If an old piece of furniture has a loose joint, examine it carefully to see how it's constructed before trying to take it apart. We tend to assume that most furniture is held together with glue, but that may not be true for an older chair or table. Instead, a leg or rung might have been turned so that it had a little wooden knob at the end that fit tightly into its hole. Or it might be held together with a pin or wedge that will break if you try to remove the leg or rung. If you decide your piece was constructed without glue, take it to a pro for repair.

Come Unglued

❖ Repairs to a damaged wooden chair or table will often require you to take the piece apart first. If the piece was held together with glue, begin by mixing together equal parts water and vinegar and brushing it onto the joints to soften the old glue. Ease the pieces out, perform any necessary repairs and clean out all the old gunk (with the water and vinegar mixture) before you reinsert the repaired parts.

Make Yourself a Key to the Puzzle

❖ As you take apart a chair or table for repair, mark the pieces (particularly chair spindles, rungs, legs and the like) so that you know which piece fits where.

Stick with Glue

❖ Whenever you plan to use glue on furniture, be sure that the temperature of the room you're working in is around 70°F. Glue doesn't work well when it is too cold or too hot. (Don't try to force the glue to dry quickly with additional heat from a hand-held hair dryer or space heater—it won't work!)

❖ When regluing a wooden chair that you don't intend to use outdoors, use yellow carpenter's glue (available at hardware stores). It is strong and sets up quickly, so have your pieces ready to assemble immediately after you apply the glue. (This type of glue is not waterproof, so don't use it on outdoor furniture.)

Glue How-To

❖ When repairing a piece of furniture with glue, mix a little sawdust with the glue to make the glue stronger.

❖ When gluing together furniture joints, apply the glue to both pieces before assembling them.

Joints: Uptight Is Good

❖ If a chair rung is loose because it's become too small for the hole it goes in, wad a bit of steel wool into the hole, apply glue to both the rung and the hole and reinsert the rung. This should give the rung a tight fit.

❖ To tighten a loose joint, cut several cloth strips just a bit narrower than the end of the leg or rung that is to be inserted into the hole. Dab a bit of glue on the center of each strip, draping the strips over the end of the leg in a crisscross pattern. When the glue has dried, trim the strips to about half the depth of the hole into which you'll insert the rung. Apply glue to both parts of the joint and assemble it.

Clamp Down

❖ When repairing chair legs, you'll need a clamp to hold them in place. Buy a piece of cloth webbing with a ratchet at a hardware store. Wrap the webbing around the chair legs, then tighten it.

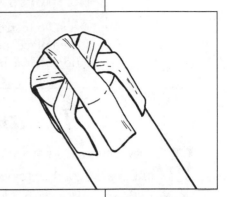

Glue overlapping strips of rag over the end of a loose chair rung before gluing the rung back in place.

❖ Alternatively, go to an outdoor-equipment store and ask for a length of climbing webbing with a plastic snap lock at both ends (these are often sold as belts). Wrap the webbing "belt" around the chair legs, tighten it and click the snap lock shut.

❖ When using clamps to hold newly glued furniture together temporarily, allow the glue to dry for 24 hours (or at least overnight) before you release them. After you remove the clamps, let the furniture sit for another 24 hours before you use it.

REFINISHING
WOODEN FURNITURE

Don't Be Afraid to Strip

❖ If you want to extend the life of a dreary-looking piece of wooden furniture and you're sure it needs more than just cleaning, your next step should be to refinish it. Stripping furniture isn't complicated or expensive—but it *is* messy and time-consuming. For your first refinishing project, you might want to try a table, which is generally easier than a chair, because it's likely to have larger areas of flat wood (as opposed to spindles and rungs).

Strippers Need Fresh Air

❖ Do your stripping and refinishing in a clean, well-ventilated place (perhaps a garage) to minimize the accumulation of dust and fumes. Cover the floor with drop cloths.

Instant Aging

WHEN WORKERS REMODELED the kitchen of our town hall several years ago, they tossed out an old unfinished kitchen chair with one missing leg. I brought it home, thinking I might fix it. The chair sat untouched for so long that I finally decided to throw it away. But an auctioneer friend said that he'd buy the chair if I fixed the leg. Naturally, I couldn't resist the offer.

It was not difficult to turn a new pine leg on my lathe. The challenge came when I tried to match the finish of the new leg to the chair. "Aging" new wood is the hardest finishing job there is, so instead of working with commercial stains, I tried an old trick I know. I mixed some wood ashes into a small can of water to make a stain—just enough ashes to give the water some thickness, but not enough to make a paste. I applied the stain to the leg with a paint brush. After it dried, I applied another coat of the stain in areas where the leg was still too light. Where it was too dark, I sanded it lightly. The new wood absorbed my homemade stain the way it would any other. In the end, you couldn't tell the new leg from the old ones.

You might find this trick useful if you ever have to stain new wood to match aged, unfinished wood.

Wearing protective gloves, brush on the furniture stripper and let the piece sit. After the stripper has softened the old finish, scrape the finish with a wooden scraper. (Don't use metal, which might gouge the wood.) Use a soft brass brush on crevices. Then reapply the stripper and repeat the process until all the old finish is gone. Rinse the whole thing down with a mixture of TSP or another product containing trisodium phosphate and water, rubbing with extra-fine-grade steel wool. (You can get the protective gloves, furniture stripper, brass brush and TSP at a hardware store.)

Sprinkle On the Sawdust

❖ Sprinkle sawdust on your furniture piece just after you've rinsed it down with TSP or another product containing trisodium phosphate. In fact, use as much as you need to soak up the water and chemicals. Then brush or wipe off the muck immediately so that the sawdust doesn't dry and cake on the wood. Let your furniture dry, scrape with a cabinet scraper and then sand the wood (always sanding with the grain) until it is smooth. (This is when you will be able to remove any discolorations that have worked their way into the wood.)

Repair before You Refinish

❖ If your piece of furniture needs repairs as well as refinishing, make the repairs after stripping and before refinishing.

❖ Also after stripping and before refinishing, check to be sure the joints are tight. Stripping can melt glue and thus cause joints to loosen. If that happens, be sure to tighten the joints before proceeding with the refinishing.

To Stain or Not to Stain

❖ Once you strip your piece of furniture, you may decide that you prefer the beauty of bare wood rather than stain. If that's the case, use a brush to apply eight or nine thin coats of tung oil (available at hardware stores) to build up a finish that is impervious to water and alcohol stains.

Choose Your True Colors

❖ If you are uncertain about what color stain to use, go light. You can always add stain to darken the color of your wood, but it's almost impossible to lighten a dark color. When you apply the stain, you'll have greater control over its hue if you wipe off the excess immediately and then continue to apply thin coats, wiping the excess off each time.

Get Tipsy

❖ If you need to stain both sides of a piece of wood and want to save time by doing the second side before the first dries, just tip the piece gently against a wall or another support so that only the edge of the wood is touching. This will prevent blotches or smears from ruining one stained side while you do the other.

One Good Coat Deserves Another

❖ After staining a piece of furniture, brush on a coat of varnish. Let the varnish dry, then sand the piece with fine-grit sandpaper. Repeat the process until you have three or four coats. Use thin coats of varnish, and sand progressively more with each coat to bring down "high" areas and fill in "low" areas. The sanding will even out the surface, making it smoother.

A Use for Those Spare Containers

❖ Whenever you use stain or varnish, pour the amount you think you'll use into a small container and work from there. That way, you won't gunk up the leftover finish in the original can with dust, dirt and stray bristles from your brush.

A Smooth Finish

❖ For a smooth surface on your refinished piece, sand the last coat of varnish with wet 600-grit wet-or-dry sandpaper. Then make a muddy mixture of ¾ cup of pumice, a squeeze of lampblack (it comes in a tube) and enough paraffin oil to make the mix soupy. (All these products are available at paint and hardware stores.) Brush the stuff on with an old toothbrush or, for wider areas like tabletops, a small floor brush. Use long, continuous strokes. Immediately clean up behind your strokes with rags. The lampblack will hide any white grit in the crevices. Switch to a clean rag for a final pass over the furniture to make sure you wipe off any residue. Then buff with the high-quality polish or wax of your choice.

A Mirror Image

❖ If you want a glassy "mirror" finish—say, for a tabletop—coat the surface with furniture wax or shoe wax and rub it in with a car buffer.

UPHOLSTERED FURNITURE

It Needs a Stable Home

❖ Push a couch or an upholstered chair up against a wall so that it stays stable instead of rocking back when someone sits down in it. If you leave the piece standing free in the middle of the room, the back will eventually separate from the seat.

Avoid Overexposure

❖ Set upholstered furniture beside or away from a window instead of directly in front of it. Avoiding direct sunlight will keep the fabric looking new instead of allowing it to bleach out.

This Could Be a Moving Experience

❖ When moving or storing a piece of upholstered furniture, avoid placing it against other items with sharp corners or edges (such as a mirror or small table), which could puncture or tear the fabric. Instead, rearrange the moving van or storage room, or wrap the sharp item in several layers of blanket before packing it near the upholstery.

PUZZLER

ALTHOUGH IT LOOKS LIKE A ME-dieval instrument of torture, this item actually helped the user with his craft.

ANSWER: *Chair maker's harness. The craftsperson wearing it could anchor the top of a brace and bit in the harness's indentation while boring a hole in a chair.*

A Clean Sweep

❖ Use a whisk broom to remove the dust that collects on top of the back and arms of upholstered furniture. This keeps the fabric looking fresh. A vacuum cleaner, even if it has special upholstery attachments, tends to pull threads.

Clay, You Say?

❖ If you find children's clay modeling compound stuck to your couch or overstuffed chair, remove the excess and let the rest dry. Use a stiff brush to loosen any residue, then whisk it away with a whisk broom. If necessary, use mild soap and water to clean any remaining spots.

A Good Night's Sleep Hangs in the Balance

MOST HAMMOCKS NOWADAYS are set up at summer cottages, but when I was a kid, it seemed every family had one in the yard. There's nothing like relaxing in a rope hammock, and a good one will last a long time with very little mainte-nance. Just bring the hammock in for the winter each year and treat the support ropes that bear the hammock's weight (not the entire hammock) with a wood preservative such as Cuprinol once a year.

EARL
remembers...

I once spent a couple of weeks sleeping in a hammock at a remote job site. I started off on an air mattress, but after it went flat, I borrowed a navy hammock and strung it between the studs in the building I was framing. It was May, and the nights were still pretty cold. The first night, I slept with my blan-kets on top of me and woke up so cold that my teeth were chatter-ing. That morning, someone put me wise: you have to have as many blankets under you as over you when you sleep in a hammock!

Easy On, Easy Off

❖ To make upholstered dining-chair seats last longer, stitch together simple covers with ties at the corners. Spray them with Scotchgard or a similar product. When the covers get dirty, toss them in the wash.

When in Doubt, Send It Out

❖ When your upholstered couch or chair needs more cleaning than soap or a whisk broom can handle, send it out to a reputable professional. (Look in the Yellow Pages under Cleaners—Upholstery.) A professional will use the right chemical cleaners, and you won't be stuck guessing whether the solution you're about to rub into that stain will leave a hole in the fabric.

A Patchwork Couch

❖ Fortunately, many upholstery tears occur along the weave of the fabric, creating a triangular flap. You can actually patch the tear with glue and another piece of heavy fabric (such as canvas, denim or muslin). First, cut a piece of heavy fabric slightly larger than the tear. Peel back the flap and slide the patch beneath it with the handle of a spoon, using the spoon to adjust the position of the patch. Then pin back the upholstery flap with a poultry skewer or an upholstery pin. Brush a thin layer of latex fabric glue over the surface of the patch and along the edges of the torn upholstery. Carefully replace the torn flap on top of the patch, adjusting the fit and patting it gently to avoid squeezing glue out the sides of the repaired area. Use more poultry skewers or upholstery pins to pin the torn flap against the patch

Fold back the torn flap of upholstery and insert a patch slightly larger than the torn area (A). Position the patch so it extends underneath all edges of the tear (B), glue the top of it and reposition the upholstery fabric. Pin the torn fabric in place (C) until the glue dries.

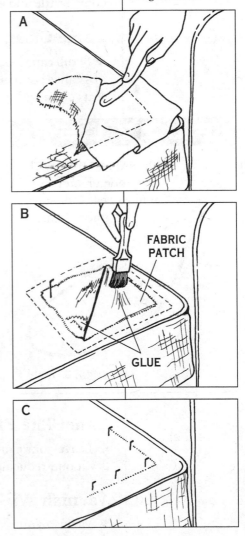

A

B

FABRIC
PATCH

GLUE

C

until the glue has dried and set properly, then remove them for a perfect repair.

RUSH, CANE AND WICKER

Keep It in the Dark

❖ Place your cane- or rush-seat chair away from direct sunlight, which will darken the color of the caning or rush. Sunlight also will dry out the material, causing it to become brittle and eventually to break.

Come Clean

❖ Scrub cane seats with a soft brush dipped in a solution of 1 tablespoon of salt and 1 quart of hot water. Wipe the seats clean with a cloth, then dry them completely with a hand-held hair dryer positioned several inches away from the cane.

❖ You can also wash your cane seats with hot water and dishwashing liquid, then rinse them and allow them to air dry.

Sit Tight

❖ To tighten a cane seat that has stretched out, use a sponge to soak the caning with hot water. As the caning dries, it will shrink back to its original shape. Be careful to avoid wetting the spline—the piece that anchors the caning in the chair. It will loosen if it gets too wet.

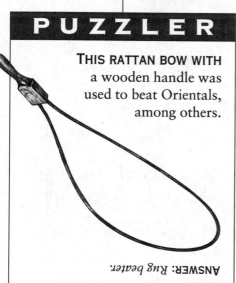

PUZZLER

THIS RATTAN BOW WITH a wooden handle was used to beat Orientals, among others.

ANSWER: Rug beater.

Cane: The Plain, Unvarnished Seat

❖ Leave your cane seat in its natural state. Varnish will dry it out, reducing its strength.

Varnish Will Hold the Rush

❖ Varnish your rush chair seat once or twice a year to double the life of the seat.

Wicker: Keep It Light

❖ To lighten up a piece of unfinished wicker furniture that has darkened or become discolored over the years, dip a paintbrush in a mixture of ¼ cup of household (5 percent) bleach and 1 quart of water and apply evenly it to the furniture.

❖ Once you've cleaned unfinished wicker furniture, you may want to protect it. Wait till the piece is dry, then spray on a clear satin urethane varnish or lacquer.

LEATHER FURNITURE

Keep It Soft

❖ To keep leather furniture soft and supple, use a cloth to rub in a good-quality leather dressing such as saddle soap or neat's-foot oil (you can buy these at a hardware store or tack shop). Let the dressing absorb into the leather for about two hours, then wipe the piece clean. For a glossy glow, finish the piece off by applying a neutral shoe polish and buffing.

Ring-around-the-Tabletop

❖ If you're bothered by water rings on your leather tabletop, just keep polishing! If you continue applying furniture polish on a regular basis, the rings will eventually disappear.

Lemon Drops

❖ Mix a solution of equal parts lemon juice and water to clean a leather tabletop. Sponge on the solution, then wipe dry.

Color It Repaired

❖ To repair a small hole or tear in leather furniture, melt a small piece of crayon that matches the color of the furniture and drip the wax into the damaged area. While the wax is still soft, smooth over the surface with your finger, blending in the edges.

Well-Preserved Legs

❖ You don't have to treat an entire piece of wooden outdoor furniture with preservative. Instead, just brush the product from the bottoms of the feet up about three inches on the legs. This will keep the furniture from absorbing water from the ground.

Table Scraps

I ONCE DID SOME WORK for a woman who had recently had a house built. The builders had left in the woods a stack of scrap lumber almost as big as the house they constructed. They didn't work to make the best use of their wood. If they cut a board wrong or mishammered a nail, the board went into the scrap heap.

EARL remembers...

The woman asked me to build four picnic tables for her grounds. Of course, I wouldn't think of going out and buying new lumber when perfectly good wood was available right on the job site. The design of a picnic table is very basic, and it's easy to build one out of scrap lumber. So I salvaged planks from the scrap heap. The woman liked the results and asked me to do some more work on her property. I went on to build a sugarhouse and a workshop for her caretaker out of wood salvaged entirely from that same scrap heap.

Unfortunately, it's common for builders to have a lot of lumber left over. So if you're planning to build a picnic table—or any other crude outdoor furniture—I recommend using lumber salvaged from the scrap heaps of job sites. Don't be shy in asking for permission; most builders are happy to let you have the wood they are discarding if you'll just cart it away.

The Nuts and Bolts of Wooden Legs

❖ When you want to replace a leg or a seat on your picnic table (or any other outdoor wooden furniture), use only stainless steel or galvanized steel nuts and bolts. Brass isn't as strong, and other hardware will rust and cause the surrounding wood to deteriorate.

The Director's Chair: Lights, Camera, Sewing Action!

❖ To refurbish a director's chair when the canvas has stretched or become bleached out, first take the chair apart by removing the screws that attach the upper half to the lower half. Slide the old canvas off and rip out the stitches, being careful not to tear the fabric. Now use the old canvas as a pattern for a new back and seat. Buy a few yards of new canvas and cut it to match the old. To complete the new seat, just hem the edges. To complete the back, hem the edges and then turn under the edges on the sides to make a "cylinder" into which the back uprights of the chair will fit. (Match the size of the new "cylinder" to that of the old one.) Slide the new pieces into place. If you're feeling ambitious, repaint the wooden portions of the chair before sliding on the new canvas—and you've got yourself a nearly new chair.

Ship to Shore

WHEN THE British navy began to dismantle World War I warships, someone realized that the teak decks were worth saving. The wood was so durable—and beautiful—that some people constructed garden benches from it, and the tradition of building garden furniture from teak was born. Many of those original benches are still used daily by Britons in their gardens.

Wrap It Up

❖ Don't throw away a porch or deck chair just because its webbing or plastic cord has stretched out. Buy new webbing or cord at a hardware store (or at a store that sells outdoor furniture), remove the old material and wrap the new material yourself. Stretch it tightly and evenly across the chair frame. (If you're not certain you'll remember the winding pattern the old material followed, leave a row or two intact until you've started with the new material.)

Walls, Floors, Doors and Windows

THE FIRST TIME I EVER LAID linoleum was at a summer house when I was working for my father and doing basic handyman tasks for the couple who owned the house. They had just had a linoleum floor laid in their large farm kitchen, and the professionals who had done the job had left a pile of large scrap pieces. The couple wanted to have linoleum laid on the long, narrow floor of their pantry, so they asked me if I could do it using the scrap pieces. I thanked them for the chance and set about it.

It was a challenge to piece together the scrap sheets of linoleum, but I matched the patterns of the pieces together as best I could. In the end, I was satisfied with my work, and, more important, the couple loved it. Their praise made me feel pretty good about doing that type of work, so soon after that, I quit working for my father and started out on my own. Before long, I was laying linoleum for five stores locally.

Which all goes to show how one thing can lead to another. That's equally true of fixing up your house to make it last. It's all too easy to start off replacing the wallpaper and end up tearing out the walls. But many times that happens when a house hasn't been properly maintained in the first place. In this chapter, we'll show you how to deal with loose door hinges, salvage old floors and use an old Yankee trick for extending the life of stair runners. And even if it's too late for preventive maintenance, don't worry. You'll find ingenious ideas for fixing doors that stick and floors that squeak, covering scratches—and even small cracks—in windowpanes, cleaning brass doorknobs and patching torn wallpaper. And when you're done with all that, skip to the very end for a fun way to clean your louvered window shutters.

PROTECTING WALLS

The Doorstop

❖ It's surprising how many walls have been needlessly damaged by doorknobs and latches hitting against them. To protect against that problem, follow the time-honored technique of installing doorstops. A standard doorstop is a wood screw attached to a brass rod with a rubber head. The rod is usually long and straight (screwed into a baseboard an inch or two off the floor, where the corner of the door would hit it) or short and curved (screwed directly into the floor). For formal rooms, consider using more decorative stops, such as turned oak or maple spindles, found in specialty hardware stores. Or use a hinge pin, a small adjustable arm that attaches directly to the hinge. Some people consider these less noticeable than stops attached to the wall or floor. They're available in the door-hardware sections of department and home supply stores.

Don't Cut Corners

❖ Protect the outside corners of plaster walls the traditional way by covering them with wooden corner beads. You can still find these wooden strips—often decorated with simple turnings—at home supply stores. They work on drywall corners, too.

The Chair Rail

❖ Those thin wooden strips of molding about three feet above the floor in many formal rooms are called chair rails. Prized now for their aesthetic quality, they are actually useful for guarding wallpaper and plaster against chips and tears from the backs of moving chairs. If you have a room that might benefit from a chair rail, consider installing one yourself. Though not advertised specifically for this pur-

Corner beads protect the edges of plaster walls and decorate them at the same time.

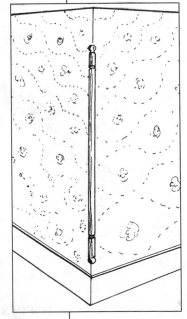

pose, inexpensive stock molding at a lumberyard is suitable for this use.

PLASTER WALLS

Paper Over Plaster

❖ If your plaster wall shows small cracks and rough, irregular surfaces, prolong its life simply by wallpapering over it. The paper will help support the plaster.

Plaster Pick-Me-Ups

❖ To smooth and repair gouges in a plaster wall, patch with drywall joint tape and joint compound, just as you would finish the joints and nail heads when hanging drywall. Both materials, found at hardware stores, come with clear directions.

❖ If your plaster wall shows large cracks or small holes, don't automatically assume that you'll have to replace or cover it. Use the same technique as above, except use fiberglass tape, found at hardware stores.

❖ If your plaster wall bulges but otherwise shows no sign of being damaged, the "keys" have broken off behind the lath. (Keys are created where oozing plaster has pushed through and hardened in the spaces between wood lath strips. Keys give plaster walls their strength.) To reattach loose plaster, locate the position of the studs behind the bulge. Then, using drywall screws and plaster washers, screw the plaster tight to them. Cover with joint compound, sand and paint, just as you would drywall.

Stress Shouldn't Show

❖ To stop stress cracks from appearing in your plaster wall, especially in areas that have been recently repaired, con-

PUZZLER

LONG BEFORE BACKPACKS from L.L. Bean, this was used by the school-yard set.

ANSWER: Book carrier, with a strap and locking handle.

sider spraying the walls with one of the new elastic coatings such as Good-Bye Cracks, available at hardware stores. Do this, of course, prior to painting or wallpapering.

Getting the Last Lath

❖ There's no reason you can't reuse old split or sawn lath, as long as the lath is still sound. Most contractors shy away from this, because old lath is extremely dry. It tends to suck moisture out of the new plaster, invariably causing cracks. But hold firm. A couple of days ahead of time, start coating the lath with water from a spray bottle. As the water is absorbed, the wood will swell slightly. There's no need for the lath to be dripping wet when the plaster goes up, but it should no longer be drinking in water.

❖ As an alternative to wetting old lath, you can coat it with a masonry bonding agent, available at most masonry supply stores. The agent is a fast-drying latex that brushes on easily and bonds to the wood, sealing it against water.

WALLPAPER

Keep It Dry

❖ If you have wallpaper in areas like the bathroom or above the kitchen stove, be sure to use an exhaust fan when cooking or taking a shower. Or, if you can, crack a window to help reduce the moisture in the air. As with so many things in the house, moisture is the biggest threat to wallpaper's long life.

❖ Keep an eye out for water stains or other signs of leaking, especially in

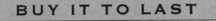

BUY IT TO LAST

Weighty Thoughts on Wallpaper

IF YOU'RE GOING to be putting up new wallpaper, choose paper labeled "medium-weight." Heavy paper tears easily under its own weight, especially when installed in high-ceilinged rooms. And lightweight paper tears easily in general. It stands to reason that medium-weight is both the most popular and (usually) the most expensive grade of wallpaper sold. If you're buying for the long term, consider buying paper with a light pattern (it shows less dirt and wear than solid papers), in a subtle or subdued color scheme that won't soon be out of fashion. And consider a vinyl or coated paper for bathrooms or utility rooms where moisture may be a problem. Vinyl looks shinier than standard wallpaper and costs more, but it won't be harmed by the moisture.

places that aren't easily visible. Likely places include ceiling edges, behind large pieces of furniture, along the tops of baseboards, below windowsills, behind radiators and on the walls below bathrooms and radiators. If you catch the problem causing the leaking soon enough, you may be able to save the wallpaper, too.

Maybe This Could Start a Decorating Trend

WHEN I WAS YOUNG, my brother and I used to hang wallpaper as a team. In the winter, when things got slow, we would occasionally work for the bank, reconditioning homes that the bank was planning to rent or sell. The houses we worked on were in horrible condition. We had to clean them out, paint the trim and wallpaper the walls.

**EARL
remembers...**

To keep our costs down, we bought remnant rolls of wallpaper at a discount. This meant that we had to plan our use of each pattern carefully. Sometimes we'd have enough of one pattern to do a whole room in the same paper, but more often we'd have only enough to cover one wall. Although it wasn't the decorating scheme we would have preferred, we did our best to keep the walls in a room from clashing with one another. The bank loved our work and gave us job after job.

If you're fussy about how your home is decorated, I don't recommend patching together different wallpaper patterns. But I do suggest that you look at remnant rolls of wallpaper when you're making your decorating choices—especially if you're papering a relatively small area. You can save a lot of money buying remnant rolls at a big discount.

Help for Aging Wallpaper

❖ Wallpaper will fade over time, but it will still outlast several paint jobs on unpapered walls. In sunny rooms, occasionally move artwork, mirrors and other wall hangings so that the paper will fade evenly. (Or once the wall hangings are in place, *never* move them.)

❖ Often wallpaper starts to look old and in need of replacing not because of age but because of scratches and dents caused by moving furniture. Take extra care when you rearrange your furniture, especially with any sharp-cornered items like filing cabinets and bookshelves. If possible, leave a little space between those items and the wall when they are finally in position.

Spare It, Tear It

❖ Make sure to hold on to spare scraps of leftover wallpaper. Down the road, they may come in handy for patching a section of torn or badly stained paper, allowing you to hold on to the original wallpaper longer. Simply tear out a replacement patch slightly larger than the area you need to cover, align it to match the pattern and paste it onto the wall using wallpaper paste. The torn edges are thinner than clean, cut edges would be and so will smooth out more tightly against the wall.

PUZZLER

THIS WAS AN attention getter in the old days—and not because of its bizarre appearance. Sailors tended to steer away from it, though.

ANSWER: Foghorn, worked by bellows.

Prepare Ye the Way

❖ "Prepare the surface well" is a phrase you hear often around home remodeling—and that's especially important if you want your wallpapering job to last a long time. Before papering, consider applying a latex wall sealer to the surface (available at most hardware stores, in formulas that vary depending on the surface being covered). It not only seals the surface against moisture but also makes the papering job easier by providing a good gripping surface for positioning the paper.

TILED WALLS

Clean the Shower

❖ One of the easiest ways to prolong the life of your shower walls is to wipe them down after every use or two. (A squeegee works well for this.) This prevents soap from building up on the surface and discourages mildew.

❖ To clean your shower curtain or sliding door, wipe it down with a sponge dampened with white vinegar.

Clean the Tile

❖ To keep your tiled walls clean and free of mildew, clean them frequently with a solution of 3 quarts of water, 1 quart of household (5 percent) bleach and 1 cup of TSP or another product containing trisodium phosphate. Just be sure to rinse well and allow time for drying.

A Touch of the Grout

❖ To get more years out of your tiled wall, seal all of your grout with clear silicone (available at hardware stores in spray- or brush-on formulas). It will not only add luster to the finish but will also seal the grout's pores against bleach. Bleach, because it kills mildew, is a common ingredient in bathroom and household cleaners. Unfortunately, it eats into porous materials like grout, causing them to deteriorate. Remember that with a tiled wall, it's rarely the tile that goes bad or wears out—it's the grout.

❖ If you are regrouting, consider using a silicone-based grout additive that contains mildewcide (available at hardware stores). The grout will last longer, and you'll have less cleanup work.

BUY IT TO LAST

Walls for Wet Places

PLYWOOD AND drywall both suffer when wet: plywood delaminates, and drywall goes soft. If you're planning to use either of these materials in a high-moisture area of your house, you'll get much longer life out of them if you specify water-resistant (W/R) plywood and special water-resistant drywall. In both cases, the sheets are both heavier and more expensive than standard sheets, but they'll save time and money in the long run.

For areas subjected to constant moisture, such as tub surrounds or showers, use concrete backerboard. Even water-resistant drywall won't stand up to water penetration from hairline cracks in tile grout.

Save for a Rainy Day

❖ If you live in an old house and have some storage space, never throw away an old board or piece of molding. A 20-inch scrap of pine wainscoting may make a replacement panel for a cupboard someday. An old wooden baseboard may be trimmed and planed for a new door casing.

I'm Waiting for a Call from Buckingham Palace

I N THE 1960S, THE CONTRACTOR I was working for was hired to tear down a castle in Northfield, Massachusetts. Yes, I do mean a castle. The building was five stories high and made out of granite. It was originally the private home of a wealthy owner, but subsequently it had been bought by a neighboring golf course and had fallen into disrepair. Unfortunately, the castle's finest interior features, such as floor-to-ceiling mirrors, had been damaged or stolen before our crew arrived. So we just went about disassembling what was left, preparing the granite for resale.

EARL remembers...

The crew did manage to salvage all the wooden interior doors, which were eight feet tall and made up of horizontal panels. They were beautifully made, and I gladly stored them away. My boss couldn't imagine how we'd ever use doors that tall, but he let me keep them.

For years after that, I used those castle doors whenever a customer needed a special door. I'd cut off one or two of the horizontal panels to make the door fit in the customer's house. All the new owners were delighted to have them.

If something is well made, I'll do whatever I can to salvage it.

A foot-long piece of molding might someday replace a damaged section somewhere else. Anything you can store and reuse may save the cost of buying antique boards or having custom millwork done down the road.

Pretreated Lumber Should Make the Grade

WHEN CHOOSING pretreated lumber for porches, decks and other outdoor uses, make sure you select the proper grade. Pretreated lumber comes in three basic categories: "Above ground" is right for sills, floor joists, decking—any section not constantly wet or directly in the ground. "Ground contact" is used for porch and deck footings and supports. "FDN," labeled for "foundation," is the most thoroughly treated lumber, appropriate for piers and other in-ground uses. For porch decking, be sure to choose a hard, dense-grained wood such as Douglas fir. Yellow pine and redwood, two other common choices, don't wear nearly as well underfoot.

Straighten the Warp

❖ When a single board such as a cupboard door or a wainscoting panel becomes warped, try an old-time remedy to save it. Lay the panel, cupped side down, on damp grass in the hot sun. Leave it there for a few hours, and the warping should disappear.

❖ An alternative approach to correcting a warped board is to lay the panel on a warm register or radiator, cupped side up, with a damp towel on top of it. Leave it for at least a few hours. If it's still warped, redampen the cloth and repeat the process.

INSTALLING FLOORBOARDS TO LAST

The Drier the Better

❖ Before you lay your finish flooring, make sure the wood has the proper moisture content. Here's an easy rule of thumb: Hardwoods should air dry one year for each inch of thickness. Softwoods dry a little faster, so the boards could be dry in about eight months per inch of thickness. (This does not apply to kiln-dried flooring, which has already been properly dried. If your flooring has been kiln dried, it should have no shrinkage once it's installed.)

The Subject Is Subfloors

❖ Consider using solid boards rather than plywood for subfloors, especially in areas likely to see a lot of water—

bathrooms, laundry areas and the floor below kitchen sinks. Wood in its natural state has a surprising capacity for water storage. Even planks stained black from water can still be structurally sound. Plywood, which has a poor water-storage capacity, expands and buckles when wet and eventually delaminates. If you do use plywood in these areas, be sure to specify "marine grade" when you place your order. That grade is treated to repel water.

Nail It to Last

❖ When nailing your floorboards to the subfloor, always drive the nails at opposing angles. This will prevent them from pulling out if the finished floorboard shrinks or warps.

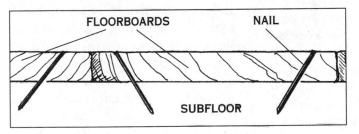

FLOORBOARDS   NAIL

SUBFLOOR

If you drive in the nails at opposing angles, they'll hold floorboards in place despite any wood shrinkage later.

FLOOR MAINTENANCE

Stop Dirt in Its Tracks

❖ The simplest way to help make modern wood floors last is to keep them free of dirt and grit. Start by tracking in less dirt. Ask family and friends to remove their shoes before entering. Brick that dirt path leading up to the house. Less dirt and grit means less wear and tear on a floor's finish—and eventually less sanding, stripping, refinishing and wearing down of the wood beneath.

❖ Use a straw carpet mat inside the door to trap much of the dirt before it reaches the floors.

The Value of Nails

TODAY OLD hand-wrought nails are valued highly for the "antique" feeling they give to wide-board floors. When those nails were first used, though, they were even more valuable. Nails, in fact, were so expensive and hard to come by in the early days of this country that some people are said to have burned their houses down before moving, just to save the nails and bring them along.

Upside-Down Floors

FRUGAL OLD-TIMERS got more life out of their floorboards by pulling them up when the boards got too worn and then flopping them over. Of course, eventually the boards would wear so thin that they'd have to be covered over—or swapped for flooring in the attic, a closet or some other lightly used area. You can occasionally find evidence of that kind of flopping if you see paint or whitewash on the undersides of boards.

There's no reason you can't follow the same principle today to extend the life of your flooring, but a more practical application might be to use the worn floorboards for some other purpose— as cupboard shelves, for example. Or lay them in an outbuilding, substitute them for broken panels in a cupboard door or hand-plane them into wainscoting.

An Old Technique That Still Works

❖ Use canvas floorcloths to protect areas that get unusually high traffic— in front of the sink and stove, next to the bathtub. They protect floors from excessive wear and moisture, they wipe clean (unlike throw rugs), and they can add light and color to otherwise dark rooms. Originally, floorcloths were made of hemp or flax, waterproofed with oil-based paint. Today you can make your own out of heavy cotton canvas. Cut out a rectangle of fabric and lay it out flat. Paint a solid background on the fabric and stencil a design over it, then cover the whole thing with a coat of varnish. Let that dry, then apply another layer of varnish. Repeat the process until you have five or six coats of varnish. The floorcloth should wear for years—with an occasional new coat of varnish—and extend the life of your floor that much more.

Investigate a Cover-Up

❖ With a little digging, you can find floorcloths for sale. Ask around at museums, interior decorating stores, local craft associations and other places that might have an interest in floor coverings.

REPAIRING WOOD FLOORS

Stop the Squeak

❖ Before doing anything drastic to squeaky floorboards (like replacing them), try sweeping some talcum powder into the joints between the boards. That may ease the rubbing that's causing the noise.

❖ If the squeaky boards happen to be over the cellar, quieting them may be as simple as driving a wooden shingle between the boards and the floor joist. Sometimes that simple step will keep the boards from moving and will thus eliminate the squeak.

A Knotty Problem

❖ If a knot has come loose in your wood flooring, there's no need to replace the floorboard. Simply glue the knot back in place with carpenter's glue.

When Looks Deceive

❖ If your floors are old, grimy or blackened, you may be able to save them. Try stripping them of their finish, then

---

BUY IT TO LAST

Finishing School

WHEN CHOOSING the finish for your wood floor, you'll need to select one of two basic types: penetrating or surface. Penetrating finishes, which include oils, permeate the wood grain. They are easily renewed, but they do require special care in waxing and polishing to keep floors strong and clean. Old-house owners with softwood (pine) floors often prefer penetrating oil-based finishes because they make the wood look softer—not shiny and plastic. Oils bring out the grain and texture of the natural wood, which is why makers of fine furniture use them, too.

Surface finishes, including varnishes and polyurethane, form a hard surface on top of the wood. They offer better protection against scratches and stains and are easily cleaned, so they're more common on hardwood floors and in newer houses. Think of the finish on a gym floor—superdurable but plastic-looking. That's polyurethane. Surface finishes can be removed if you change your mind later, but the process of stripping and refinishing is time-consuming.

Here's a loose rule of thumb: consider oils in formal and fancy rooms that get light use, and surface finishes in the kitchen, hallway and other high-traffic areas. Choose your finish according to your circumstances and preferences.

REPAIRING WOOD FLOORS

scrubbing them with a stiff-bristled brush and repeated doses of extremely hot water and ammonia (an ounce or two per gallon of water). When they're treated this way, floors may reveal a pleasing color and grain and provide you with years more of service.

❖ Another way to attack an accumulation of dirt or grime on old wood floors is with a combination of 1 gallon of extremely hot water and a few ounces of TSP (available at most hardware stores) or another product that contains trisodium phosphate.

A SECOND LIFE

Turn Your Floor into a Workbench

HOMEOWNERS often replace vinyl or asphalt-tile flooring not because the floor has worn out, but because the pattern or style has gone out of fashion or no longer fits the decoration scheme of the room. If you're going to replace your own still-usable flooring, think twice about discarding it. Take up the tiles carefully by heating small areas with an iron or hand-held hair dryer and working a broad-bladed putty knife underneath them. (If the flooring is old, wear a mask and be extra careful not to breathe in any asbestos the tiles or backing might contain.) The flooring can now be glued down to make a smooth, waterproof surface for your workbench or storage shelves. Scraps from new vinyl flooring can be used the same way.

FINISHING WOOD FLOORS

Paint: Make It Tough Enough for Traffic

❖ If you're painting a wood floor, make sure to use an alkyd-resin paint. That provides a strong, durable finish. Add an extra coat or two in any high-traffic areas, especially where traffic is concentrated or gets "funneled." There's no rule that says you have to have the same number of coats on an entire floor.

The Finish: Put On an Extra Overcoat

❖ A lot of people put off the job of re-finishing floors because they assume it involves the tedious work of stripping the entire surface. But there's no need to recoat the whole floor if it's wearing in only one or two spots. Instead, sand just the worn areas with medium-grit sandpaper, then put on a new coat of polyurethane or varnish. Repeat that process for added protection. The new finish will blend right into the areas around it, and you'll have a good looking floor with a minimum of extra effort.

Glossy Strength, Satin Look

❖ When varnishing a floor, you don't have to compromise between the durability of a gloss finish and the softer look of satin. Make the first two coats glossy, then finish with a final coat of satin. That will produce a harder surface, but with the soft finish many folks prefer.

Fair-Weather Finish

❖ To ensure a long-lasting finish on your floor, do the work during dry weather. Never apply a sealer or surface finish like polyurethane when it's damp or humid. Moisture will hinder the even drying and bonding—and the ultimate longevity—of the finish.

LINOLEUM FLOORS

Don't Replace; Paint!

❖ Before you replace your dingy-looking or out-of-fashion linoleum floor, consider this: you can create a brand-new look by abrading the surface with a rotary sander, then painting with a good-quality floor enamel. (Do not try this if you suspect the flooring contains asbestos. Floor tile made of asbestos is harmful to your health if abraded.) You can brush or roll on the paint, add stencils if you want or experiment by applying the paint with a sponge or an old rag. Or find some leftover paint and create multicolored speckles by dipping your brush and snapping it at the floor. Add a coat or two of polyurethane, and your old linoleum will look and work just like a new floor!

The Mixed Blessing of Central Heat

THE CONCEPT OF central heating was surely one of the most significant home living improvements of the Victorian era. For the first time in history, homeowners in cold climates had convenient control of their environment. But those furnaces created a problem unknown to earlier settlers: termites. Termites, which are tropical in origin, cannot survive in nature where there are severely low temperatures. Once cellar furnaces began warming the soil beneath northern houses, though, termites established year-round nests, expanding the range of one of the worst threats to the long life of a house's wooden frame and walls.

CARPETING

Keep Your Antique Rug Aging Gracefully

❖ Most conservators recommend against using a vacuum cleaner on antique Oriental rugs. The wearing caused by the beater bar and strong suction will actually reduce the life of the rug, not prolong it. Instead, contact a local professional who can clean the rug properly. To find such a person, look in the Yellow Pages under Carpet and Rug Cleaners, then check the fine print of the ads for the key word *antique* or *Oriental*.

Better Endurance for Stair Runners

❖ Stair runners—long, narrow carpeting laid on stairs—can add comfort to a home while reducing wear on

If You'd Rather Conceal Your Past

I RECENTLY REARRANGED the furniture in my living room. If you weren't familiar with the old arrangement, it wouldn't be hard to figure out what it used to look like, because you can still see dents in my rug where the chair and table legs used to stand.

EARL remembers...

Yankee readers must be big furniture movers, because I frequently get letters from readers with the same problem. They all want to know how to get furniture dents out of a rug. I tell them first to comb the dent to loosen the rug's fibers, then hold a steaming iron over the dent for a few seconds to soften the fibers. Don't touch the rug with the iron, because it could melt the fibers if they are synthetic. Then brush the dent with a clean, stiff brush.

Someday soon, I'll have to follow my own advice!

wooden treads. When laying a stair runner, here's a trick to make the runner last longer. Calculate the length you'll need as if there were two more treads on the staircase. Fold half of the extra material under the top tread and half under the bottom. When the edges of the stair runner start to appear worn, simply shift the placement of the runner.

DOORS IN GENERAL

Make Those Brass Doorknobs Shine

❖ Clean your old brass hardware with fine bronze wool and brass cleaner. Using bronze wool rather than ordinary steel wool does make a difference. It's more expensive, but it produces fewer splinters, won't rust and lasts longer than steel wool. You can find it at marine supply stores.

The Case of the Loose Hinge

❖ A loose door hinge probably doesn't need to be replaced. To make the existing hinge last, try replacing the loose screw with a longer screw of the same diameter.

❖ If the screw hole is too large or has become stripped of its threads, stick a wooden match or toothpick in the hole, snap the match off flush with the surface and screw the hinge back tight. The screw should hold fine in the new wood.

Paint the Edges

❖ It's easy to forget to paint the top and bottom edges of an exterior door—and easy not to notice the oversight

Dead as a Doornail

EARLY COLONIAL doors were usually made two boards thick. In a typical exterior door, two long vertical boards would form one layer, while four or five wide boards would form the other. The two layers were held together by nails that were driven through and then clinched over. The clinching was said to "deaden" the nail—fixing it permanently in place. And thus "dead as a doornail" became a phrase that described anything that had no chance of ever moving again.

Those early doornails weren't going anywhere . . .

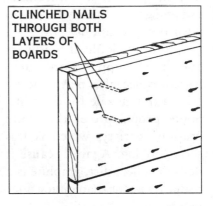

CLINCHED NAILS THROUGH BOTH LAYERS OF BOARDS

once the door is hung. (It's also likely that if you've had wall-to-wall carpeting installed, the folks doing the work trimmed away the painted edge of the door.) To see if your top edge is painted, simply get a chair or stepladder and look. To check the bottom edge, slide a small mirror beneath the door and look at the reflection. If the edges haven't been painted, remove the door and correct the oversight. It's important that all unfinished surfaces are painted, especially where the wood's end grain is exposed. Otherwise moisture can seep in, at best causing swelling and fitting problems, at worst rotting the wood.

COMMON MISTAKES

Oil Is Not Good Medicine for Door Locks

NEVER PUT OIL into a lock to lubricate it. Although the oil will initially provide good lubrication, over time it will collect dirt and grime, causing the lock to wear out. Instead, use powdered graphite, available at hardware and home supply stores in a handy, squeezable plastic bottle with a thin nozzle for tight fits. Some people prefer the white graphite variety, which is less dirty-looking. Again because it doesn't collect dirt, graphite is a better lubricant than oil for door hinges, too.

Abused Doors

❖ If you have a door that gets extremely heavy use (or abuse) or whose bottom section is in poor condition, reinforce it with a solid brass or stainless steel kickplate from a hardware store. The plate can also strengthen a panel door in which the joints have worked loose. Screw the plate to both stiles and the bottom rail. That one repair can make all the difference in a door's longevity.

Sticky Situations

❖ To repair—and thus hold on to—a door that sticks or binds in its frame, rub chalk or a crayon on the edges of the doorjamb and close the door hard. The chalk or crayon will be transferred to the door in the spots where it's binding. Use a hand plane to plane off the marks. A rule of thumb for proper clearance between a door and its jamb is just enough room for a nickel to slide between them.

Warped Doors

❖ If you have a warped door in an area where appearances matter, try a trade-off. Swap the warped door for a similar one—in good condition—from a part of the house where perfect fit is less important.

Exterior Doors Need Extra Protection

❖ When applying varnish to exterior doors, be sure to use a product made specifically for outside use. One example of such a product is durable spar varnish, so named for its original use on the spars of ships. It will last longer than ordinary varnish.

Good for Another Hundred Years

THIS IS WHAT HAPPENS to a door hinge after 100 years of swinging. Gradually, the metal wears down on the top hinge, which bears most of the door's weight. The top corner of the door hits the frame. The bottom corner of the door drags on the floor. And the latch does not catch right.

I recently came upon this situation in a friend's old house. She was frustrated because she wanted her door to swing properly, but she didn't want to replace her original antique hinges, nor did she want to plane the door so that it would close.

I came up with a simple solution. As is the case in many nineteenth-century homes, only two hinges supported this door. The top hinge

EARL
remembers...

had worn so severely because it was doing nearly all the work. (Today doors are almost always hung with three hinges, which distributes the load much more evenly.) Since the top hinge was carrying most of the load, I figured the bottom hinge would be in good condition, and I was right. I swapped the top hinge for the bottom one, and the door fit perfectly again.

Of course, 100 years from now, the house's owner will have a problem that's a little more difficult to solve!

❖ If your exterior doors are varnished, apply a new coat frequently—at least once a year, more often if the door is exposed to intense sun—to combat flaking and deterioration. Sand the old finish well, remove dust with a tack cloth and then apply new varnish with a clean brush.

SCREEN DOORS

The Right Screen

❖ If you have inherited a door with ripped or patched screening or you have young kids or pets around, the best way to make your screen door last longer is to replace the screening. Screening is available in different materials, including aluminum, coated aluminum, fiberglass and bronze. Of these materials, bronze is the most expensive and the one best suited to withstand abuse.

❖ Heavy-duty screening is another option for making your screen door last longer. A lot of people use this on the bottom portion of the door. It's more expensive than regular-weight screening and is noticeably thicker and heavier, so it takes more abuse.

Protect Your Screen from Pushy People

❖ You can prolong the life of a screen door by adding—if the door doesn't already have one—a "push guard" that keeps people from pushing directly on the screen to open the door. Originally, push guards were made of heavy-gauge steel wire and were formed in intricate and decorative patterns. Today they're commonly made of aluminum. Primed and painted, they can pass for steel wire—which is important to restorers and others who care about the look of a place.

A Little Tension Is Good for a Door

❖ To straighten out a warped wooden screen door, install a tension rod with turnbuckle braces. Mount the rod

> ## PUZZLER
>
> THIS WAS A BOON TO the person who didn't have a leg to stand on.
>
> ANSWER: *Three-legged crutch.*

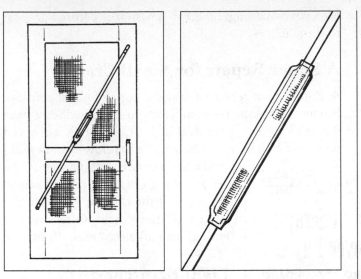

*A tension rod (left)
with a turnbuckle
brace (closeup,
right) will help a
warped screen door.*

diagonally on the door and tighten the turnbuckle as
needed.

Closing Lines

❖ If you're more concerned with long life than with nos-
talgic sounds, install a small hydraulic rotary closer on
your screen door. It will slowly and smoothly close the
door into position. This avoids slamming the door shut—
a process that's probably the fastest way to wear it out, as
each slam shakes the joinery loose. Traditional spring
closers are notorious offenders in the door-slamming department. The ubiquitous piston-type returns (found on
most aluminum screen and storm doors) are better than
springs, but they allow the door to open only 90 degrees,
and they lose their effectiveness over time. A rotary closer,
mounted correctly—fairly close to the hinge, rather than
in the middle of the door's edge—allows the door to open
all the way.

WINDOWPANES

Glass Pane Storage: Keep 'Em on Edge

❖ Always store glass windowpanes on edge, as you
would phonograph records. For extra protection—especially if the glass is old or thin—it's a good idea to wrap

each pane in a single sheet of newspaper before adding it to the stack.

A Super Repair for Small Cracks

❖ Rather than replace a cracked pane of glass, consider leaving it in place. (A small crack in a glass windowpane doesn't let out a great deal of heat, although a cracked pane will break more easily if the window is slammed.) Add a drop or two of super glue to the center of the crack. Capillary action should pull the thin liquid along the length of the crack. Often this is enough to make the crack disappear.

Light Scratches: You Can Skip the Floss

❖ To touch up light scratches on your window glass, rub the scratches very lightly with a mildly abrasive toothpaste (not the gel type). Use a cotton-gloved finger or soft flannel cloth to apply the paste. The method also works on light scratches on mirrors.

The Aged Can Be Thin and Irregular

❖ When cutting old glass to use or recycle, practice on scraps first. Old glass is no more brittle than new glass, but it is often thinner and more irregular. Because of that, applying smooth, even pressure with the glass cutter is crucial.

Cutting Glass: Even the Score

❖ When cutting old glass, first make sure the surface is completely free of dirt. Put a drop or two of lubricating oil on the cutting wheel. Make one smooth score, using a straightedge as a guide. Then use the ball end of the cutter to tap the underside of the score, starting in the middle and working out toward both sides. This will cause the break to run along the score.

A SECOND LIFE

The Best Paint Scraper You'll Never Buy

DON'T DISCARD broken panes of glass. Turn them into scrapers. The straight edge of a scrap of glass will cut well but not too deeply if you draw it toward you at a slight angle. A piece about one by three inches is easy to handle. Cover the noncutting edge with tape for safety, and slightly round the corners with a glass cutter so that they don't cut into the wood. When one edge gets dull, flip over the glass and use the other edge.

Cut Them Down to Size

❖ Don't throw away large panes of glass that have broken or chipped near their edges. Instead, use a glass cutter to cut the pane down to the next-smallest-size glass you use in your house or outbuildings. You'll have it on hand the next time you need a pane that size.

Putty in Your Hands

❖ True Yankees like to salvage as much glass as possible from broken windows in order to put it to other uses. Often that's a difficult chore, because the putty will have turned hard as cement. To deal with that problem, spray oven cleaner on the putty and allow it to soften, then remove it with a putty knife.

WINDOW SASHES

The Proper Way to Putty

❖ You can prolong the life of your window sash by brushing a coat of boiled linseed oil onto the wood before you putty. Let the oil soak in for about half an hour, then wipe off any excess before applying linseed oil putty. Because the oil will prevent the oil in the putty from being sucked into the dry wood, you'll be prolonging the life of the sash and the putty.

The Proper Way to Paint

❖ When you paint the outsides of your window sash, extend the paint beyond the putty so that it goes just barely onto the glass. That will keep water from getting down in back of the putty, prolonging the life of the wooden sash.

❖ Seal the bottom window rails and sills with boiled linseed oil before repainting. Those are areas where moisture

PUZZLER

JUST AS FOLKS ARE STILL TRYING to build a better mousetrap, they've been trying for years to improve on this invention. It was especially helpful in areas where the screen windows were in bad shape.

ANSWER: *Glass flytrap. The user would place sugar and water in the base to attract the flies, which would enter through the opening at the bottom and then be trapped under the glass dome.*

often collects and causes problems. Mix ½ cup of boiled linseed oil, ½ cup of paint thinner and a few drops of Japan drier to make the linseed oil dry properly. Scrape off all the loose paint. Brush on the mixture liberally, then allow it to dry for 24 hours. Repeat a second time (and a third for badly weathered wood). Wait 2 to 3 days, lightly sand, apply an alkyd primer and then finish with alkyd or latex paint. Wood painted this way, even when exposed to repeated moisture, should hold its paint for up to 10 years or more.

Magic Muntins

❖ Among the most fragile parts of a window sash are the thin glazing bars of the muntin. Especially when windows get old or stubborn glass is removed, those strips often break or snap off. If that happens, you don't have to re-place the entire sash or pay for a custom repair, and you don't have to compromise by creating a new bar out of

There's a Reason Window Frames Are White

EARL
remembers...

AS A KID, I HELPED my father maintain the local school buildings, which were brick. The window frames in the schools were painted dark green—because green and red are complementary colors, I suppose. So I learned early on why you should *not* paint window frames a dark color. The dark green absorbed the heat from the sun more readily than a light color would have, and therefore the putty in the windows dried and cracked more quickly. I was constantly working on the schools' windows.

It's pretty rare that you see windows painted a dark color today—and that's one trend you shouldn't be tempted to buck!

glazing. Instead, use a utility knife to cut a comparable strip out of the thin end of a spare clapboard. Attach it with small finish nails or brads, then reglaze as usual.

WINDOW CASINGS

You'll Wonder Where the Water Went

❖ If you have a chance to build new window casings, design the lower sill to slant away from the window, allowing water to run off easily.

❖ When you build your new window casings, add a thin strip of wood on the top, just over the window sash. Make sure it extends out over the window, forming a "hood" that will keep water off the window itself. This will prolong the life of the window's wooden frame.

HOOD

A hood on a window casing helps to prevent water damage.

The Low-Tech Way to Straighten a Lead Frame

❖ Often old lead frames (found in stained-glass windows) will bow or sink over time. To straighten them out, first soften the putty and remove the glass. Then wait for a hot sunny day and lay the bowed section on an asphalt driveway. Weight it down carefully with flat slates or a heavy board. During the course of a few hours, the gentle pressure of the weight and the reflected warmth from the asphalt will gradually straighten out the frame. Then you can put the glass back in place.

Alternatives to Replacement

❖ Before deciding to replace your old windows in favor of more efficient modern ones, consider the (usually cheaper) options: installing storm windows, thoroughly weatherstripping and caulking or creating "movable insulation" such as interior folding shutters, insulated panels or quilted drapes.

STORM AND SCREEN WINDOWS

Weeping Is Good for Them

❖ If you have the common triple-track aluminum combination storm windows, make sure the weep holes aren't plugged. Those two little gaps at the bottom edge of the frame are designed to let rainwater drain from the sill. If the holes are blocked, your windows will not drain properly—and the wooden sill below will rot from moisture damage.

Make Plastic Last

❖ Shrink-wrap plastic sheets taped across the inside of a window work tolerably well to create insulating dead-air space. Although they won't last as long as permanent storm windows, they're considerably cheaper, and you can get several seasons' use out of them if you remove and store them carefully. When winter is over, remove the plastic and roll it up. Place it in cardboard tubes or long, skinny boxes, secured by tape or string, and store it out of dirt's and harm's way—on the rafters of a garage, for example.

Adapt a pair of pallets to store your storm windows safely.

CONNECTING BOARDS

PALLET

STORM WINDOWS

PALLET

Storm Window Storage Stacks Up like This

❖ Here's a tip for storing seasonal storm windows. Construct a simple wooden crate with a slot for each window. Or pick up a couple of wooden pallets and mount them so that the slots line up—as long as the windows fit in the slots. Like all glass, storm windows should be stored on edge, as you would store books or records. If possible, keep them in a warm, dry place.

Keep Window Frames Looking Good

❖ You can keep the frames of aluminum combination windows looking good by maintaining them. To remove

I Had to Reconstruct the Problem

WHEN I WAS WORKING for my father right after high school, he won a contract to provide and install about 30 big storm windows for a commercial building. He sent my brother to measure and order the windows. When the windows were delivered, we got a rude shock. My brother had reversed the dimensions on all the windows. Instead of being four feet wide by six feet tall they were six feet wide by four feet tall. We couldn't use the windows turned on their sides, because they wouldn't work properly in the frames. I won't tell you what my father said!

EARL
remembers...

Since the windows were very expensive, I was assigned to rebuild them. As I started each window, I took out all the putty and window points (the tiny pieces of flat metal that you stick into the window frame to hold the pane in place for puttying). Then I removed the glass and took apart the frames. I rebuilt the frames in the proper dimensions and reassembled each window, reusing all the original materials. It took me about six weeks to finish the job, but it was satisfying to know that we weren't forced to throw away the windows.

When you're working on your home and you make a mistake, stop and think for a minute before you throw out the materials from the job. Lots of times, a little extra effort—and a touch of inventiveness—can salvage the project.

the white pits caused by oxidation, rub screen and window frames with aluminum jelly, a product sold in hardware stores for just that purpose. Kept free of oxidation, frames should last for many, many years.

Five Steps to Painting Storm Windows

❖ To ensure a long-lasting paint job on your aluminum storm windows, make sure to prepare the surface properly. After removing the dirt and grime, wipe down the aluminum surfaces with vinegar and let them dry. Use a primer coat specifically designed for metal surfaces, then apply at least two top coats. (If your aluminum storm windows are one of the new brands that come with a baked-on enamel surface, you can skip the paint job.)

SHUTTERS

The Most Fun Way to Clean Shutters

❖ To prolong the life of the paint job on your shutters—and therefore to prolong the life of the shutters themselves—you need to thoroughly clean off all dirt and debris at least once every two to three years. (The frequency depends on the location of the shutters. Incorporate a shutter check in your spring or fall cleaning ritual, and you'll be sure to know when they need cleaning.) That includes the tedious, usually time-consuming job of cleaning each side of every louver. Here's a better, quicker way to do that. Load your shutters into the back of your truck or station wagon and take them to the nearest do-it-yourself car wash. Spread them out, standing them

---

A SECOND LIFE

Turn Old Screening into a Scrubber

ONE GOOD WAY to remove rust and scour metal is to use a wire wheel spun by an electric drill. Old metal window screening is perfect for this. Cut out about a dozen five-inch-diameter circles of old screening. Drill a quarter-inch hole through their centers, slip them onto a bolt with washers on each side and lock them tight with a nut. Chuck the end of the bolt in the drill and secure the whole thing in place. You're ready to scour!

Cut circles of screening and bolt them into place on the end of a drill.

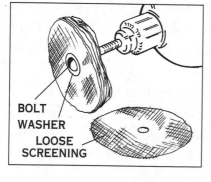

BOLT
WASHER
LOOSE
SCREENING

---

upright. Wash them as you would your car: spray them with warm soapy water, holding the wand about six inches away from the wood, then rinse well. Let them air dry before putting them back in place on the house. This is a lot faster and easier than doing the shutters by hand. Cost? About eight quarters.

Make Them Stiff in the Joints

❖ A quick way to extend the life of a shutter with loose joints is to pull the joints tight, then screw narrow L-shaped metal plates on the backs of the shutters to secure them in that position. Paint the plates (called mending plates in most hardware stores) the same color as the shutter.

Mending plates hold loose shutters tight.

Improve Their Sagging Posture

❖ If your louvered wooden shutters sag, strengthen them with a wire secured diagonally across the backs. Since the shutters tend to sag away from the support pins, the wire should pull the lower outside corner up and back toward the window.

Your Home's Exterior

W HEN I WORK ON A JOB, I want the result to look good. If it doesn't—even if the customer is happy with it—it bothers me. I've always felt that way. My father was different. If the customer was happy, he was happy—no matter how the job looked.

Once my father had me build an addition onto a building that had a hip roof. He told me to build a shed roof on the addition and to tie it into the hip roof above the eaves. I thought this would look awful, and I warned my father and our customer about it. The customer didn't care, so my father told me, "Titrivate it!"—which was his expression for "make it work." I did what he said, and both my father and the customer were satisfied with the way the job turned out. But the look of that building used to bother me every time I drove by it. After the building changed hands, the new owner tore down the addition I'd built and put up another one. If I'd been in his shoes, that's what I would have done, too.

In the form versus function debate, my father would choose function every time. But I say you need both if you want something to last.

In this chapter, perhaps more than in any other, making things last crosses the line from desirable to downright necessary. The exterior surfaces of our houses and outbuildings are what protect our biggest investments from the onslaught of weather and time. No paint, no wall—and no wall, no house! We'll take a look here not only at exterior walls but also at roofs, gutters, decks and all the other things that make a home a house, always with an eye toward the frontline defenses that make repairs less drastic and costly—and make a place look better, too.

EXTERIOR PAINT

The Band-Aid Test

❖ Considering applying new paint directly on top of old but concerned that the old stuff may not be sticking well enough to hold a new coat? Here's how you can find out: Take an ordinary adhesive bandage, stick it to the old paint surface and then rip it off just as you would from a healed cut. If the paint stays put, it's still well attached to the surface. If the bandage takes paint with it, go sharpen the scraper.

Paint Scrapers: Look Sharp!

❖ The longevity of your paint job is often determined by the thoroughness of your scraping job. There's no way around the work involved in doing it right, but this tip will help: don't skimp on your scraper's sharpness. Supply yourself with extra blades, or bring a file up on the ladder with you and sharpen your blade frequently.

Get Rid of That Gray

❖ When working with weathered, gray wood that hasn't seen a coat of paint in a while, sand down to bright wood—wood that looks nearly freshly sawn—before applying paint. The gray wood consists of fibers that have been broken down by the sun to a soft, spongy material, just right for collecting any moisture that makes its way under the paint film and causing more damage. By sanding it away, you give the remaining wood a better shot at a longer life.

Keep after It till It Stops Drinking

❖ After sanding any old, weathered wood on your home's exterior, but before applying primer, take the time to treat the freshly sanded areas with a solution of equal parts boiled linseed oil and turpentine. Make sure the wood is dry, then paint the mixture on with an old brush, reapplying it in particularly needy areas as the wood drinks it up. Allow the mixture to soak in, then return the next day and repeat the process until the area no longer drinks up

Paint: More Than Just a Pretty Face

PAINT MAKES the outside of your home look attractive, but its main purpose is functional, prolonging the life of wood or metal by protecting it from exposure to the elements. The paint binder blocks rain and water from attacking your home's exterior, and the opaque pigment in the paint shields the surface from the sun's ultraviolet rays, which break down wood fibers. Clear varnishes and other finishes don't provide this pigment, so outdoor wood treated with them turns gray from exposure to the sun's rays and is likely to show age by the second year. (Most such wood shows some blisters and is ready for refinishing by year five.) A properly prepared and applied paint job will hold up for at least five to seven years—longer if you follow the tips on these pages.

the liquid. (Areas to watch particularly are the old, neglected wooden parts of a house that have been exposed to a lot of sun but haven't seen any paint in a long time. The wood here is usually raw, chapped and dried out, and it will drink up the mix readily. Window frames, windowsills and door trim are particularly likely candidates.) Wait 24 hours, then apply a coat of primer. The treatment presaturates the wood, saving primer and helping it anchor better to the surface.

Moisture— The Old Enemy

❖ Before painting a windowsill, set of steps, porch deck or any other place where snow or rainwater tends to stand, treat the area with a paintable water repellent such as Woodlife, then prime and follow with a finish coat of paint. The repellent contains a waxy substance that repels moisture, keeping it away from the wood so that it won't lift the paint. These products are sold in paint stores, home centers and lumberyards. Check to be sure that the one you buy is paintable; some are made solely for use without paint.

Latex or Oil?

❖ If you have a surface that needs to breathe—that is, release moisture—as much as possible, choose an acrylic-latex paint system over oil-based or other paint. Areas of the house exterior where this might be the case are hollow porch columns, wooden siding near kitchens or bathrooms, and masonry walls. Of the common architectural coatings, latex paint is the most permeable to water vapor. That means there's a greater chance that it won't peel or blister as the moisture rises through it.

Time for a Change?

❖ Wondering about applying a water-based latex paint to an older house that's been protected with oil-based paint up to now? No problem. Just follow these keys to success: wash and prepare the surface well, and before starting to paint, apply an oil-based primer made specifically to work with latex paint. Typically, the safest bet is to stick to the same manufacturer for the primer and paint.

❖ Never try to apply oil-based paint over latex. You'll cause paint adhesion problems for sure.

Good-Bye, Old Paint

❖ If you have a house with very thick and old accumulations of oil-based paint—layers that go back, say, 100

Watch Out for Sprayed Paint

I WAS WORKING AT A WOMAN's big clapboard house when she called me over one day and said, "Earl, my house looks like it needs painting, but it was done just last year. What's wrong?" She was right about the paint job, which was peeling badly. I guessed, correctly, that the painters had used a sprayer.

Spraying paint on your house is one of those "shortcuts" that winds up costing you money. To spray paint, you need to thin it so much that most of what you're applying is thinner. A coat of paint should be just that—a sturdy seal against the elements. What's more, sprayed paint does not adhere well to the surface of your house. When you brush on paint, you are brushing it in at the same time.

EARL
remembers...

Some people prefer to spray-paint their houses, but I'd advise against it if you want your paint job to last.

---

years or more—be cautious about investing in a new latex paint job over the existing paint. When you're dealing with many layers, the first coats of paint—the ones that are the oldest—are also the critical coats that bond all the others to the wood or masonry. Oil-based paint loses its elasticity over decades, and these first coats may be very brittle. If you add a fresh, flexible latex coat outside these old brittle coats, the new paint can actually pull the old paint off the building as it moves with changes in the weather.

A Great Method for Procrastinators

❖ If you're worried that a new layer of latex may have this effect on an old building but you're not anxious to start stripping off all that old paint, here's an alternative: paint a test strip on the side of the building with the oldest, thickest paint and see how it holds up over at least six months (two changes of season). That sounds like a long time, but why rush into a whole-house paint job when the only indication that it won't fail is hope?

Matchmaker, Matchmaker

❖ Always stick with compatible systems when doing a two-coat paint job. That is, use a primer and a top-coat paint that are made to work together. The easiest way to do this, of course, is to stick with the same manufacturer for both products. This advice is more than just a bit of brand-loyalty salesmanship. Although most paints of a type are basically the same, each manufacturer includes its own set of additives for shelf life, performance on the building, mildew resistance and so on. If you mix brands, there's a chance the additives may clash and cause your good work to fail prematurely.

The Secret of Its A-peel

Y OU CAN MAKE a new paint job last longer if you first solve the problems with the old one. Before you start prepping or painting, take a long look at the surface and analyze why it's failing. One rule of thumb divides peeling paint into two types. Paint that's peeling between coats suffers from a poor prep job (usually a dirty or chalky surface) or incompatible paints (paints from different manufacturers, for example). Paint that's peeling down to bare wood is often being "blown off" by moisture problems behind the paint. If you have this problem, check for water entering the wall (such as roof or gutter leaks from above), condensation in the wall (from improperly installed insulation) or high moisture levels in the house (say, a shower and teenagers on the other side).

When You Prime, It's Time

❖ To avoid intercoat peeling problems in a season or two, be sure to apply the top coat of paint within a week or two of applying the primer—48 hours is actually ideal. Never prime new work in the fall and then come back in the spring to finish the job. The primer not only will get dirty but also will develop compounds on its surface that will resist bonding with the top coat.

Painters' Weather

❖ Paint exterior siding in hot, dry weather, when the wood is as dry as possible. Your paint job will last longer. (And choose the sides you work on according to the shade: west side in the morning, north side at midday, east side in the afternoon, for instance. Painting in the heat is hard enough—give yourself a break.)

❖ Never paint on a cool surface that will be in hot, direct sunlight in a few hours. You'll get temperature blisters—those noteworthy (up to deviled-egg size) bubbles in the new coat of paint—within a day or two. Temperature blisters form when the sun warms liquids (such as water or thinner in the paint itself). The rapid change in temperature causes them to expand under the new, still very elastic paint film.

❖ Don't paint when the temperature is below 50°F. You'll risk poor bonding between coats and the chance of intercoat peeling down the road.

Dews and Don'ts

❖ Never apply latex paint in the early morning, before all the dew has lifted, or in the evening of a cool spring or fall day. If you do, you'll risk streaking and discoloration as the fresh dew mixes with the water in the still-wet paint.

EXTERIOR STAINS

Paint That Ain't

❖ When you're working with a difficult paint surface—say, weathered wood or shingles, or siding with moisture problems—consider using a semitransparent stain instead of paint. As the name implies, these coatings are half opaque paint, half clear stain. They penetrate the wood well, so they have good adhesion on hard-to-paint or porous woods like rough-sawn lumber. To a much greater extent than true paint, they can be permeated harmlessly by moisture. The downside is that they don't give the same protection as paint and they have to be renewed more frequently.

❖ Don't bother trying to use semitransparent stains on composition and "engineered" wood building materials. The glues and waxes in waferboard, oriented strand board, chipboard and even hardboard will keep the stain from penetrating. The same holds true for staining over paint or opaque stains (which contain a higher level of pigment). Most plywoods will accept stain, but test first if you suspect otherwise.

Double Protection

❖ When applying a stain, use two coats of stain for longer-lasting protection. For the best penetration, apply the second coat before the first is completely dry—which generally means you should start on the second coat within 20 to 30 minutes after beginning the first. On a big job, you'll have to watch your timing a little to pull this off—or have a second painter follow you by 20 minutes.

SIDING BASICS

After the Rain Is Gone

❖ Inspect your house's siding after it's stopped raining. Darker areas will indicate a potential problem where water either is being directed or is collecting. Check around front and back steps, around electric meters, near gutter seams

---

PUZZLER

THIS SEVEN-FOOT IMPLEMENT, popular with undertakers, made everyone come out even.

ANSWER: *Casket leveler. After a casket had been set down in the grave and one side was found to be higher than the other, the hook would be slid under the low side and the casket lifted. A little dirt would be thrown in to keep things level, then the hook would be pulled out.*

and around propane tanks or anything else standing close to the house. If you can't figure out how to reduce the water hitting those areas, add an extra coat or two of stain or paint—and be prepared to maintain those sections a bit more frequently than other parts of the siding.

The House's Raincoat

❖ An old-time solution to the problem of splash back of rainwater onto a house's siding was to reduce the "exposure" of the clapboards toward the bottom of the wall. (Exposure is the amount of clapboard exposed to the weather.) Although this is not commonly done anymore in this age of gutters, synthetic siding and good in-ground drainage, the concept is still sound. Simply start with a very tight exposure—say, an inch and a half. Gradually, over the first eight to ten courses, increase this to the uniform exposure you've chosen for the main part of the house—say, four inches. The exposed part of those lower clapboards will be thicker and therefore will last longer before needing to be replaced. The graduated exposure, incidentally, creates a very pleasing aesthetic effect.

WOODEN LAP SIDING

High and Dry

❖ Wooden siding will last longer if you let it dry at least several months before putting it up. This allows the pores in the wood to open fully. Open pores mean deeper penetration and a better bond with the paint or stain—in other words, better protection against moisture and less maintenance for you.

❖ To dry wooden siding or other lumber, the key is to stack the lumber with good air circulation in mind. Keep the wood off the ground, and use three-quarter-inch strips of wood called stickers, spaced about two feet apart, between courses of boards. Stack clapboards (which have a tapered thickness) in married pairs.

Wooden siding must be air-dried before installation. To allow the air to get at the wood, stack the clapboards in pairs, separating the rows with smaller sticks of wood and being sure to keep the boards off the ground.

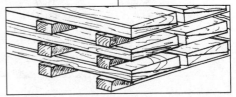

Perfect Mates

❖ A joint between two clapboards is an opportunity for water to enter behind the siding and start decay problems. Ideally, the clapboards on a house are carefully planned so that all boards end at a window, door or corner, but you can't always be that lucky. Where joints are inevitable, it's good practice to make the seam as watertight as possible. Here in New England, the traditional technique is to make a skived joint—that is, to taper both boards so that one laps onto the other like a pair of mating wedges. If you don't want to go that far, at least install some flashing under the joint before butting the boards. A six-inch-wide piece of roofing felt will work fine.

Clapboards: A Radial Idea

MOST CLAPBOARDS today are flat-sawn—cut out of the log in a quick and economical fashion. The grain in those boards varies greatly, resulting in differing degrees of drying and, over time, warping or twisting. But a few small and specialty clapboard mills still cut them the old way—radially or quarter-sawn. Each board is cut out of the log perpendicular to the grain. The result? Straight, even grain in each clapboard, which eliminates warping and twisting and which accepts paints and stains extremely well. Properly applied radially sawn clapboards can last more than a hundred years. While many of these specialty mills charge a premium, catering to the restoration market, the clapboards are so superior to off-the-shelf clapboards that they actually save money over the life of the job.

Radially sawn clapboards (A) last much longer than the more common flat-sawn ones (B).

A

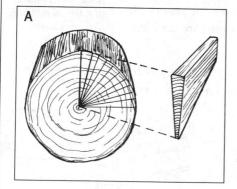

B

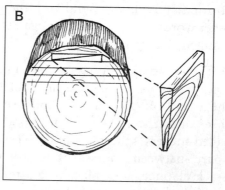

The Great Escape

❖ If you suspect that you have high moisture levels in your walls, it's worth your while to increase the ventilation through the clapboards. One way to do this is to slip wedges between the clapboards at regular intervals to open up the space. You can use plastic or metal spacers sold for this purpose. Or you can make your own out of shingles or thin hardwood strips—even cut nails (used for flooring and masonry) will work. Just tap them in wherever the boards are free. The goal is to create a gap of one-quarter inch or so.

Nail Head Rust Relief

❖ To avoid rusty nail heads on a clapboard house, use hot-dipped galvanized nails. Prime the nail heads with a white metal primer for more protection. Then set the heads and fill the holes with putty to add another shield and simultaneously hide the nails. Rusty nail heads can be unsightly on a clapboard house and can even encourage deterioration in the siding.

❖ If you're especially concerned about rusty nails destroying the appearance of your house in the future, do what the old-timers did: drive the nails in at a slightly uphill angle so that if they do get wet, gravity won't carry the water into the wood!

Clapboard Caulking Has Its Limits

ALTHOUGH IT'S a good idea to caulk the vertical joints of clapboards where they meet door and window trim to reduce wind and rain penetration, you should never try to caulk the horizontal joints where one clapboard lies on another. Clapboards, being wooden, have to move with changes in moisture levels. If you seal them together, they may split. Furthermore, sealing these joints can trap moisture inside the walls behind the clapboards, causing paint and decay problems.

WOODEN SHINGLES

Aging, Weather or Not

❖ After they've repaired parts of a shingled wall to make it last longer, most folks look for a way to make it match. A simple way to get new brown cedar shingles to look weathered is to dissolve 1 pound of baking soda in 1 gallon of water. Spray the mixture onto the shingles, and after a few hours in the sunlight, the shingles will turn ash-colored.

Wanted: Flat Shingles

❖ Cedar shingles larger than eight inches wide are likely to cup over time and need replacing. Avoid that problem by using a utility knife to split those wide shingles in half before nailing them up. They'll lie flatter that way and last longer.

Victoriana

A FTER THE GREAT New England Hurricane of 1938, I worked for my father for an entire year patching up damaged houses. Right after the storm, we rushed around and took care of emergency repairs. Then we did another round of the homes of his regular customers, putting everything in order.

EARL
remembers...

The most challenging job my father gave me after the "Big Blow" was repairing the Victorian home of his old boss. My father wanted the job to come out perfectly. The problem was that the high winds had blown the ornamental detail from the Victorian's quarter-circle porch all over the neighborhood. I had to chase around and find all the pieces I could. Even back then, it was hard to get ornamental work like that—hand-planed curved moldings, all of them custom. After lots of searching, I found most of the pieces of the porch and fit them back together. It was like doing a giant puzzle.

Of course, the craftsmanship on buildings has declined considerably since then. If you have nice, old ornamental work on your house, don't let it fall into disrepair. It's irreplaceable.

A Swell Idea for Cedar

❖ Cedar shingles have a tendency to swell when they get
wet, so be sure to leave a slight gap (about one-eighth inch)
between them as you lay them up. That space will allow
for swelling without buckling and lead to a longer life for
the siding.

Nail It Right

❖ When installing exterior siding, always use either stainless steel or hot-dipped galvanized nails. Either of these
will last as long as the siding does, and neither will create
rust stains.

❖ When nailing wooden siding shingles in place, drive the
nail until the head just barely touches the wood; don't let
it go deep into the wood. This approach leaves the shingle free to expand and contract without splitting around
the nail head.

MAN-MADE SIDING

Paint the Siding, Not the Dirt

❖ Before painting any man-made siding, be sure to wash
the surface thoroughly. Use a scrub brush and a household or commercial detergent mixed with warm water.
Failing to remove dirt, oils, mildew and chalking pigments
is the major reason a new paint job will start to peel between coats and not hold up as long as it should.

❖ If the siding you plan to paint is particularly dirty, you
might prefer to clean it with pressure-washing equipment,
available from equipment-rental firms.

Don't Dent Your Siding

❖ It doesn't make much sense to risk denting or buckling
man-made siding with a ladder while you're trying to paint
or otherwise improve it. Take care to support the ladder
ends on nonsiding areas like windowsills, or cushion them
with a wrapping of rags.

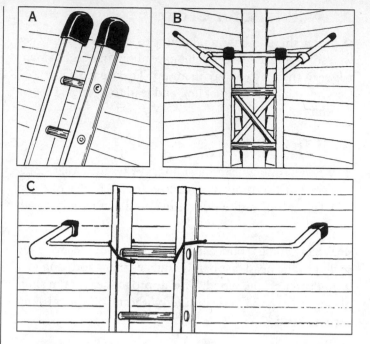

Ladder caps (A) help protect your home's siding while you're working on it. So do stabilizers, whether used in the ell portion of a house (B) or on a straight surface (C).

❖ If you're going to be doing a lot of work on your siding, you might want to invest in accessories such as the ladder caps (protective coverings for the ends) or stabilizers made by most major ladder companies. The stabilizers are U-shaped devices made of tube aluminum that clamp onto the ladder so that it is supported some distance out at either side. Stabilizers come in many models—fixed sizes (48 inches is the standard span), adjustable and even angled versions for leaning on building corners or round walls.

Aging Aluminum

❖ If your aluminum siding has developed flaking paint, oxidation of the bare aluminum or chalking (a powdery surface), it's especially important to prepare the surface before painting it. Use medium- or fine-grade steel wool to clean the siding down to a stable substrate. Aluminum siding is metal that's been coated with a prepared finish at the factory, so as it ages, it's not unusual for the finish to develop these problems.

❖ If the siding has seen some weathering, stick to a flat finish when selecting your paint. Glossy finishes will highlight any dings and scratches in the metal surface.

❖ Prime aluminum siding with a good-quality exterior acrylic-latex primer, followed by an acrylic-latex finish coat in the color of your choice.

Vinyl Victories

❖ To clean mildew or occasional chalking from vinyl siding, just wash it with laundry detergent mixed with water and applied with a scrub brush.

❖ Don't try to sand vinyl siding; you'll only damage the surface. Vinyl siding is plastic with color incorporated throughout the material. It will fade on exposure to the sun's ultraviolet rays, but since it has no paint, it won't peel. Therefore sanding is unnecessary.

Keep It Light

❖ If you decide to paint your faded vinyl siding, be sure to choose a tone that's lighter than the original siding color—never darker. Vinyl siding is sensitive to heat, and repainting in a new, darker color, which will absorb radiant energy, can cause the siding to warp and buckle irreversibly.

MASONRY WALLS

Don't Paint Over Your Problems

❖ If the masonry walls of your basement or garage are damp, have started peeling or have efflorescence (white marks or crystal "flowers" of salts blooming out of the surface), inspect them carefully to figure out where the water is coming from. You may need to change the pitch of your gutter or add more downspouts. (See index for tips.)

❖ Don't ever paint or seal below-ground garage floors or walls if you have moisture problems. Moisture that is migrating through the masonry won't be stopped by a thin

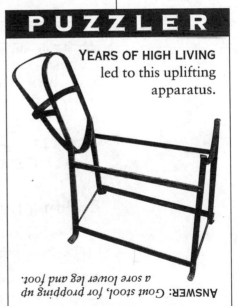

PUZZLER

YEARS OF HIGH LIVING led to this uplifting apparatus.

ANSWER: Gout stool, for propping up a sore lower leg and foot.

Drop Out of the Ivy League

IVY GROWING ON the outside of your house can give the building a traditional look, but your stucco and masonry exterior wall surfaces will last longer if they aren't hosts to such distinctive vegetation. Ivy and other vines growing on the sides of houses—like those living on roofs and gutters—can be the source of premature failure. Although some people argue that the leaves shield the siding from water, on many houses the vines hold moisture near the building. Walls should not be trellises. Ditch the plants.

To do this, cut the ivy away a few square feet at a time, leaving the suckers, pads or roots that connect the plant to the building. Allow these remnants to dry for a week or two, then remove them with a stiff brush and laundry detergent mixed with water. Don't use acids (which can stain) or wait until the suckers turn very hard. And, tempting as the idea may be, don't try to pull the greenery down. Most climbing plants are anchored to the masonry with those deceptively innocent-looking bits of greenery, and pulling the vines away can take weak mortar or brick with them, causing severe damage to the wall.

film. It will simply move the paint or sealant out of the way and create blisters. (In fact, coatings on indoor surfaces can do real damage, allowing moisture to build up in the wall or floor to the point that it becomes completely saturated.)

PORCHES, DECKS AND OUTDOOR STAIRWAYS

Building (and Repairing) Basics

❖ When building or repairing a porch or deck, make it last longer by using galvanized nails.

❖ Lay floorboards directly on top of joists and allow for plenty of ventilation underneath. Don't use a subfloor.

Perfect Pitch

❖ Slope the floorboards one-eighth inch for every foot they run away from the house. (The boards, naturally, run in the direction of the slope, allowing water to run off down the cracks.)

For a Finished Floor

❖ For a finished porch or deck floor, use caulked tongue-and-groove joints. (Put a small bead of caulk along the tongue before inserting it into the groove.)

A Simple Spacer

❖ For a camp or other informal porch floor, lay the floor-boards with a small (one-quarter inch or less) gap between the boards, allowing water to run down through the floor. Here's a simple way to create a uniform gap as you nail down the boards: drive a twelvepenny nail through each end of a piece of scrap wood. Use the nails as a gauge, butting each new floorboard tight against the nails before fastening it. Some people use a nail alone for a spacer, but driving a pair of them through a block of wood makes both nails easier to hold, easier to find and less likely to drop through to the ground.

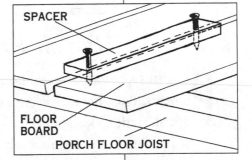

SPACER

FLOOR BOARD

PORCH FLOOR JOIST

This simple spacer—which you can easily make from a piece of scrap wood and a couple of twelvepenny nails—lets you position porch floorboards evenly.

Keep Things Free and Open

❖ Don't defeat the purpose of careful construction. Clean the spaces between floorboards regularly with a putty knife and garden hose. Do this often enough to keep the spaces open and free of dirt and leaf debris.

Do You Really Need Risers?

❖ One way to ventilate outdoor wooden stairs is to skip the vertical riser board behind the tread. Although the riser will make for a more refined-looking staircase, it will trap moisture in the space under and behind the staircase.

To make outdoor stairs last longer, cut decorative shapes in the risers. This will improve ventilation behind the steps.

Artistic Talents on the Rise

❖ If you simply can't live without risers on your outdoor stairs, at least perforate them—say, with decorative cutouts such as stars or half-moons.

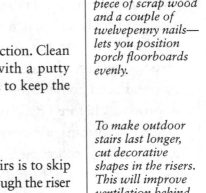

Don't Frustrate Your Vents

❖ If you need to restrict access to the space underneath a porch, deck or outdoor stairway, screen the area with open-mesh wooden lattice or a similar material that permits free airflow. Never enclose or box in the space. These features sit near the ground, where constant moisture and lack of sunlight encourage the growth of wood-eating organisms. Good ventilation is the key to keeping them around longer.

Porch Protection

PORCHES ARE PRONE to rot because they are so exposed to the elements. Back before the days of pressure-treated lumber, it was a real battle to keep a porch from falling apart.

The biggest porch repair job I ever tackled was on a porch that wrapped around three sides of an old cottage. The porch was so badly rotted that I had to rip out most of it and start from scratch. After I had laid new joists, I covered their tops with roofing felt so that water seeping through the porch would not rot them, as it had before. I oiled both the tops and bottoms of the floorboards before I nailed them on. This protected the bottoms of the boards from the moisture that would collect there. Then, when I nailed the boards in place, I left a crack between the floorboards so that water could seep through.

E A R L
remembers...

Some builders think that they can lay flooring tight on a porch, because the structure is covered by a roof. I disagree. Water will always find its way onto a porch—even if it's covered—and the porch needs to shed that water if it's going to last. Even with pressure-treated lumber, this should be your guiding principle for porch construction.

Cut Down on Cupping

❖ Avoid cupping in outdoor stairways by using two or three narrow boards rather than one large board for each step.

❖ Another way to cut down on cupping is to prime and paint the bottoms of the tread boards (or the floorboards of a porch or deck) so that they won't absorb moisture from the ground and swell more than the exposed, drier tops.

Jack Up the Low Spots

❖ If you notice any low spots where water collects on the porch floor, rent a hydraulic or screw jack to lift those areas, then support them with four-by-four posts. Although this is a dirty job, it's a fairly simple one, and may add years to the life of the floor.

Mats Aren't Welcome

❖ As a rule, don't use carpets or mats on porch or deck floors. They trap moisture below them.

Time to Replant?

❖ An easy way to make your porch last longer is to hang your plants from the outer—not the inner—edge of the eaves, where they won't drip water onto the porch railing or floor. Or use plant pots that have saucers to catch the dripping water.

PATIOS

Hold the Salt

❖ In the winter, use sand or cinders to cope with the ice on your masonry patio. Avoid using rock salt, calcium chloride and other salt-based ice-melting products. Salt is a natural enemy of all masonry, as it deteriorates cement mortar and concrete.

It Worked with the Pyramids

❖ When building a flagstone patio on a sand bed, you can make it hold up better over the years if you use large, thick stones with flat tops and bottoms and relatively square edges. Large stones resist shifting more than small ones. They're also less time-consuming to lay and grout.

This Is No Time to Be Shallow

❖ In constructing a flagstone patio to last, be generous with the mortar joints. Make them at least one inch wide and deep. Thin, shallow mortar joints tend to break up after a few seasons of expansion and contraction, while the mass and surface area of larger joints increase their longevity.

A Better Bond

❖ Mortar joints are likely to fail in a short time on a brick patio laid on a sand base. You'll have better luck—and looks—with a sand-mortar fill. Combine one part cement and four parts sand in a dry mix, then pack all joints around the brick (start with a push broom, then follow up with a trowel). Moisten the grout with a light misting from a garden hose for half an hour. Repeat the misting every day or so for several days to keep the patio damp and allow the grout to bond and cure. Keep the spray light, and be careful not to wash away the grout. Regrout the patio at the beginning of each year or as needed.

Noodling Around

❖ Where a flagstone patio meets the house, you'll often have a major joint that will inevitably expand and contract as the two surfaces move. When caulking large joints like these, fill most of the joint first with plastic backer rods—spongy caulking "noodles" sold at lumberyards.

PUZZLER

THIS 31-POUND IRON OBJECT was used for fancywork—but not necessarily by the lady of the house. The bottom leaves a zig-zag pattern, as shown, if hammered into soft material.

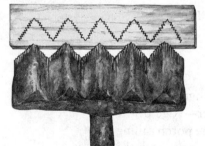

ANSWER: Leather worker's tool. It was used to cut designs on leather jackets or give a fancy edge to other items.

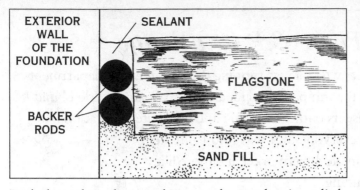

EXTERIOR WALL OF THE FOUNDATION

SEALANT

FLAGSTONE

BACKER RODS

SAND FILL

Use plastic backer rods to fill most of the space between a flagstone patio and your home's foundation. To create a joint that will last, add sealant only on top of the backer rods.

Pack the rods in the gap almost to the top, leaving a little less than the distance across the gap unfilled. Then caulk the rest of the way with sealant. Using this method saves sealant and produces a limber, hourglass-shaped seal that will flex with both materials. Don't succumb to the expedient solution of filling the cavity with sealant. You'll not only consume a lot of sealant, but you'll also get a big, inflexible band that will soon pull away from one side of the joint and defeat its purpose.

WOODEN ROOFS

Fight Cavities

❖ Your wooden roof will last longer if you give it a regular clean sweep. Before the wet season begins, or anytime you see an accumulation of litter, brush away all leaves, pine needles, sticks and seeds with a stiff broom. Pay particular attention to the "keys"—the gaps between shingles. Like the spaces between your teeth, they trap foreign matter that can start deterioration. "Floss" them clear with an old screwdriver if they're full of debris. Then rinse with water from a garden hose.

Wooden Shingle Preservatives

❖ Your new wooden-shingle roof will last longer if you apply a wood preservative to it when the roof has weathered for three to four months but not more than a year. The goal here is to fight off the mosses and wood-eating fungi that do in many wooden roofs before they are ten years old. At a lumberyard or hardware store, pick up a

The A&P Challenge

AT ONE POINT WHEN I was running the maintenance department at Yankee, the company bought an old A&P supermarket building to house its data-processing and computer operations. Before we moved everyone in, I was told to make it look less like an old supermarket and more like a nice office building.

EARL remembers...

It was easy enough to renovate the interior of the building, but the exterior was a real challenge. First we took down the old A&P sign and replaced it with a beautifully crafted wooden sign of our own. Then I took on the round metal columns that supported the flat roof over the building's entrance. I boxed these in with fancy wooden panels, which helped to give the entrance a more traditional look. We landscaped the entrance, planting all sorts of trees and shrubs in a granite-bordered area.

But still the building looked like an old A&P supermarket, and I knew why. A trademark of old A&P buildings is their cupolas, which are set distinctively at an angle to their bases. So on a day when there was no wind, I climbed up through the attic, stood inside the 12-foot-high cupola and loosened the bolts that secured it. I moved pretty gingerly inside the cupola, because I would have been in trouble if it had tipped over. A helper on the roof carefully turned the cupola until it was square with its base. Then I bolted it down.

That slight change made all the difference in the appearance of the building. It didn't look like an old A&P after that. The management of the A&P chain later sent a photographer to record the alterations we'd made so that they could show the potential of their old buildings to prospective buyers.

Sometimes it's not making the change that's the problem. It's knowing what to change.

wood preservative (in either an oil-based or a water-based form) that contains one of these active ingredients: copper naphthenate, zinc naphthenate or copper 8 quinolinolate. Using a thick-napped paint roller or a sprayer, apply the treatment to a dry, clean roof in several even, light coats. The idea is to make sure the wood absorbs as much of the liquid as possible. You'll know when you've gone far enough. As the wood becomes saturated, it will accept less and less of the preservative.

You Could Always Repaint the House to Match the Roof

❖ When applying a wood preservative to a new roof, be sure to test the treatment for appearance in a small area before doing the whole roof. Some compounds may alter the color of the wood—copper naphthenate, for example, imparts a greenish tint—in ways that some people don't find pleasing.

Flash! Help for Wooden Roofs!

❖ You can let Mother Nature help with some of your wooden roof preservative treatments. Installing 2-inch-wide strips of copper or galvanized flashing along the ridge of your roof will often keep mosses and lichens under control. (If you have a big roof, run a strip horizontally every 15 to 20 feet up the roof.) You may have noticed that mosses and lichens almost never grow below the flashing around a chimney or dormer. That's because the rain running over the metal leaches out chemicals that retard the growth of the organisms. Copper flashing creates copper

Install a 2-inch-wide strip of copper flashing along the ridge of your roof to deter moss (A). If the roof is large, add more strips of flashing at 15- to 20-foot intervals (B).

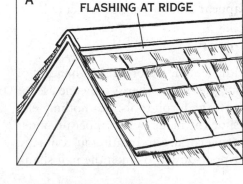

A **FLASHING AT RIDGE**

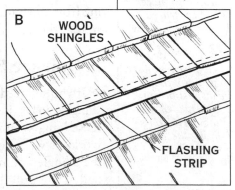

B **WOOD SHINGLES**

FLASHING STRIP

compounds similar to those in copper naphthenate. Galvanized flashing releases zinc, another effective retardant.

A Little off the Top

❖ Use a hammer and chisel to remove one or two damaged wooden shingles without disturbing others in the course. Position a one-half-inch chisel on the butt of the first faulty shingle about one to one and a half inches in from the side—approximately where the nail is hidden at the top—and start splitting the shingle apart. Repeat on the other side, extracting pieces as you go, until the shingle is free of the nails and falls out.

Replace a Single Shingle

❖ Once you have the damaged shingle out, you'll want to replace it with a new one. Cut and plane a new shingle so that it fits the opening fully, but without binding or lifting the course on top. Slide the shingle into place, tapping it in until it has about one-quarter inch to go before the butt is flush with the neighboring shingles, but no farther. Now, take two tenpenny galvanized finishing nails and drive them in at an angle at the top of the shingle, right where it meets the next course. Set the heads just slightly below the surface with a nail set. Finally, take a block of wood and, working from the butt, tap the shingle all the way into position so that the nails disappear and the shingle is secured.

A Quicker Ripper

❖ If you're faced with removing more than a handful of shingles, invest in a shingle ripper. There's only one use for these long, swordlike forged-iron tools, but nothing else works as well. You slide the blade of the ripper up under the shingle and maneuver it around until you contact a nail. Then pull the ripper down to cinch the nail shank

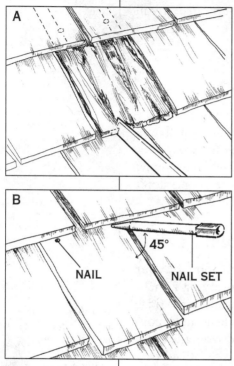

Use a chisel to split a faulty shingle (A), then remove the pieces. Slide a replacement shingle almost into place (B), then drive a couple of tenpenny nails into the top of it at a 45-degree angle. Use a nail set to position the heads just below the surface of the shingle. Finish by tapping the shingle completely into its place.

MAKE IT LAST

with the forked tip. Once you've hooked a nail, drive the ripper down with a few blows of a hammer, and it will pull out the shingle, nails and all. If you can't find a shingle ripper at a hardware store, look for one at a roofing supply house.

Scrub Those Shingles

❖ If you find dirt, light stains or a little mold and mildew on your wooden shingles, a good scrubbing with a cleaning solution will probably get rid of them. Mix together 3 ounces of TSP or another product containing trisodium phosphate, 1 ounce of powdered laundry detergent, 1 quart of household (5 percent) bleach, and 3 quarts of warm water. Apply the solution with a broom or soft brush. Rinse clean with fresh water.

A Healthy Roof Gathers No Moss

❖ An old-time, but still practical, way to remove heavier accumulations of moss from wooden roofs is to apply a good dose of copper sulfate (bluestone)—the same crystals you buy at a hardware store for root problems in plumbing lines. Mix ¼ to ½ ounce of copper sulfate in 10 gallons of water. Then use a watering can or pump sprayer to shower the solution on the moss. Go back over areas with particularly heavy moss accumulation a second time, or douse them with a stronger mixture. Then rinse off the mixture with a garden hose or power sprayer. Use copper sulfate carefully, as it can corrode some metals and harm plants. Keep it away from children and pets. Avoid spraying gutters, flashing and plants, and as soon as you finish the moss treatment, rinse all of these thoroughly. (You may want to cover

Nothing else is quite as effective as a shingle ripper. Place the blade under the row of shingles and move it around until you hook a nail. Use a hammer to drive the ripper down and pull out both shingle and nail.

A Word of Caution

CHEMICALS POWERFUL enough to kill green growths on roofs are strong enough to be treated with respect. Keep them out of the reach of children and pets, and dress appropriately when using such materials. Gloves, goggles, long sleeves and pants are prudent gear to wear when using copper sulfate or even common household (5 percent) bleach. Also, avoid breathing the fumes or dust of such chemicals or splashing liquid on the skin.

When Is a Shingle Not a Shingle?

SOMETIMES YOU HEAR people using the terms *shingle* and *shake* interchangeably when they're talking about wooden roofs. It's enough to give a roofer a case of the shakes (or even the shingles). There's an important difference.

Wooden shingles have been around for hundreds of years. In colonial days, they were handmade by splitting single shingles out of oak, cedar or cypress logs with a mallet and froe, then dressing them (smoothing the surface) with a drawknife. In the nineteenth century, when steam-powered saws and shingle mills appeared, shingles could be split or sawn out by machine (then sometimes resawn to produce two shingles). With either process, the shingles were always relatively flat and smooth on both sides.

Wooden shakes, however, are pretty much a creation of this century. As ranch houses became popular in California in the 1950s, so did the wooden roofs that typically covered them. These roofs, made of shakes, were characterized by a heavily textured appearance that added visual interest. The shakes were thick and purposely split to produce an uneven, washboard-type surface that was left undressed. While these look rustic to us today, our ancestors probably would have thought such roofs were unfinished and would never have used them. (In some areas, people aren't allowed to use them today. Some localities now have fire regulations restricting the use of wooden shingles and shakes.)

any shrubs, flowers or grass in the area before beginning this procedure.)

Moss Murders

❖ An alternative way to get rid of moss on a roof is to apply one of the products—known generically as moss killers or biocides—made for keeping green growth off masonry patios. These moss controllers, available at garden and lawn supply stores, are safer for plants, animals and humans (and they don't corrode metals). Many are potassium salts of fatty acids—biodegradable soaplike chemicals that break down the cell walls of the moss. However, they also should be used with care. Follow the same precautions as for copper sulfate.

Take the Weight Off

❖ Never walk on a slate roof if you can help it. If you must work on one, stand on a ladder laid over the roof to distribute your weight.

A Roof to Last a Lifetime

A MAN ONCE CALLED ME to ask for an estimate to build a garage and a breezeway. The barn that was attached to his house had recently burned, but it had not been totally destroyed by the fire. He wanted to replace the barn with a garage, and he wanted the addition to be in keeping with the style of his well-kept old house.

I won the job because I told him I'd salvage the slate tiles off his old barn roof and use them on the new garage and breezeway. My plan saved him money, because he didn't have to pay for new roofing material. But he was most pleased by the fact that the "new" slate roof would match the existing slate roof on his house.

EARL
remembers...

A good slate roof, when properly maintained, will last several lifetimes. All you really need to do is replace slates when they crack or begin to absorb moisture. The better the quality of the slate, the longer it will resist moisture. And slates crack infrequently—usually when a roofer or chimney sweep has been walking on them the wrong way.

If you don't want to spring for the cost of a new slate roof, look for a roofing concern that specializes in salvaging slates from old buildings. One of these outfits can install a slate roof for you. The cost will still be high, but your roof will last longer than you will.

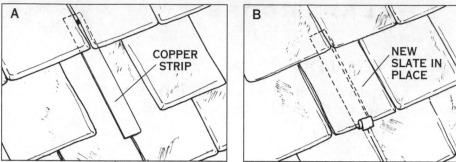

A **COPPER STRIP**

B **NEW SLATE IN PLACE**

To install a replacement slate, first nail a copper supporting strip to the deck boards (A). Position the new slate, then bend the copper up (B) to secure it.

Keep Tabs on Your Slate Roof

❖ If you need to repair an individual slate on a roof, you may want to use the metal tab method. First, remove the damaged slate with a shingle ripper, available at a hardware store or roofing supply house. Next, install a copper strip that extends an inch or so beyond the butts of the slates. Nail the strip to the deck boards (the wooden surface over the rafters that supports the roof) by inserting the nail between two slates. Slide the new slate into place, then simply bend the tab up like a hook to secure the slate in place.

Careful Keystrokes

❖ Other people prefer the nail method of repairing slates, because it leaves no metal tab to be dislodged by ice and snow. After fitting a new slate in place, mark it for a nail hole. This will be in the space, or "key," between the two slates in the course on top and high enough so that the nail will pass through only the replacement slate—not those in the course below. Drill a hole in the slate at this spot and secure it with one fourpenny copper slater's nail. (You'll have to trim the sides off the nail head to get it through the

Alternatively, drill a hole in the slate (A) and secure it with a trimmed-down slater's nail (B). Cover the nail with a copper strip to prevent water damage.

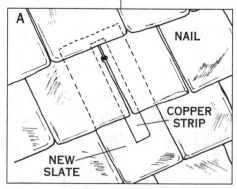

A **NAIL** **COPPER STRIP** **NEW SLATE**

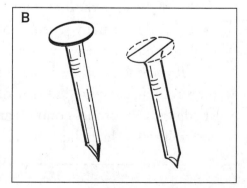

B

key or nibble away parts of the slates on either side.) Finally, slide a strip of copper up on top of the slate so that it covers the nail by a couple of inches. You can bend the copper so that it is slightly crowned and stays in place by itself, or you can adhere it with some silicone caulk.

Slipping and Sliding

❖ When roof slates are basically intact but there still seems to be a water problem, you can solve it with copper or aluminum slips. Cut several rectangles of the metal you prefer, each roughly half the size of a slate, and slide them under the slates and keys in the problem area. Use a medium-size drywall taping knife to "weasel" them in as far up the slates as possible. Try a few at first, but be prepared to come back with more until the leak is fixed.

TILE ROOFS

You're Not Running a Hostel

❖ The open ends of Spanish and barrel tiles at the eaves of a roof are favorite nesting places for birds and small critters. To keep out these creatures (as well as their nests, which can be tinderboxes), mortar the ends closed with ready-mix cement or install prefab metal bird stops (available at good roofing supply houses).

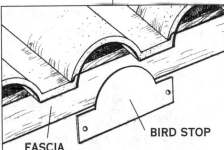

A bird stop will keep small creatures from moving into the ends of a tile roof.

Say Good-Bye to the Old Bat

❖ If you see bats leaving the eaves of your tile roof at dusk and notice droppings along the trim at the entrance, you're probably sharing your roof with a bat colony. Make sure all the flying tenants are evicted, then close up the entrance. (Mature bats leave the colony every night to feed, so this is your best time to act. Otherwise you can just wait till winter in cold-weather regions, as most bat species migrate south.)

❖ One way to discourage bats from returning to a tile roof is to mount a metal rain gutter under the entrance tiles.

The bats will be able to exit, but they'll find landing on the slick aluminum offensive and won't return.

Bat-Exclusion Zone

❖ Another animal-friendly idea for bidding bats good-bye is to rig up an exclusion device. Take a section of one-half-inch plastic bird mesh (used for protecting fruit bushes and available at any garden supply store) and rig it up over the entrance. The mesh should hang down past the opening by at least two feet. With this arrangement, the bats will be able to crawl out from under the mesh to leave the nest, but they won't be able to get back in.

The Standards Should Be As High As the Roof

THE ASPHALT SHINGLES are curling on the back roof of one of Yankee's office buildings. Pretty soon the tabs will start to break off, and then we'll need a new roofing job. I'd guess that the last roofer must have put lightweight shingles on just the back of the roof. The shingles on the front of the roof, which look to be heavier weight, are fine.

EARL
remembers...

Many people aren't aware that asphalt shingles come in different weights. When you hire a roofer, be sure he uses heavy-weight asphalt shingles; they'll hold up better over time. Watch, too, to see how the roofers are nailing the shingles. The proper way to nail a three-foot strip of shingles is with six roofing nails, placed on either side of the slot. Some roofers will drive only one nail directly over each slot—not a good idea. Shingles nailed this way will have a greater area that can be blown in high winds and thus are more prone to cracking.

If you want your roofing job to last, it pays to see that your roofer holds to these standards.

ASPHALT ROOFS

Look for the Handwriting on the Roof

❖ How do you know when you need a new asphalt roof—that is, before it starts to leak? Watch out for one of two telltale signs of aging asphalt: curling and loss of mineral. If you see shingles that are buckling or otherwise not flat, or areas of black patches because the shingles are no longer fully covered with colored granules, you better start planning for a new roof.

It Helps If You Have Friendly Neighbors

❖ To inspect an asphalt roof—or any roof—without getting up on a ladder, use binoculars. Walk around the house at ground level, repeating the process at different times of the day so that you check things out under all kinds of light conditions. Or take advantage of a neighbor's attic or second-floor windows for a roof-level perch. Be especially sure to check the south-facing side of the building. This is the area that usually gets the most exposure to the sun's ultraviolet light, so it tends to have the shortest life span. (You may be able to replace just the south side rather than the entire roof.)

METAL ROOFS

An Old-Fashioned Paint Job

❖ A standing-seam metal roof is one made of sheet-metal panels, about 24 inches wide, that run vertically down the roof. They are bent up at the edges to form upright seams about 1½ inches high that look like ribs. Such a roof can last a lifetime, but if it's made of the material called terne (see box on page 174), you'll have to give it regular help with a paintbrush. Paint your terne roof as soon as it's installed, and

COMMON MISTAKES

The Repair That Isn't

NEVER TRY TO repair a terne roof with black roofing cement or asphalt coatings. The asphalt corrodes the terneplate, which exposes the iron or steel underneath to water and air. Together they create a galvanic action between the two metals that will corrode the roof.

on a regular basis thereafter, with tinner's paint. This is old-fashioned stuff—linseed-oil paint with an iron oxide pigment—that dries very slowly so that it bonds well with the pores in the metal. Start a new roof with a primer coat, then follow several days later with two or more finish coats. Be sure to prime the undersides, too, to protect the metal from condensation. Repaint periodically, well before any primer shows through the finish coats. Tinner's paint comes in traditional colors (gray, green, red, brown), but you won't find it at a hardware store. Order it from a terne supplier; you should be able to get an address from a local roofing supply house.

It Looks Fine on the Statue of Liberty

❖ Don't assume that you should try to make your old copper roof look new. The gray-green patina that copper develops actually protects the metal from the elements. Even black stains (often the result of air pollution) are more unsightly than harmful.

Use the Old Nut

❖ If you're determined to clean a copper roof, you'll need to call in professional help to avoid permanently damaging the metal. Check the Yellow Pages for metal-cleaning contractors that do glass beading or "agriblasting." They'll blow the top layer of crust off with walnut shells and the like, which is much safer for the metal than sandblasting.

The Fountain of Old Age

❖ If you can't wait for your new copper roof to look old, try making your own patina. Clean the copper well (it

Cat on a Hot Terne Roof

W HAT'S IN A NAME? Quite a lot if you're talking about metal roofs. You'd be hard-pressed to find one that's truly nothing but tin. While fairly durable, tin is a soft metal and too weak to stand alone as a roofing material. When tin was first used in roofing, it was used primarily as a coating for iron plates or steel sheets, which were fastened to the roof and then soldered together to make a waterproof surface.

In the nineteenth century, manufacturers started adding another ingredient to "tin" roofs. They still started with sheets of iron or steel, but the coating was an alloy of tin and lead called terne or terneplate, which looked much like tin and made a very long lasting roof. The latest step in the evolution of the old-fashioned tin roof was the application of this terne to stainless steel, creating a roofing material that is still used today.

But we're still waiting for the debut of *Cat on a Hot Terne-and-Stainless-Steel Roof* . . .

usually has a slight coating of oil when new) and sprinkle it with salt water. (You can get the water from the ocean if you live along the coast or just keep stirring ordinary table salt into fresh water until the crystals won't dissolve anymore.) Allow the copper to dry, then repeat until you get the look you want. A watering can with a fine spray works well for this, or you can spatter the solution on with a broom or whitewash brush. Generally, whatever equipment is kicking around the garage will do just fine.

GUTTERS AND DOWNSPOUTS

New Construction: Don't Mix and Match

❖ Always stick to one metal when installing or repairing gutter systems. Never attach, say, copper gutter pieces to aluminum or galvanized-steel sections. As soon as a little water starts flowing through the system, it will set up a battery-like galvanic action that will corrode both metals.

❖ The "like metals" rule applies to fasteners, too.

Proper Placement

❖ Often gutters become damaged by falling ice and snow and have to be replaced prematurely. Old-time roofers knew the usual cause of this problem: the gutter was installed too high. Instead of tucking the gutter up tight to the roofline, hang it at least an inch below the plane of the roof. It will catch rain and meltwater, but snow and ice will slide right by without damage.

Keep Your Mind in the Gutter

❖ Make sure you're using the right size gutter. As a rule of thumb, a 4-inch gutter can handle roofs up to 750

If a gutter is installed too high (A), snow and ice drain into it, clogging the gutter and causing it to wear out prematurely. Hang a gutter at least an inch below the plane of the roof (B), and snow and ice will slide on by.

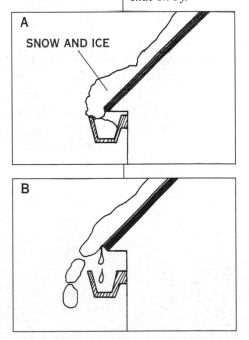

A
SNOW AND ICE

B

square feet in size, a 5-inch gutter takes care of roofs up to 1,500 square feet, and a 6-inch gutter is best for roofs larger than 1,500 square feet.

Say "Ahhh"

❖ The best thing you can do for your existing gutters is to give them a regular checkup twice a year. Look for leaks, storm and ice damage and debris buildup. The ideal times to inspect and clean are early spring (before the rainy season) and late fall (after the leaves are down). Gutters that don't get regular care are soon leaking water down the side of the house as if they never existed or lying in pieces among the shrubs after they've fallen off. Good gutters and downspouts are important to the health of a house, especially where rainfall is heavy. They collect roof runoff and channel it away from the building so that water doesn't splash back against the foundation walls and find its way into the basement.

Clutter in the Gutter

❖ When you inspect those gutters, you need to clean them, too. Gutters that are clogged with roof minerals and debris, leaves and seeds not only don't collect and move water, but they also stay wet and heavy and eventually disintegrate into a mess of rusting metal or rotting wood. When gutters are left uncleaned for a couple of seasons, small plants start growing in the fertile muck—and once a gutter has found a new life as a garden, it's unlikely that it's still doing its original job.

COMMON MISTAKES

Don't Screen That Gutter

N EVER COVER an entire gutter with metal or plastic screening. Although it sounds like a good idea—a mesh that prevents material from entering the trough—in many cases leaves just pile up on the screen in a "roof" that defeats the purpose of the gutter, while fine sediment accumulates inside with little water to flush it away. (Downspout strainers *are* a good idea, however, especially the old-fashioned copper or galvanized wire "spider" kind. They stop debris before it can clog the spouts.)

Wooden Gutter Preservation

❖ To prevent wooden gutters from absorbing moisture (and thus to keep them lasting longer), treat the wood once a year or so with a water-repellent wood preservative.

After making sure the gutters are dry, apply the preservative with a paintbrush. Allow the gutters to dry for 24 hours, then repeat the process. Wood preservatives are sold anywhere paint is sold—typically at good hardware stores, lumberyards, paint stores and home centers.

❖ An alternative is to make your own mixture for treating unpainted wooden gutters. Combine equal parts raw linseed oil and turpentine and apply just as you would the commercial product. This mixture will repel water but allow moisture to escape from the wood.

Help for Galvanized Gutters

❖ If you have galvanized-steel gutters rather than wooden ones, your best means of preserving them is a plain old paint job. Paint protects the zinc coating (which keeps the steel from rusting) in the area that is most exposed to water. Use a good-quality metal primer, followed by a coat of finish or metal roof paint, and keep the coating intact by touching it up every year.

Wait before You Paint . . .

❖ New galvanized gutters should not be painted until they are a season or two old. Sounds like the opposite of good preventive maintenance, but there's a reason. When fresh from the factory, galvanized gutters have a smooth and oily surface that will cause paint to flake off in short order. Letting the metal weather for a while etches the surface and provides some "tooth" for the paint to grab on to.

. . . Or at Least Prep First

❖ If you really can't wait to paint your gutters, you can get rid of the surface-oil problem by wiping down the gutters with vinegar. Or use a metal paint–prep solution made for this purpose (available at auto body shops).

PUZZLER

IT LOOKS LIKE A GATE, BUT IT actually was used to show someone (or something) the door.

ANSWER: Dog tongs, used by the sexton to remove parishioners' dogs when they became too noisy during church services.

You Don't Have to Solder

❖ Gutters that leak aren't very good for the house, and they'll wear out faster than ones in good repair. If you want to keep your galvanized-steel gutters in shape but aren't too keen on soldering the joints (the traditional approach), try applying butyl-rubber caulk. This material—a little stringy, but cheap, easy to use and available at most hardware stores, lumberyards and home centers—is an all-purpose product that has a life span of five to ten years. You can use it on wooden gutters, too. Butyl-rubber caulk comes in a cartridge. Just place the cartridge in a hand-held gun made for the purpose, then squirt out the caulk.

COMMON MISTAKES

Don't Paint Yourself into a Predicament

NEVER COAT the inside of a wooden gutter with paint or asphalt compounds. They'll only trap moisture in the wood once water gets under or penetrates through the paint film, which it eventually will. The moisture will lead to decay, and that means your gutters will soon be gutted.

Now Here's the Pitch

❖ To make gutters last, it's important to keep them draining freely by maintaining their proper pitch. Ideally, gutter pitch is tailored to the individual house and depends on roof size, gutter size and average yearly rainfall. (Professional roofers have tables to calculate this value.) But you can get a general reading on your home's gutter pitch with a simple test. Get up on the roof and pour a good volume of water into the gutter to see how it flows. If the trough doesn't empty quickly or fully, proceed to the next tips. It's a particularly good idea to check gutter pitch after a house has settled over a number of years or after an icy winter, when gutters can lose their pitch.

❖ If your gutters fail the test, you'll need to adjust their pitch. To determine the right pitch for your house, you can call a professional roofer, pull out your slide rule—or follow a simple rule of thumb. On the average house, the gutter should fall about one inch for every ten feet of its length.

Rethink the High Points . . .

❖ If you have a long gutter and the pitch you need to keep it happy and healthy means that it will run at a conspicuous and unattractive angle across the front of the house, don't worry. You just have to rethink the gutter system a little. One solution is to have the gutter pitch in two directions—that is, have the high point somewhere in the center and a downspout at either end. Such a scheme takes more parts but also provides better drainage.

. . . Or the Low Ones

❖ If gutters still don't drain properly after their pitch has been adjusted, consider adding more downspouts.

Why (and When) I Water My Foundation

M Y HOUSE HAS a concrete block foundation that is exposed on one side, and occasionally it needs painting. When it's time for this chore, I prepare the surface with a wire brush and get my paintbrushes ready. Next I stir up a can of latex floor enamel, which is made for concrete. Then I go and get the garden hose.

Unless you wet concrete before you paint it with latex paint, the paint job won't last. Dry concrete will suck the water out of latex paint as soon as you apply it, so the paint won't harden properly and seal the concrete. Concrete blocks are even more absorbent than poured concrete. So I spray my concrete block foundation lightly with water and wait a short while until the blocks are merely damp. (As important as it is to wet things down, it's equally important to avoid applying so much water that it puddles. A careful washing is usually adequate.) Then I begin painting.

EARL remembers...

You can avoid the need to wet concrete before painting by using oil-based paint. But I like latex better because it cleans up so much more easily.

The Water's Going *Where?*

❖ To preserve the life of your house, make sure down-spouts and leaders take water away from the building and not into it. A gutter-downspout system that stops at the foundation line and dumps water there is almost worse than no gutter at all. Unfortunately, this is just the situation on many houses where the lead-out pipes have been lost or never installed.

❖ If your downspouts enter a tile or ceramic pipe that goes into the ground, check to see where that pipe is going, and make sure the operation is not clogged or leaking—say, into your basement. Some old systems drain into the city sanitary sewer—illegal now in most communities. It's more likely that your system was designed to empty into the storm sewer, a dry well or a network of polyvinyl chloride (PVC) or corrugated plastic pipes on the property. In any case, you need to make sure the water's going where it's supposed to.

Go with the Flow

❖ If you suspect that a leaky dry well is the source of water in your basement, here's an easy way to check: Pour a bottle of food coloring into the dry well, along with a stream of water from a garden hose. If a red or green wet spot appears in the basement, you'll have a good idea of the source.

❖ If you want to confirm the flow of a field pipe outlet, flush some Styrofoam packing "peanuts" down the pipe. If they come out the other end, you can assume the pipe is not blocked. The peanuts work well because they're easily identified for retrieval later and they won't create a logjam.

DRIVEWAYS

Stir before You Seal

❖ Be sure you thoroughly stir any driveway sealer before applying it, especially if it has been stored for any length of time. These products are emulsions, and the heavier parts sink to the bottom over time. If you don't remix them, you'll get uneven coverage, funny looks and poor protection.

Breaking Up Is All Too Easy to Do

❖ Left alone, significant cracks in a blacktop driveway will be the start of larger problems. The water that enters can freeze and expand, opening up the cracks and starting the pavement on the road to breakup. Before coating a driveway with a sealer, fill small cracks (under one-quarter inch) with a liquid driveway crack filler (available at hardware stores or home centers). Larger cracks (up to one-half inch) should be repaired by troweling in a patching mix.

Grease Grief

❖ Oil and grease stains may not directly shorten the life of concrete and asphalt surfaces, but they certainly can ruin the area's appearance and make you want to replace the surface sooner than you otherwise might. To remove a grease stain from a driveway or a garage floor, try scrubbing with a scrub brush dipped in TSP or another product containing trisodium phosphate (available at hardware stores) or in sodium metasilicate. For example, use an all-purpose powdered woodwork cleaner (from a hardware store) or a product made for brightening whitewall tires (from an auto parts store). Or use dishwasher detergent, which contains trisodium phosphate. A mixture of ½ cup of cleaner per 1 gallon of water should do the trick.

Driveways: Three Ways to Seal the Deal

MOST FOLKS GRASP the advantage of sealing a blacktop driveway—it helps the pavement resist oil and water and improves the look—but not the advantages of the different types of sealers. The two most popular types are coal tar sealers and modified asphalt sealers. Coal tar costs a bit more than modified asphalt, but it usually lasts longer. It does give off a strong odor as it's applied, though, and it will burn if it contacts skin. Modified asphalt is popular because it is odorless and less expensive than other types; however, it's not quite as durable. Pure acrylic-latex sealers are the top of the heap. They cost more than either coal tar or modified asphalt sealers, but they give close to three times the coverage, and they're easy to apply (you can use a paint roller).

Lawn and Garden

I'VE ALWAYS LIKED FOUNTAINS. So after I finished building the house I live in now, I set about building a fountain for the patio—and that meant scrounging the parts. (I didn't want to go out and *buy* them!)

One day when I was at a steamfitter's shop, I told the manager, "The next time you cut up a big old boiler, I'd like to have the end to use as a pool for a fountain." The man smiled and led me into another room, where he showed me a giant round stone sink that had been shipped to the college in town. They had refused it because it was cracked, so the steamfitter gave me the sink. I got some help, trucked it home and positioned it in my patio. It was easy to seal the crack with some caulking compound.

Not long after that, I had a job adding onto the concession stand at a racetrack. In the process of renovating the stand, I came across five recirculating pumps that had been used in the stand's beverage service. The owner explained that they were broken but that he'd never gotten around to throwing them away after he'd replaced them. He was sick of tripping over them and gladly let me have them. I managed to repair one of the pumps. Then I installed it in my basement and hooked it up to a pipe to the pool, with a return pipe back to the pump.

So now, thanks to a little careful recycling, I have my fountain. And I proved that, when it comes to your lawn and garden—maybe more than anywhere else around your home—a little creativity can save you a lot of money.

The deep-rooted Yankee sensibility that favors economy and recycling is easily shaken by today's world of glitzy lawn and garden products.

But as anyone who's been gardening for a while knows, it's often the simple things that last longer, are easier to use and cost less in the long run. Over the next few pages, we'll take a look not only at the hardware that helps our green thumbs along but also at plants, shrubs and garden crops themselves, and how we can make *them* last longer, too.

LAWN MOWERS

Avoid Grass Buildup

❖ Before mowing your lawn, spray the underside of the mower with a nonstick cooking spray to discourage clippings from sticking. A buildup of debris can prevent the mower from cutting properly and encourage rust.

It's All in the Oil

❖ Every time you go to start your power mower, check the crankcase first to make sure it's full of oil. Crankcase oil is the lifeblood of any engine: it lubricates, cools, cleans and seals the internal moving parts. It is a particularly critical component of mower engines, which are usually too small to have internal pumps to move the oil around or radiator systems to help with cooling. (Most use a simple oil slinger or connecting-rod dipper to keep the oil in motion.) Since the oil volume in a mower engine is already pretty small—seldom more than 20 ounces—running the engine with a less-than-full crankcase means the remaining oil will be hotter, dirtier and less likely to bathe the parts of the engine. All this leads to premature engine wear. If you're mowing all day, continue to check the oil every five hours of engine use.

Keep It on the Level

❖ When you check the oil, make sure the mower is on level ground so that you get an accurate measurement. And read from a freshly wiped dipstick— not from the stick when you first pull it out.

A Word of Warning

BEFORE YOU WORK on any part of your mower, tiller or other piece of power equipment, disconnect the spark plug wire and tape it to make sure the engine cannot start accidentally while your hands are near blades, belts or other moving parts.

Oil: Enough Is Enough

❖ Never overfill the engine crankcase. An excess of oil puts a strain on the piston and engine seals, because there's less air and room for expansion inside the engine. In fact, the oil fill plug in many walk-behind mowers is idiot-proof—that is, designed so that oil will overflow rather than overfill the crankcase. However, some riding mowers use an extended oil-filler tube that makes it possible to add too much oil. You'll know if you've done that as soon as you start the engine. The exhaust will smoke heavily as the engine tries to burn off the excess oil. If that happens, stop the machine immediately and drain off the excess.

Changing Times

❖ Always keep your engine oil clean. It's the easiest and least expensive thing you can do to maintain the health and extend the life of your engine. Old oil can't lubricate

Gentlemen (and Ladies), Start Your Engines!

WHEN YOU GO TO WORK on any small gas engine, it's important to know the crankcase from the carburetor. Here's a quick reference for the novice.

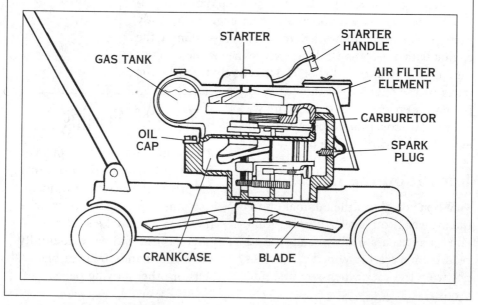

GAS TANK · STARTER · STARTER HANDLE · AIR FILTER ELEMENT · CARBURETOR · SPARK PLUG · OIL CAP · CRANKCASE · BLADE

the metal surfaces properly, and circulating dirty oil means you're bathing bearings and piston rings with dust particles from the air and microscopic pieces of metal from the engine itself. They cause friction and abrade the machinery like sandpaper.

❖ Don't wait until the oil looks like black paint or runs like tar to change it. In fact, if the owner's manual says to change the oil every 25 hours of operation, change it at 20—or even, if you want to be really safe, 12—hours. The few extra dollars' worth of oil is an insignificant expense when compared to the life of a $400 to $2,000 mower. Also be sure to change the oil when it is still warm from operating the engine. That way, the oil will run readily and will take a maximum amount of dirt and combustion by-products with it.

A Mower Is Not an All-Terrain Vehicle

❖ Common sense is hard to heed when you're a kid mowing lawns, but it's always a good idea to avoid running over roots, rocks or high grass that will slow or stall the engine. Impeding or stopping the blade on power mowers puts tremendous stress on the engine, especially if there is no drive belt connecting engine and blade that can absorb some of the shock. In most small mowers, the blade is bolted directly to the vertical crankshaft. You create a problem if you halt its rotation while the piston is in the power stroke and trying to move the blade. This can cause the connecting rod—the weakest link in the power train—to fail and destroy the engine.

Renew That Spark

❖ For best mower engine power and performance, clean and regap the spark plug twice a season. Gapping a spark plug is the process of adjusting the electrodes to a clearance recommended by the manufacturer so that the plug will produce a spark of the right size and intensity for best ignition. In practice, this simply means hand-bending a little metal arm, then checking the clearance with a gauge. Don't use a wire brush or sandpaper to clean the plug contacts. You run the risk of leaving metal or grit in the recesses of the plug, and these substances can find their way into the engine and cause wear. Use a spark plug file for this part of the process—or better yet, start over with a new plug.

Clean-Air Acts

❖ If your mower engine has an oil-foam air-cleaner element—as most of them do—check and clean it after every 25 hours of mowing. Do this much sooner if you've been mowing in a dusty area. Simply remove the element from its housing (without knocking dirt into the carburetor), wash it in liquid laundry detergent and water and then wrap it in an old towel and gently wring it dry. Last, pour some engine oil on the foam until it's saturated, squeeze out the excess and reinstall the air cleaner. The air cleaner prevents the engine from drawing in the chaff and dirt particles that can instantly begin to wear and grind away its close-fitting internal metal parts. However, when the air filter becomes dirty and blocked, it can starve the engine of air, causing it to run rich and perform poorly.

Nobody Wants to Be Dull

❖ If the blade on your rotary mower is dull—and mower blades get dull quickly—it will chop rather than cut the grass. Not only will this make for ragged tops on plants (and open the door to brown or sickly lawns), but it also will slow the mowing process and put an unnecessary strain on the engine. Check your mower blade regularly for sharpness.

In Case of Overheating, Take a Load Off

❖ If your mower engine should overheat, take the load off the engine by disengaging cutters or drive wheels. Then throttle the engine down gradually and shut off the ignition. Afterward, move it to a shady spot. Never try to cool an overheated engine by spraying it with a hose or dunking it in water. The sudden thermal shock will cause the metal castings to distort, crack or become brittle.

❖ Once you have corrected the problem causing an overheated engine, change the crankcase oil before restarting the engine. Heat breaks down oil.

The Cycles of Lawn Mowers

SMALL GAS ENGINES—the kind used on nearly every piece of yard and garden power equipment—are of two types. **Four-cycle engines,** the most common design in mowers, are basically miniature versions of automobile engines. With this principle, the engine requires four strokes of the piston (specifically, the intake, compression, power and exhaust strokes) to complete one cycle. It takes two revolutions of the crankshaft for all these events to occur. Also essential are many small moving parts (such as valves, springs and timing gears) to control the sequence of these events and a reservoir of oil to keep them operating at high speeds.

Popular in small mowers, and almost universally used in chain saws and string trimmers, are **two-cycle engines.** Although these engines do not have as high a power potential as four-cycle engines (and have more problems with clean-air requirements in areas where pollution is a problem), they have many practical advantages in the field. For one, they are much less complicated mechanically and so can be made much smaller and lighter. Two-cycle engines are miserly on internal parts (they have ports instead of valves and little else besides a piston), and they need no heavy flywheel to keep them rotating through a long cycle. Another advantage to these engines is that, because they use oil in the fuel (which becomes a mist to lubricate the cyclinder), not in a reservoir, they can be operated in almost any position.

Two-cycle engines also combine intake and power in one stroke, exhaust and compression in the other. This is not as efficient a use of fuel as the four-cycle principle. However, two-cycle engines make up for it because they have a power stroke at every rotation of the crankshaft—in other words, at the same rpm, they complete two cycles for every one of a four-cycle engine.

Sharp Talk

❖ To sharpen a rotary mower blade, first disconnect the spark plug wire (to prevent the engine from starting) and unbolt it from the shaft. Then remove the blade. This is not difficult mechanically—the blade is usually attached with just a bolt or two—but sometimes the bolts are rusty, and you'll need a little penetrating oil and muscle to free them. (Watch out for spilled gas when you turn the mower on its side, and check the crankcase oil level when you're finished.) Clamp the blade in a vise and renew the cutting edge with a medium-size flat bastard file. File into the blade, rather than off it, to get the sharpest cutting edge. Work at the original angle—typically 30 degrees. Don't waste your time trying to remove large amounts of metal, however. If the blade is very dull, bent, heavily nicked or out of balance, you'll make out better buying a new one.

A Balancing Act

❖ If you're sharpening your own rotary mower blade, you should make sure it's balanced. Even a small mower engine runs at around 3,000 rpm, and if the blade is heavier on one side, it will cause the mower to vibrate. This makes it hard to handle and starts premature wear on the engine bearings. You don't need laboratory equipment to balance a blade, just some sort of fulcrum. A good hardware store or mower shop—any place that sells tune-up parts—will have a simple cone-shaped gadget made for this purpose. Or go low-tech and balance the blade on a pencil, or on a nail stuck in a wall. Place the center of the blade on the fulcrum, and if it doesn't balance, file or grind off metal on the heavy side until it remains horizontal.

Fueling Around

❖ Always use clean, fresh gasoline in a mower or any engine. Buy it in small quantities, and don't store it for more than 30 days. Old gas can produce gum deposits that will clog the carburetor, and it won't provide the same amount of power as fresh gas.

Your Battery Could Use a Little Baking Soda

❖ Keep the top of the battery clean. The mixture of dirt and condensate from the cells can make an electrical bridge across the terminals that will run the battery down when it's not in use. Clean corrosion and dirt from the ter-

PUZZLER

HERE'S A BACKPACK WITH A LOT of moving parts. The wearer moved the bow, the bow turned the wheel, and . . . well, let's say it had to do with an earlier form of broadcasting.

ANSWER: Seeder. The rotating wheel broadcast the seed carried in the bag.

minals regularly to make sure you get the best electrical connection. (A poor one means that the battery can't deliver full power to the starter or motor, and the battery, in turn, can't receive a good charge.) The old baking-soda-and-water wash is still a good way to clean, but be sure not to splash any into the cells. A wire brush is ideal for cleaning the terminals.

Before Storing That Battery, Charge It!

❖ When you put a battery into winter storage, always make sure it is fully charged. A battery that is partially discharged not only stands a greater chance of becoming sulfated (chemically and electrically inactive), but it is also susceptible to freezing. When the battery is completely "up," however, the electrolyte is in its most acidic state and unlikely to freeze under normal winter conditions. Check the cells with a good, calibrated hydrometer battery tester to evaluate their condition. One of these testers will give you a much better picture of the charge than will a cheap one with those little balls, and it will cost only a couple of dollars more.

CHAIN SAWS

Mixing Matters

❖ Since two-cycle engines depend on the oil you add to the fuel for proper lubrication, you can easily harm or kill them if you don't do a good job of mixing. Make sure you use the exact proportions recommended by the manufacturer—ratios vary from one brand to another. (Mixing is easier, too, if you stick with the premeasured cans of oil sold by the toolmaker.) Keep the fuel for the chain saw in a specially marked one-gallon gas can, and give the can a shake before you refuel in order to remix the oil and gas. (This applies to string trimmers, too.)

Unbridled Power Can Be Dangerous

❖ Never rev up a chain saw to a high rpm when you're not cutting wood. Normally, the wood will provide enough load to keep the engine within its safe operating speed—typically 6,000 to 9,000 rpm. Running wild without a load is no good for any engine because the combination of high speeds and slight variations in timing can cause instant internal damage.

The Best In-Tensions

❖ On a saw with a round-nosed guide bar, adjust the chain tension so that there is up to three-eighths inch of slack. For a saw with a roller-nosed guide bar, adjust the chain so that there is no slack but it is still loose enough to be pulled evenly around the bar by hand. Maintaining the correct chain tension is an important element in prolonging the life of both the chain and the guide bar. If the chain is too tight, you'll not only prematurely wear out the chain, but you'll also burn up the pivot bearing at the

The Logger Missed a Lesson

EARL
remembers...

AN OLD ACQUAINTANCE of mine used to work as a logger, so I've never understood why he didn't treat his chain saw properly.

A chain saw won't work dependably unless you keep the teeth sharp, clean the sawdust out of the air filter regularly, avoid getting sawdust in the gas tank and keep the chain well oiled. On this last point, my acquaintance was especially negligent. He'd run the saw until it was out of bar oil. Then, instead of stopping to refill the saw with oil, he would continue to saw, occasionally dipping the bar into a can of oil for lubrication. It seemed this fellow was always taking his saw to be repaired, and it's no wonder.

A chain saw is one of the most temperamental power tools you can own. Maintain it by the book, and it will serve you well. Ignore routine upkeep, and you'll end up with costly repairs.

nose of the guide bar or the bar itself. If the chain is too loose, the bar may be damaged at the drive end, and the chain may jump off the bar.

Chain Reactions

❖ To get the maximum life out of a new chain, before you install it, soak it overnight in a bath of motor oil—SAE 20 or 30 in warm weather or SAE 10 in cold weather. The oil you see on the chain when you remove it from the package is just a rust preventive and not enough to keep it lubricated in the first critical hour or so of use. Each link in the chain is, in essence, a bearing, and without lubrication the chain will soon fail.

Buck Up!

❖ When you're sawing, it goes without saying that you shouldn't let the chain come in contact with stone or metal. But don't ever let the chain touch soil, either. It will cause rapid dulling of the cutters and drag on the engine. If you're cutting felled timber, first buck it (support it with another log) to give yourself clearance underneath.

Clear the Port

❖ If your chain saw has an automatic oiler, be sure to keep the oiler port clear of wood chips and sawdust. Use a stick or rag, not your finger. The automatic oiler is near the drive sprocket on most saws.

Don't Chuck That Chain

❖ Sometimes a chain gets fouled with pitch and resins from certain evergreen trees. When this happens, instead of chucking the chain, first disconnect the spark plug wire, then back off on the chain adjuster until the chain is loose enough to be worked off the guide bar and drive sprocket. Once you've removed the chain from the saw, try soaking the chain in a bath of liquid laundry detergent or ammonia and water, then scrubbing it with a soft brush. When it's clean, dry it thoroughly right away. Before putting it back on the saw, soak the clean chain in oil to prevent rusting.

Garden Coils

IF YOU'RE SHOPPING for a new hose, here are the features to check:

• **The couplings on each end.** Brass is best; if the hose has brass couplings, it's likely to be high quality.

• **The edge on the couplings.** A flattened octagonal or hexagonal edge makes it crush resistant.

• **The material of the hose itself.** Top-of-the-line hoses are made of rubber, which is wear resistant. With proper care, they can last a lifetime. New reinforced vinyl or combinations of vinyl and rubber have their own advantages. They stay flexible at low temperatures, are knot and crimp resistant and endure abrasion well.

Newspaper: It's a Wrap

❖ If you're putting up your chain saw for a while, wrap it in clean newspaper, which will allow it to breathe. Don't wrap it in plastic. Although plastic appears to offer good protection from the elements, it will seal the saw in an environment of moisture and corrosive gases.

The Story on Storage

❖ Before storing your chain saw for any length of time, brush and wipe the saw clean of any dirt and debris, then give the chain and bar a good oiling.

GARDEN HOSES

Out of Sight, Out of Trouble

❖ One of the main secrets to getting a long life out of a garden hose is to take it out only when you're using it. Discipline yourself to roll up the hose after every use. If it bakes in the hot sun, ultraviolet rays can damage it by breaking down the fibers that give it strength. And a hose that is tucked away won't be tripped over, crushed by the wheels of your car or accidentally cut by the lawn mower.

Hose Hang-Ups

❖ If you don't have a reel to hang your hose on, attach an old metal bucket to the barn or garage wall by nailing it through the bottom. Wrap the hose around it and store the nozzles and sprinklers inside.

A Stand-Up Act

❖ Before a hard frost, drain all standing water out of your hose and hang it up to dry. To do this, stand on a chair and slowly pull the hose up, foot by foot, to chest height.

Get a Good Grasp of the Subject

❖ When unrolling a hose, never grasp it by the nozzle or coupling. These are its weakest parts and the places where it will often spring a leak.

Rigid Procedures

❖ This do-it-yourself technique for mending serious hose gashes or rips seems to last longer than any hardware store fitting. Cut out the damaged part of the hose and discard it. That will leave you with two good sections. Slide a piece

When It Comes to Hose, the Fireman Knows

NOWADAYS, MOST GARDEN HOSES are made of plastic, but it wasn't too long ago that hoses and hose washers were made of real rubber. I remember making my own washers from old sections of rubber hose. I'd slice the washers off the end of the hose with a single-edge razor blade. New hose washers are so inexpensive now that I've stopped making my own. But I suspect I've still got a few old hand-cut rubber washers in the hoses around my house.

EARL remembers...

The new plastic hoses are less prone to cracking than the old rubber ones were, but even with today's stronger hoses, it makes sense to take precautions against accidents. Have you ever noticed that firefighters don't stretch a hose straight across a road? This is so vehicles can't run over the hose with two wheels at once. I once ran over an old rubber hose at a construction site, and the pressure of the water in the section that was pinched between the two wheels of my pickup split the hose.

If you've got a hose stretched across your driveway, take a moment to check that it's on a strong diagonal.

of six- to ten-inch copper tubing (use a diameter slightly smaller than that of the hose) into one section of hose, about three to five inches deep. Slowly insert the other end of the tubing into the other section of hose, bringing the two hose pieces together as close as possible to the center of the copper tubing. Secure the pipe inside the hose with three hose clamps—one in the center where the two hose pieces meet and the other two about an inch from each end of the copper tubing.

A Swell Solution for a Leaking Hose

To plug a pinhole leak in a hose (A), insert a toothpick into the hole (B), then cut off the toothpick flush with the surface. Wrap the area with electrical tape (C) to complete the repair.

❖ If your hose develops just a minor leak or two, try to patch it before you buy a new one. If you notice a pinhole leak, insert a pointed round toothpick into the hole from the outside, just penetrating the hose wall. Snip it off flush on the outside. Wrap the hose with electrical or duct tape that covers the pick and a good inch or two on both sides of the repair. As water flows through the hose, it will cause the toothpick to swell and fill the hole.

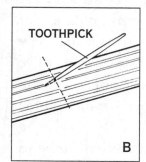

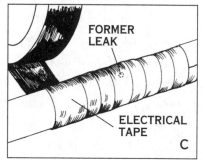

SPRINKLERS

Keep Moving!

❖ Pay attention to where the water from your oscillating sprinkler is landing, and move the sprinkler occasionally to correct the imbalances. These sprinklers provide broad coverage, but stretches of lawn closest to the sprinkler often get neglected, while those at the outer edges get well saturated.

An Impulse Buy

❖ If you live in a windy area or have an irregularly shaped lawn, use an impulse sprinkler—which delivers water forcefully—rather than an oscillating type. Invest in a model that can be adjusted for various shapes and patterns.

GARDEN TOOL MAINTENANCE

Care for a Tool?

❖ If your tools are caked with mud after a garden work-out, hose down their metal parts and then dry them thoroughly. Pay special attention to hollow places in the backs of crimped shovels where dirt tends to clump, encouraging rust and loosening the blades at their weakest point.

❖ To keep tools in good condition, fill a pail or old milk carton with sand and saturate the sand with used motor or crankcase oil or kerosene. (Because the fumes can be dangerous, store this setup in the garage, barn or tool-shed—never in the house.) Dip shovels, spades, forks, trowels, hoes and any other blades into the bucket several times to remove mud and grit after use.

Fight Rust

❖ To remove rust from a garden tool, scrub it with a steel wool soap pad dipped in kerosene or turpentine. (Do this outdoors, away from heat. Both of these materials are dangerous if inhaled and are highly flammable.) Then rub the tool with a ball of aluminum foil.

Kill the Cooties

❖ If you use pruning tools to cut away diseased stems or branches, disinfect them after each pruning session with a solution of three parts household (5 percent) bleach or rubbing alcohol and one part water. Keep the mixture in

PUZZLER

HERE'S A DEVICE THAT was used for getting to the kernel of the matter. Might be the symbol for Nebraska's college football team.

ANSWER: Corn husker.

a clearly labeled spray bottle, soak cutting surfaces with it and then wipe the pruners dry with a cloth to prevent rust.

SHARPENING GARDEN TOOLS

Extend a Knife's Life

❖ If you're working in the garden and you realize your pruning knife or shears are dull, use the edge of a clay flowerpot as a handy sharpening stone.

❖ When your pruning or grafting knife gets dull, position it so that when you strike it across the sharpening stone,

---

BUY IT TO LAST

A Guide to the Best Garden Tools

IF YOU'RE READY to invest in a garden tool that you hope will last a while, here are a few quick points to check before reaching for your wallet:

1. Try out the tool right there in the store. Pick up that shovel, open and close those shears, to find ones that feel right. Consider the weight. Is it appropriate for the task—and for you? You want something strong enough to hold up, but a tool that feels heavy in the store won't get lighter as you work with it, and you won't last long using it in the yard or garden.

2. Inspect the paint job—not for its aesthetic value, but to see what it might be hiding. Sometimes design or construction flaws in cheaper, less durable tools are disguised by thick coats of bright paint. Be wary and don't buy a tool

unless you can see clearly how it is held together. If you want to buy tools that will possibly last you a lifetime, choose top-of-the-line closed-shank tools without seams and welds.

3. Give it the wiggle test. Grab hold of the tool head and wiggle it. If it bends or feels loose, that tool is not meant as a garden workhorse. (The cheapest, least durable items are stamped out of one flat piece and then crimped just below the socket, creating a hollow back.)

4. Look for parallels. Check to be sure the wood grain in a handle is free from knots or other defects. On the best tools, the grain of the handle will run parallel to the direction of the force you'll apply when you use the tool.

5. *Now* **you can reach for your wallet.**

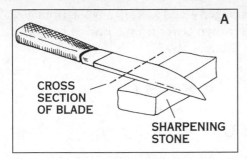

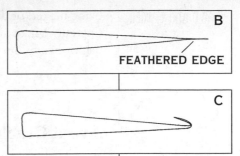

the edge is leading. If you sharpen it with the edge trailing, you'll create a feathered edge that may *feel* sharp but that will fold over and become dull as soon as it is used.

Sharp Remarks

❖ Use a file to sharpen spades, hoes and shovels. Use a whetstone to hone shears, scythes and other cuttingly sharp blades.

SCYTHES

Don't Be a Grim Reaper

❖ Keep a scythe blade razor sharp as you work. This may mean sharpening it every 20 minutes or so. Stabilize the end of the blade in the ground and hold the handle with one hand. With a glove on your sharpening hand, use just-mowed grass or a cloth to wipe the blade clean. Then sharpen with a sharpening stone, keeping the stone flat against the blade. Begin at the base of the blade with the base of the stone.

A Rule of Thumb

❖ To avoid damaging your scythe blade, never use it to cut anything larger in diameter than your finger.

Protect Your Scythe and Yourself

❖ After each use, wipe the blade of your scythe carefully with cut grass or a cloth to dry it and prevent rust.

❖ When you're finished using a scythe, cover it with a sheath that can be securely tied to keep the blade from being nicked or damaged—and to keep anyone from getting cut. Make your own cover from a burlap bag, feed bag or heavy-duty laundry bag.

AXES

Avoid Crack-Ups

❖ To keep your ax or splitting maul handle from cracking when you overswing it and strike with the handle instead of the head, wrap an inner tube a few times around the shaft by the ax head. Tie it tight so that the rubber protects the handle at the point of likely impact.

❖ An alternative is to wrap the first five to six inches of handle beneath the ax head with a dozen or so layers of electrical tape to cushion mislaid blows.

A SECOND LIFE

What Goes Around . . .

SOME OF THE BEST garden helpers come from your kitchen, workshop or garage. Here are but a few of the many ways to practice Yankee thrift and the gentle but important art of recycling.

• Wooden handles from brooms or sponge mops make good stakes for tomatoes.

• If you need to replace a shovel handle, save the old one and cut it down to a length of about eight inches to make a dibble, a useful tool for poking holes in the ground to plant seedlings. If the shovel has a grip, include that portion.

• Make your own plant markers by cutting strips from the sides of white plastic bleach bottles.

• When seeding a new lawn, drag a flexible doormat over the prepared area to mix seeds into the top one-quarter inch of soil.

• Cut old T-shirts into strips and use them to tie delicate plant stalks to stakes in the garden. They're soft and somewhat stretchy, so they won't harm the stems the way string can.

• If you have an old, worn-out hose, save it and use it to design new flower beds or herb gardens. Lay it down and curve it into the shape you want. You'll create a prettier, more natural looking garden than if you use straight lines.

• A long-handled kitchen fork makes an excellent weeding tool.

Early Re-tirement Protection

❖ Another good trick for protecting your ax is to set logs to be split in the middle of a couple of old tires. They will hold the logs upright and also keep the ax blade from plunging into the dirt if you swing short.

Keep Your Head

❖ To prevent an ax head from loosening, drill a one-quarter-inch hole about two inches deep into the butt of the handle. When you store the ax, place it on its head and pour the hole full of boiled linseed oil. This will soak down the length of the handle and help prevent shrinking. Whenever you notice that the oil level has dropped, replenish the oil. (The oil won't spill out. After a while, it will harden, just like beeswax.)

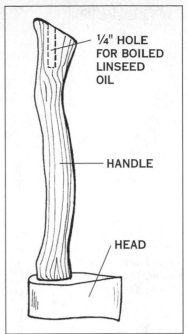

¼" HOLE FOR BOILED LINSEED OIL

HANDLE

HEAD

Pouring boiled linseed oil into a hole in an ax handle will keep the ax from losing its head.

WHEELBARROWS

Wooden Treasure

❖ If you're lucky enough to be in possession of an old wooden wheelbarrow with removable sides, take care of it by routinely oiling or staining the wood.

Second-Best Behavior

❖ If you can't get into the habit of putting your wheelbarrow under a roof after every use, do the next best thing and store it upside down so that rainwater won't pool in the bottom.

Arrest That Rust!

❖ Should your metal wheelbarrow begin to rust, sand the affected areas and touch them up with rust-inhibiting paint.

BUY IT TO LAST

Look to the Bottom of the Barrow

WHEN BUYING a wheelbarrow, choose one with a pneumatic tire, designed to make it easier to move heavy loads over both rough and soft terrain. Opt for sturdy construction, heavy-gauge steel with a smooth exterior and heavy-duty bearings. Carrying loads puts a lot of stress on the wheel.

TREES AND SHRUBS

Branch Surgery

❖ If a tree branch gets broken or damaged, cut it carefully away from the tree, making sure you do not lop it off so close that you cut into the tree trunk itself or so far out that you leave a big stub sticking out.

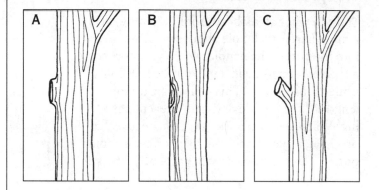

When removing a tree branch, be careful to leave just a small nub (A). Cutting too closely (B) can damage the tree, and leaving too much (C) is unsightly.

Extra Effort Won't Pay Off

❖ Use hand shears to prune branches up to one-half inch in diameter, lopping shears for those from one-half inch to one-and-a-half inches and a pruning saw for larger branches. Never use a small pruning tool on a large branch. The proper tool should cut through the branch or stem easily. If you have to twist and wiggle the tool to make a cut, it is the wrong size for the job, and you risk damaging both it and the plant.

No Ointment Necessary

❖ After you remove a limb from a tree, let the air get to the wound and speed the healing process. Do not apply tar, paint or anything else. Sealants often do more harm than good, encouraging diseases in the wood that stays moist under the covering.

Weathering Winter

❖ Protect a small tree or shrub from extreme cold and the uneven temperatures of freezing and thawing by surrounding it with a cylinder of snow fencing. Fill the space

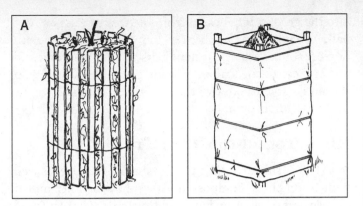

A   B

Encircle a tender young evergreen with snow fencing (A) to protect it from the harsh winds of winter. Or drive four stakes into the ground around the tree, and wrap protective material around the stakes to form a windbreak(B).

between the tree and the fencing with straw or dry leaves for insulation.

❖ To protect a dwarf or young evergreen from winter damage, drive stakes into the ground at four corners around the plant. Wrap burlap, nylon or heavy black plastic around the stakes and secure it top, bottom and center with twine.

Provide an Anchor in the Storm

❖ An alternative way to protect a dwarf or young evergreen is to anchor three stakes in the ground and connect them with burlap, creating a right angle to deter prevailing winds.

Hang Out the "No Vacancy" Sign

❖ Place mothballs around the base of wrapped or covered evergreens to deter mice and other rodents from setting up winter quarters in the shelter—

and nibbling away on the bark. *Mothballs are poisonous if eaten, however, so use them only if you're sure that children and pets will not get at them.*

Support Young Trees

❖ To help a young tree grow straight and tall and survive high winds or top-heavy growth, use two stakes, each approximately two-thirds as tall as the tree. Drive the stakes

If you have only three stakes available, position them this way around the plant and connect them with protective material.

into the ground far enough from the tree to miss its root ball. About halfway up the tree, loop strips of heavy cloth or pieces of old elastic garment belts around the trunk and fasten them to the stakes. Within 12 to 14 months, you should be able to remove the support system and let the tree grow on its own.

Ring-around-the-Tree-Trunk

❖ Create a ring around a tree or shrub and cover it well with wood chips, composted leaves, hay or other mulch to keep grass from growing up to the trunk. (Grass planted right up to the trunk of a tree can turn lawn mowing into a tremendously painstaking job and can compete with the tree for water and nutrients.)

❖ An alternative approach is to plant a ground cover such as pachysandra or vinca near the tree. These ground covers are less competitive than grass.

Minimize the Shock of Moving

❖ If you decide to move a large bush or shrub, cut around the root ball to a depth of 12 inches or more with a shovel to sever the feeder roots. Let the plant stand this way for a week or more and then move it. You'll reduce the shock it would otherwise suffer with the move.

Take the Plunge

❖ Once your tree is established, keep it healthy for years by aerating the soil several times during each growing season. Do this by plunging your spading fork into the soil in two or three places in each square foot of soil, all the way out to the drip line. This will help keep the soil from compacting and depriving the roots of oxygen.

❖ If an older tree's roots break out above ground and make bumps in your lawn, it's time to call in a professional tree surgeon who has power tools that can aerate the lawn to a depth of two feet.

PUZZLER

PRESS DOWN ONCE, AND YOU were ready to start six plants. The tears came later.

ANSWER: *Onion planter.*

The Proper Diet

❖ Fertilize your hedge each spring with well-rotted manure or compost, or mix in two to three tablespoons of superphosphate fertilizer for every five feet of row. Feed it with a balanced fertilizer every six weeks during the growing season. Hedge plantings require more fertilizer than shrubs planted any other way, since their closely spaced roots constantly compete with one another.

Keep It in Trim

❖ Prune your hedge so that the base is wider than the top. This will ensure that the lower portions of the hedge receive adequate light and air, and it will help snow slide off the plants.

❖ Rejuvenate a seriously overgrown hedge (if the plants are healthy) and extend its life span by cutting it uniformly back to as little as a foot from the ground. When plants such as lilacs and privet are let go for a number of years, they get very straggly. Often you can see right through the lower branches. When you drastically cut back these old hedge plants, their huge root systems encourage a lot of low new branches, which you can then prune for denser overall growth. This treatment works best for deciduous hedges—including privet, ninebark, pyracantha, lilacs, barberry, spirea, buckthorn, and potentilla—and for a few evergreens such as yew and boxwood. It is not a good approach for elderly fir and hemlock hedges, which are likely to die in the process.

Cosmetic Gardening

FRANK LLOYD WRIGHT, the architect as famous for his ego as his designs, once quipped that "the physician can bury his mistakes, but the architect can only advise his client to plant vines."

LAWNS

The Lawn and Short of It

❖ For a long-lasting and healthy lawn, mow according to the needs of the grass, not of the calendar. Cut the grass only when it threatens to be too much for your mower—three to four inches high—and bring it down to two and a half to three inches to conserve moisture, encourage healthy roots and discourage weed growth. (Bluegrass cut to one inch in height will have close to ten times as many weeds as the same grass two inches high.) Needless to say, your mower will last longer if it isn't overworked by giving your yard a crew cut every few days.

❖ Cut grass only when it's dry. If you try to mow when it's wet, the grass won't cut evenly, and it will quickly clump on the lawn's surface and clog your mower.

Grass-Cutting Directions

❖ Alternate the direction in which you mow the lawn to encourage even growth and avoid compacting the soil. Mow in a north-south pattern one week and in an east-west pattern the next.

Let Him Have All the Fun He Wants

EARL
remembers...

NOWADAYS, I USE a riding mower to cut my lawn. But for most of my life, I used a manual push mower.

Push mowers have been gaining in popularity because they are environmentally friendly. My son favors them. He remembers—apparently with some fondness—mowing the lawn with a push mower when he was a teenager. My son is planning to move back home, and he called recently and asked if I still had the old push mower. I didn't have to check; I knew it was still out in the shed. (I would never throw away something that was still in working order.)

But I was glad he asked. If he enjoys the old mowers so much, far be it from me to deprive him of the pleasure.

Save Yourself Some Work

❖ Leave those clippings where they fall, and they'll fertilize the lawn with nitrogen-rich organic fertilizer as they break down. Within a week of mowing, they should be completely decomposed. Rake them up only if they form a thick, heavy layer on top of the living grass or if your mowing pattern produces big clumps that might kill the grass underneath.

The Footprint Test

❖ If footprints show up when someone walks across your lawn, it needs to be watered. Give it approximately one to two inches of water about once a week rather than a series of brief, shallow waterings. A thorough soaking encourages good root development.

The Coffee-Can Test

❖ To determine how much water your lawn is getting, set a coffee can in your sprinkler's path and measure the depth of water in it.

Sort of Like Hansel and Gretel

❖ When seeding large patches of ground, mix grass seed with sawdust so that you can tell where the seed lands and what places you may have missed.

Avoid Thatched Roofs

❖ If you notice thatch buildup—an accumulation of undecomposed plant debris on the soil's surface—give your lawn a good raking to remove the thatch and let water penetrate the soil. The best tool for this job is a thatching rake, available at garden centers. The best time is spring. If the lawn has had a snow cover, wait until all the snow is melted and the lawn is reasonably dry.

Chinch Bug Wars

❖ Round patches of yellow grass can mean an infestation of chinch bugs—winged creatures with a dark triangular marking between their wings. (They can also be identified

THIS GIZMO WAS NOT used for pulling corks, unless the bottle was as big as a barrel. It was a lifting tool, and in its "heyday" it was a big help on the farm.

ANSWER: *Hay lifter.*

by the terrible smell they release when crushed.) To find out whether they're doing the damage, remove both ends from an old coffee can and push one end of the can two inches into the sod. (Use a knife to cut the ground or hammer the can into place.) Fill the can to the top with water and keep an eye on this contraption for several hours. If you have chinch bugs, they'll float to the top.

❖ To get rid of an invasion of chinch bugs, soak the afflicted parts of the lawn with a mixture of 2 tablespoons of dishwashing liquid and 2 gallons of water. Stretch an old flannel sheet over the soaked area to catch the bugs as they emerge. Leave the sheet in place for about 20 minutes, then wash it in soapy water to kill the bugs. Repeat the entire process as necessary until no more insects appear.

WALKWAYS

Green, Green, It's Green They Say

❖ Get rid of moss on a damp walkway by scraping it off with an old putty knife. Keep it from coming back by soaking the area with a solution of equal parts water and household (5 percent) bleach and allowing the solution to dry. Repeat the bleaching treatment every two weeks during periods of prolonged damp weather.

Keep Weeds off the Walkway

❖ If weeds start to flourish in the spaces of your brick or stone walk, here's a good way to combat them: Fill a teakettle with water, bring it to a boil and pour the boiling water over the weeds. Immediately cover the area with a piece of burlap or an old blanket to hold in the heat. This treatment should kill emerging weeds before they break up your walkway.

❖ Use an old screwdriver to strip weeds from cracks between paving stones or bricks. Dig down to loosen the roots and pull up the entire plant. If uneven spaces remain, fill them in with loose soil or sand.

The Right Place, the Right Thyme

❖ If you like the look of greenery in your walk but want something that will endure foot traffic, plant thyme or other low spreading herbs in the spaces between the stones. Each time you step on them, they'll release their fragrance.

THE VEGETABLE GARDEN

Recipes to Combat Pests

❖ Deter insects that damage beans, squash and other plants with a spicy spray. In a blender, combine 4 heads of garlic, 1 chopped jalapeño pepper or 1 tablespoon of crushed red pepper and ½ cup of chopped onion. Add 3 cups of water and let the mixture sit overnight. Strain to remove the sediment, then combine ¼ cup of the spicy solution per 1 gallon of water in a sprayer. Apply morning and night for four days.

❖ To keep cabbageworms from devouring your cabbage, sprinkle the heads of the cabbages with sour milk or buttermilk, then dust them with cornmeal or hot pepper. Repeat after each rainfall.

No More Midnight Snacks

❖ Strew leaves of lettuce or cabbage, or slices of raw potato and used halves

COMMON MISTAKES

Tomatoes: Turn Out the Lights

IF YOU HAVE some green tomatoes that need to ripen, don't place them on a sunny windowsill; they don't need light to turn color, and the sun will burn them. A refrigerator is not such a hot solution either; they won't ripen after they've been refrigerated. Instead, keep them in a dark place that is 65° to 70°F. Or place them on a shelf and cover them with several sheets of newspaper. Check regularly for reddening and remove any that have rotted.

Once tomatoes ripen, store them at room temperature on a shelf or table away from direct sunlight. Don't stack them in baskets or put them in the refrigerator.

of grapefruit, around the garden in the evening to collect night feeders such as slugs, beetles and other pests. Conduct a search-and-destroy mission in the morning, dropping any bugs that you capture in a jar of soapy water to kill them.

Those Awful Aphids

❖ Aphids hate tomato juice. To get rid of the bugs, grind 8 large tomato leaves in a blender with 2 cups of water and strain the mixture. Combine 3 tablespoons of this "tomato juice" per 2 cups of water in a sprayer. Apply twice a day to any plants infested with aphids. Keep up the routine until the bugs are gone.

A SECOND LIFE

Container Gardening

YOU KNOW ALL those containers you've been saving because they just might come in handy someday? Well, you were right . . .

• Place tuna fish cans with the tops and bottoms removed, as well as paper seed packets, around transplanted seedlings to keep cutworms away.

• Use plastic gallon jugs to mix fertilizer. Or cut several small Xs in the bottoms, then fill them with water and place them next to tomato plants as a weekend drip irrigation system.

• Plastic gallon jugs also work as mini greenhouses. Remove the bottoms and use the rest of the jugs as "hot caps" over tender seedlings in the spring.

• Stack several old tires, fill the hole in the center with rich soil and compost and use the contraption as a planter for potatoes, tomatoes, melons or other plants. The black rubber absorbs the sun's heat and warms the soil, giving these heat-loving crops a boost.

• Save large plastic nursery pails, containers for drywall joint compound or any institution-size food containers. Plant invasive garden favorites such as mint and violets right in the pails to curb their spreading habits.

• After cutting potato eyes for planting, put each piece of tuber in a section of an old egg carton. Keep the carton out of the sun but warm for a few days to encourage sprouting. Once the eyes have sprouted, plant them in soil.

No Holding On

❖ To remove potato beetles and bean beetles from plants, place old dish towels or strips of old cotton sheets under the plants and shake the stems vigorously in the early morning to dislodge the bugs. Crush them as they fall.

Strange Brew

❖ Every three weeks, spray potatoes, tomatoes and rose-bushes with manure tea. To make the tea, combine one part well-rotted manure and ten parts water in a covered container and let sit for one week. Strain outdoors (it will smell terrible) before applying. This preventive medicine will ward off problems such as potato blight, yellowing tomato leaves and black spot on roses.

Tomatoes: No More Blight on the Subject

❖ Keep tomato plants free from soil-borne blight by mulching all around them so that no water can splash up from the soil.

Hair Care

❖ Negotiate with your local beautician to see if she is willing to exchange a supply of human hair—a great source of nitrogen for plants—for a few baskets of fresh vegetables. Provide your benefactor with a trash can, and stop by regularly to pick it up. Add the hair to your compost pile, spread it on the ground before applying mulch and put it in planting holes and under fruit trees. This is a great way to beef up the nitrogen content of your soil.

Second Comings

❖ Extend your harvest of fresh vegetables by planting a second crop of carrots, leeks, parsnips and radishes in early summer. All of these crops can be left in the ground after the first hard frost (many cooks say their flavor is sweeter after a frost) and harvested during the winter, or even the following spring.

COMMON MISTAKES

Rhubarb Is Not an Ornamental

DON'T LET RHUBARB develop flowers. The plant does so at the expense of new stalks, so flowering will cause a poor crop the following year.

GARDEN CONTRAPTIONS

Support Your Vigorous Veggies

❖ Make a long-lasting and easily reusable support for peas and beans with wire mesh fencing approximately four feet high. Drive five-foot stakes into the ground at four- to five-foot intervals, attach the fencing to the stakes and then lace thin dowels or bamboo poles through the mesh at the top and bottom. Nail the dowels to the stakes—or drive in a nail at the end of each dowel, rest the dowel on it and lash the dowel to the stake. At the end of the season, remove the dowels and roll up the wire to use next season.

Create an easily reusable trellis by driving five-foot stakes into the ground, connecting them with wire mesh and securing the top and bottom with dowels.

Be Kind to That Vine

❖ Come painting time, it's easy to damage a trellis that's attached to your house, to say nothing of the plant that calls it home. Think of a trellis not only as a support for a climbing plant but also as a freestanding screen, which you'll want to take down and put up now and then. To allow for good air circulation and prevent your climbing or twining plants from damaging exterior woodwork, attach the trellis to your house with two- to three-inch lengths of narrow copper tubing. Screw the trellis to the house through each tube. When you need to move it away from the house for painting, unscrew it and pull it back.

SEEDS

Save Your Seeds

❖ If you use only some of the seeds from a packet, save the remainder for another year. Store them in an airtight container in the refrigerator—preferably in a wide-mouthed jar with a rubber ring.

Munch, Crunch—They're Ready

❖ How do you know when seeds are dry enough to store? Take a bite. If they crunch, they're ready.

A Little Milk
Will Keep These Babies Healthy

❖ Here's a trick to help absorb humidity in the jar where you save your seeds. Place 2 heaping tablespoons of fresh powdered milk in a stack of 4 facial tissues. Fold and roll the tissues to make a small pouch and secure it with tape or a rubber band. Place the pouch in your jar of seeds. Replace the powdered milk once or twice a year. Dried milk

A SECOND LIFE

New Uses for Old Trash Cans or Barrels

• IF YOUR PLASTIC TRASH can develops a hole in the bottom, scrub it well and use it as a mini root cellar. Patch the hole with a sheet of plastic and duct tape. Fill the bottom with several inches of sand or peat moss, then add alternating layers of carrots or other root vegetables (spaced so that they don't touch) and sand or peat moss. Store in a cool (40°F), frost-free location. An old barrel can be used in the same way.

• If your old trash can doesn't have holes in the bottom, practice an old-time trick for making your own fertilizer: turn the can into a pot for compost tea. Set the can out in the garden and shovel into it eight to ten inches of well-rotted compost. Fill it with water and use the liquid to water your plants. Leave the can uncovered so that rainwater will help maintain the level, and add a little more compost from time to time, stirring now and then to keep the best part from settling on the bottom.

• A trash can or barrel makes an ideal potato garden, especially for patios or other limited areas. Make sure the can has a few holes in the bottom for drainage. Fill the can with about eight inches of good soil. Plant several potato sets in this layer, water them and let them grow. When they have developed leaves and before they flower, add another layer of soil and plant another group of potato sets. Continue layering and planting until the barrel is filled to within about four inches of the rim. Water routinely. When the recommended growing time for that variety has passed, empty out the bin and harvest your crop.

is hygroscopic, which means that it will soak up moisture from the air when you open the jar. So be quick about it when you remove seed packets, and promptly recap the jar.

Toward the Perfect Tomato

❖ For best results when saving tomato seeds, wet-process them using a simple technique of fermenting, washing and drying. First, squash a dead-ripe tomato into a glass or plastic tub. (Find a tomato that looks appetizing enough to eat and squeeze out just the seeds and gel.) Set the brew someplace where you won't forget it, and stir it once or twice a day for three or four days. (It should bubble up, begin to smell and grow a layer of whitish mold.) On the fourth or fifth day, spoon or pour off the mold and any pulp and lifeless seeds that have risen to the top. Strain, rinse and dry the heavier seeds on paper towels. When they're thoroughly dry, store them in a tightly sealed container, and they'll be ready for planting next spring.

That Everlasting Compost Bin

NO NEED TO INVEST in a fancy, expensive, manufactured compost bin that will fill up in a week. Make your own practical and cost-free bin with five hardwood pallets—the kind you can find discarded around loading docks or at nurseries and home improvement centers.

1. **Collect five pallets that are the same size**—generally either 42 or 48 inches square.

2. **Put one pallet down on the ground** to serve as the floor of your bin. (The bin's pallet floor provides the aeration critical to composting.

This base will rot after about two years, at which point you can throw another pallet on top of it as a replacement.)

3. **Lash the remaining four pallets together** with old coat hangers, rope or wire. Make sure the front pallet can be easily detached for access.

The finished five-pallet bin holds two cubic yards and is at least twice as large as any model you can buy. Individuals tending large yards and gardens generally need a two-bin system using nine pallets. To camouflage the bin, plant tomatoes, sunflowers or vines around three of the four sides. These plants will enjoy their close proximity to the rich organic matter.

The Kindest Cuts

❖ Carry a bucket of warm water down to the garden and immerse flower stems as soon as you cut them. The stem of a flower begins to draw in air when it's cut, and this can cause a blockage and prevent water from getting to the flower when you put it in a vase.

❖ When arranging flowers in the house (especially roses, which have bent necks), cut the stems again underwater to help them get a good drink and keep them from wilting.

No Cold Baths

❖ When placing flowers in a vase, fill the vase with warm (not hot) water. Don't use cold water. Warm water is more rapidly absorbed and prevents air bubbles from blocking the stems. Approximately 80° to 110°F is ideal.

Strip, Please

❖ Before placing flowers in a vase, strip off all leaves that would otherwise end up underwater. Foliage that sits in the water will rot quickly, give off a terrible smell and produce ethylene gas, which shortens the life of cut flowers.

They Like a Mixed Drink

❖ To help your bouquet last longer, add a dose of lemon-flavored soft drink to a vase of water—any combination up to equal parts soft drink and water will do. The soda contains lemon to lower the pH level, sugar to replace glucose the plant has lost—and needs—and carbonation to keep the bacterial growth in check.

❖ An alternative floral preservative is 1 teaspoon of gin or vodka added to the water in a vase.

Help Perennials Live Up to Their Name

❖ Divide perennials when they begin to show signs of age—fewer flowers and lots of leaves. Most will live longer if you divide them every three to five years, and their off-spring will thrive, providing you with plants that you can use to expand your garden or give away to friends.

It's Ugly but Effective

❖ After bulbs have flowered outdoors, let their foliage wither, yellow and die on the plant. Don't cut it off, or you'll rob the plant of nourishment it needs for the next year.

Annuals: Think of Future Generations

❖ Before your garden annuals are killed by frost, take cuttings from them. Remove the flowers and buds, dip the cuttings in rooting compound and plant them in vermiculite or a mixture of vermiculite and peat moss. When they're established, repot them in standard potting soil. Place them in bright light, water and feed them regularly and pinch them back to keep the plants bushy. Future generations of begonias, coleus, fuchsias, impatiens, marigolds and portulacas are among the easier annuals to grow indoors by this method.

Forced Flowers

❖ When alyssum, ageratum and Johnny-jump-ups start to set seeds and stop producing flowers, snip off all the old flower heads with garden shears to force them into another flowering cycle. They will flower right up until the first frost if you keep after them.

When staking a tall plant, leave at least an inch of space between stake and plant. Wrap the material around the plant first, forming a U, then tie it around the support, forming an O.

Don't Strangle Your Stems

❖ Tall flowers will endure through high winds and heavy rainstorms if you stake them. When tying them, be careful to leave at least one inch of space between the stem and the stake so that you don't restrict their growth. For nonslip staking, form the tie into a double loop: first take it around the plant stem to form a U, then wrap it around the stake to form an O. Secure the tie on the stake, not the plant.

Strawberry Fields Once Again

❖ To renew a strawberry bed after harvesting, mow it with a lawn mower set on high. The goal is to remove the plants' leaves without damaging the crowns. Thin the plants so that they're four to six inches apart. Water and weed them if necessary. Cultivate them in the middle of each row and throw about one inch of fresh, loose soil over the beds to provide a new rooting medium for the old crowns. A well-maintained bed should last for three to five years. After this, start over in a new location.

Traps for Fruit Pests

❖ To help reduce populations of flies and moths that want to enjoy your tree fruit as much as you do, make a trap of the following ingredients: 1 cup of water, ½ cup of apple cider vinegar, ¼ cup of sugar, and 1 tablespoon of molasses. Pour about an inch of this mixture into open containers. (Individual yogurt containers or soup cans with the lids removed are about the right size.) Hang two to three traps on each fruit tree. Clean them out every few days and refill as necessary.

PUZZLER

WE'LL BET THERE ARE STILL A few of these tucked away in barns in Maine and Idaho. Their purpose was to lift a crop onto a wagon without bringing up a load of dirt.

ANSWER: *Potato shovel.*

OUTBUILDINGS

Leave Them Cold

❖ Never insulate an unheated building such as a storage shed. Although it may be tempting to throw a little insulation in a toolshed or garden shed for those cold fall or winter days, you'll run the risk of condensation buildup and long-term damage for short-term benefits.

Don't Invite Termites

❖ To termiteproof a small outbuilding, try lifting the building up with a heavy-duty jack and shimming it with a few more stones or blocks to get extra clearance.

A Hostile Environment?

❖ If your shed backs up into a hill, dig a swale (channel in the earth) to divert rain runoff and snow away from the structure and thus avoid water damage.

FENCES

Hardware That Keeps on Holding

❖ No matter how good the wood, no fence will last long if the hardware that holds it together can't stand up season after season. When repairing a fence, never use less than hot-dipped galvanized nails or screws. Electroplate galvanizing is much thinner and doesn't protect the steel from rusting nearly as long. Galvanized or stainless steel deck screws are made for the outdoors and are ideal for fences.

Help Them Wear Like Iron

❖ Paint is the traditional protector for cast-iron and modern "wrought-iron" fences, and keeping up with spot painting needs is the best way to maintain them. These fences are made of ferrous metals that will rust and deteriorate if left unprotected outdoors. (While true wrought iron actually resists corrosion because it includes some slag in its makeup, it's rare today, and the mild steel typically used for fences oxidizes readily.) Hand-chip, scrape or wire-

Protect That Outdoor Lock

HERE'S A GOOD USE for an old inner tube. Latches and padlocks on garden sheds and garage doors are prone to getting rusty and sticking. To keep them in good working order, cut a flap from that old inner tube. Make the flap big enough to cover the lock by several inches on each side (and below, if there's room), leaving enough clear space so that you can open and close the door easily. Use a row of small galvanized nails to secure the flap to the door just above the lock, then lift the flap when you need to get at the lock.

brush all rust spots and paint blisters down to the bare metal, then apply an oil-based rust-inhibiting primer and top coats.

Curb Your Fence

❖ Stone or concrete supports are an excellent, long-lasting way to keep a metal fence upright—but only if you keep up the area where metal meets masonry. If your iron or nongalvanized-steel fence is supported by stone or concrete blocks or curbing, be sure to keep the fence posts painted where they enter the support sockets. If the metal is allowed to rust or the cavities are permitted to collect water, the metal will exfoliate (expand) and eventually crack and spall the base.

Galvanizing Isn't Forever

❖ Modern steel wire fences, such as woven Cyclone fencing or decorative versions with patterns, are manufactured with a galvanized coating that's meant to be maintenance-free protection for the metal. However, the galvanizing will eventually start to wear off. If you want your metal fence to last, let it weather for at least six months to allow the galvanizing oils to wear off, then paint it. Acrylic-latex primers have been showing good long-term performance on the galvanized surfaces of new fences.

Inappropriate Companions

❖ Keep oak, sweet chestnut, cedar and redwood trees away from galvanized steel fences. When any of these comes in contact with the zinc in the fence, the tree is likely to encourage corrosion.

Artwork, Valuables and Electronics

O NCE WHEN I WAS BUILDING an addition onto the local American Legion hall, I overheard the manager talking to some junk dealers about an old broken-down player piano he wanted to get rid of. The dealers were going to charge him to haul it away, so I offered to take it off his hands for free, and he accepted.

Player pianos use suction to "play" the keys. When air is sucked through a particular hole in the piano roll, it triggers a bellows that plays a certain key. The tubing that should have been transferring the suction throughout my piano was all cracked. The piano sat in my garage for about a year before I had time to work on it, but as soon as I installed new tubing, the piano worked just fine. I began collecting old piano rolls and played the instrument frequently.

The air motor that regulates the flow of air in the piano began to wear out next, so I rebuilt it. That got the piano back on its feet, but the sound still wasn't as good as it could be. Some of the bellows, which drive the individual keys, had failed. That's when I ordered a book and, following its instructions, rebuilt all 66 of the bellows. For a while when I had the piano apart, I was wondering whether I'd ever get it all back together. But in the end, the piano played as if it were new.

It's funny how your standards can rise to meet the challenges of a project. Bringing a player piano back to life is probably about as far as a layperson can go to revive something that is delicate and finicky by nature. But even if an item is rare or valuable, or so complicated that you can't imagine taking it apart, there are often maintenance and restoration techniques you can follow without getting in over your head. In this chapter, we'll take a look at some of these procedures, ranging from bringing the luster back to Aunt Sophie's handmade quilt all the way to keeping your VCR out of the electronics graveyard. Let's begin with . . .

OIL PAINTINGS

Don't Be Overprotective

❖ When framing an oil painting, leave its surface open to the air. Don't cover it with glass, which can trap moisture next to the artwork.

Hang It Up

❖ When hanging a valuable painting, try to place it in a spot that's relatively cool and away from any direct source of heat and light. The best spot is on a south wall—or any dry, cool wall that doesn't receive a lot of direct sunlight. Don't hang a valuable painting over a heat register, radiator or fireplace. The paint will become dry and brittle, and dirt carried by rising warm air (especially over fireplaces) will end up on the painting. Avoid hanging a painting in direct sunlight, where it will surely fade. And as much as possible, keep the artwork away from fluorescent lights, because these can also cause fading.

We Could All Use
a Little Extra Support

❖ When hanging a heavy picture, you need more than wire and hooks alone. Install a couple of angle brackets to hold up the bottom edge of the frame. If they're small enough, they won't show.

Let 'Em Lean

❖ Hang your pictures with a slight forward tilt instead of flush against the wall. This will reduce the amount of dust that settles on the surface and will let air circulate behind the artwork, preventing condensation.

Angle brackets provide extra support for a heavy picture.

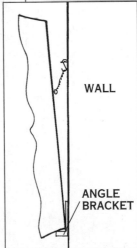

WALL

ANGLE
BRACKET

Rolling Right Along

❖ If you need to roll an oil painting on canvas to store it, roll it so that the image faces out. Paint is supple and can withstand being expanded, but it will crumble and flake if it's compressed. Place the canvas with the image facedown on a sheet of acid-free paper (available at good art supply stores). Roll it up around the paper, then roll it again in plain brown kraft paper. Tuck the ends of the kraft paper into the roll but don't seal the ends, because air needs to circulate in and around the painting. Store the canvas on its side in a dark, cool, dry place.

❖ An alternative is to roll the artwork up without the acid-free paper and then wrap it in a sheet of Mylar. Again, don't seal the ends. Mylar, available from good art supply stores, is a plastic product that has no polyvinyl chloride (PVC), a chemical found in some plastics that can damage artwork.

PICTURE FRAMES

Clean with Care

❖ When cleaning the frame around a painting, spray a common household cleaner such as Windex or Fantastik onto a soft cloth, then wipe the frame with the cloth. Don't spray cleaner directly onto the frame, as some of the spray will get on the painting. (The same holds true when you're cleaning protective glass, as the spray can get behind the glass and harm the picture.)

Not Gilty!

❖ Clean gilded picture frames with a dry feather duster. Don't use liquid cleaners; they will dissolve the gesso (a gypsum-and-glue substance used as a base coat on gilded frames).

There's Gold in Them Thar Fills

❖ Hide a scratch in a gilded picture frame by applying a little burnt umber watercolor to the damaged spot. Treasure Gold, a wax that has bronzing powder in it, works well, too. Both are available at better art supply stores and hobby shops.

Ding-a-Ling

❖ You can hide a dent or ding in a wooden picture frame. If the hole is deep, fill it in with a little wood putty. Then color the putty with a marker designed to disguise scratches in wood. These markers are available at larger hardware stores and home centers and come in a variety of colors.

WATERCOLORS AND PRINTS

Patch As Patch Can

❖ To mend a torn print, first make sure that the seams of the tear meet on the front. Spread a thin layer of boiled wheat paste over the tear on the back of the print, then place a sheet of Japanese paper over the paste. Both boiled wheat paste and Japanese paper (acid-free paper made especially for mending paper items) are available at better art supply stores.

Of Mounting Concern

❖ If you frame your own prints, be sure to mat them, to avoid direct contact between the print and the glass of your frame. While glass is important as a dustcover, it also creates a static charge that can lift ink, pastels and charcoal right off the paper.

❖ Choose mat boards that are "acid-free" or "museum quality." They are made from 100 percent rag fiber and

Let There Not Be Light

WHEN IT COMES to paintings, textiles, books, photographs and other valuables, light—especially sunlight—is one of your worst enemies. The electric lights in your house can damage those items, but sunlight is doubly harmful because it creates heat as well as ultraviolet (UV) radiation. Try any of these steps to keep light from sending your valuables to an early grave.

• Consider keeping a room that contains artworks or collectibles dark when it's not in use. Close the drapes, blinds or shutters and turn off the lights.

• Install venetian blinds to keep sunlight from falling on a particular area during the day.

• If you use spotlights, put them on a dimmer and keep them off the highest setting.

• Paint your room a lighter color so that you won't need so much window or artificial light.

By taking a few sensible precautions, you can enjoy your objects for a long time to come.

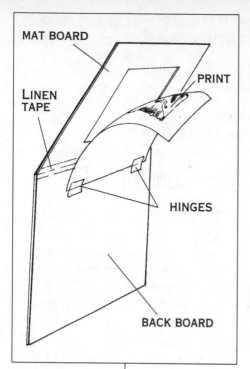

MAT BOARD

PRINT

LINEN TAPE

HINGES

BACK BOARD

A good mounting job requires two sets of hinges. Attach the print to the backboard with Mylar or Japanese paper, and connect the front mat to the backboard with white linen tape.

are reasonably safe from the bacteria and fungi that cause mildew and brown spots called foxing. Cheaper mat board is made from wood pulp, which disintegrates quickly and leaves brown stains on paper.

It All Hinges on This

❖ When attaching a print to the backboard, use hinge strips of Mylar or Japanese paper (from an art supply store) glued to the print and the backboard with rice starch glue. Place these strips at the top of the print so that gravity will pull down on the strips and the print will hang freely, allowing it to expand and contract. Don't use rubber cement or adhesive tape, which will cause stains that are impossible to remove.

❖ Hinge the "window" of the mat to the backboard with gummed white linen tape, then protect the back of the print in the frame with acid-free mat board. Use gummed linen tape to seal the back and help keep out dust. Both the tape and the mat board are available at good art supply stores.

Handle with Glare

❖ When framing prints, use single-weight window glass to protect them from fingerprints and dust. Avoid nonglare glass, which usually has to be pressed directly against the art to work properly.

Store Prints the Right Way

❖ When they're not hanging on your walls, store matted prints and watercolors in a low-humidity environment.

❖ Store prints flat—never rolled—in a portfolio. Or store them in presentation boxes from an art supply store. Ask for boxes made of two- or four-ply acid-free rag.

Build Your Own Box

❖ If a print is especially precious, store it in a box you've made yourself. At an art supply store, purchase linen tape and acid-free mat board coated with barrier paper and build your own storage boxes. The barrier paper offers the best possible protection from acid.

FINE TEXTILES

Be a Dust Buster

❖ Whether it's a seventeenth-century sampler or your grandmother's lace hankie, display fine fabric away from direct sun or artificial light and behind glass, which protects against dust. A glass storage case in an unlit corner, for example, is an appropriate home for such pieces. The case should have openings for ventilation so that condensation won't build up inside.

How to Clean Up

❖ Clean old textiles with a small hand-held vacuum cleaner. Such a unit has just the right amount of suction for delicate fabrics. Don't dust these fabrics, as this will simply move the dust around.

❖ If you don't own a hand-held vacuum or prefer to use a more powerful canister model, avoid damaging the textile by securing a piece of nylon stocking over the nozzle of the vacuum before using it on the fabric. During vacuuming, it doesn't matter how far from the piece you hold the nozzle, but avoid letting it come in direct contact with the fabric.

Make That Sampler Hold Still for Cleaning

❖ Cleaning a small textile piece such as an old sampler can be tricky. It's tough to hold a piece in place to vacuum

A bit of old nylon stocking, placed over the nozzle of your vacuum, will prevent the suction from damaging fine textiles.

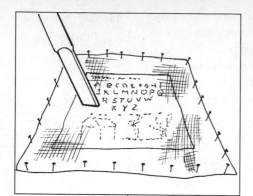

To protect a small textile piece while cleaning, secure it with a sheet of netting, then vacuum over the netting.

off dust. Here's the solution: First, lay the piece flat on a piece of acid-free mat board. Cover the cloth with nylon filament net or an old piece of clean window screen to hold it in place, then attach the netting and the textile to the board with straight pins. Gently vacuum over the netting. Acid-free mat board is available at art supply stores and frame stores. You can pick up nylon netting at any fabric store.

Keep an Eye Out for Uncontrolled Bleeding

❖ Some textiles that aren't antiques can be washed, but only by hand and only if they're colorfast. To test fabric for colorfastness, place it on a piece of white blotting paper. Dip a cotton swab into a mild solution of dishwashing liquid and water, then dab a little on the textile in an inconspicuous area. Wait 20 minutes, then check the swab and the blotting paper. If you see any color on either, don't wash the fabric.

And It Prevents Cradle Cap, Too

❖ If your sampler isn't an antique and you're confident it can stand light washing, clean it by hand with a little baby shampoo and water, mixing the soap in the water before immersing the sampler (some soaps will stain if they're used undiluted). Rather than wringing the sampler—which breaks down the fibers—roll it gently between two towels to remove the excess water. Lay the sampler flat to dry. If it needs ironing afterward, place a pressing cloth (a cotton rag dampened with water) over the sampler and press lightly with an iron turned to its lowest setting. Don't bear down too hard, which will flatten the stitches, or use too much heat, which can damage the fibers.

Flat on Its Back

❖ Store fragile samplers flat in a drawer that you've lined with white, acid-free, unbuffered tissue paper. This is the paper that textile conservators use because it doesn't break down the fibers in fabrics. You'll find it at better art supply stores.

Fold Me Not

❖ If you have the space, store your needlework and fine linens flat (not folded, which can break the fibers in the piece). Unused pizza boxes (available from your local pizzeria) make an inexpensive alternative to cumbersome flat files. Line the boxes with acid-free paper, which you can find at an art supply store.

Roll, Don't Fold

❖ If flat storage is impossible, roll fine linens around a polyvinyl chloride (PVC) tube (a piece of drainpipe will work fine) that has been covered with a clean white cloth.

❖ If you must fold linens or other fine textiles for storage, do it without ironing, and don't place anything heavy on top of them. It also helps to crumple up some acid-free tissue (never use newspaper, which will stain) and place it between the folds to minimize permanent creasing. Refold the piece periodically so that it's not always folded along the same line, which can weaken or break the fibers.

Less Is Best

WHEN DEALING with artworks, antiques or collectibles, it's often better to do nothing than to do the wrong thing. If in doubt about how to handle a valuable item, always take it to a pro. The most damage to antiques comes from owners trying to clean or repair them without the proper know-how.

QUILTS

A Salty Tale

❖ Keep the dyes in a new quilt from bleeding by soaking it in a mixture of washing soda and water. You can get washing soda from large grocery stores. If you haven't any handy, soak the quilt for about two hours in a large washbasin or clean bathtub in a mixture of cold water and 3 to 4 cups of salt. Rinse the quilt well. To dry it, lay it flat outdoors, preferably out of the sun, on a dry day.

Wait till the Dust Settles

❖ Before you put a quilt through the stress of cleaning, try the less wearing approach of simply vacuuming off the dust every six months or so. Use the lowest setting on your vacuum cleaner and fit it with the small brush attachment. It's a good idea to wrap a piece of cheesecloth or old panty hose around the end of the hose to prevent small, loose pieces from getting sucked in.

Spot Cleaning

❖ To clean a spot on a white section of a quilt, mix up a paste of cream of tartar and all-fabric bleach. Put a dab of paste on the spot and allow it to set. After it dries to a powder, brush it off.

Mil-don't

❖ To remove mildew from a quilt, wash the piece gently in lukewarm water to which you've added a little Orvus—an animal shampoo available from feed stores and veterinarians. Do this in a clean bathtub rather than in the washing machine, where the quilt is likely to get balled and knotted. Rinse the piece and lay it outside for a few hours on a dry day. It's best to put it in the sun, mildew's worst enemy, but leave it there only until it's dry. Remember that sunlight can fade fabric if it's left too long in the sun.

Taken to the Cleaners

❖ In general, clean a modern quilt made of wool and silk by dry cleaning. You can wet-wash (by hand) those made of linen or cotton.

❖ If you want to clean a valuable old quilt, especially one made from a fragile fabric such as silk, satin or velvet, it's probably best to leave the job to a professional—but not your neighborhood dry cleaner. Find a cleaner who specializes in large and delicate textiles by asking the textile curator at a local museum or a quilt shop owner. Or look in the Yellow Pages under Quilting, Cleaners or Draperies and Curtains, and get recommendations from the establishments listed there.

You Perborate!

❖ Brighten a quilt that has yellowed with age by soaking it for an hour or so in a solution of 1 tablespoon of sodium perborate and 1 gallon of lukewarm water. Sodium perborate is a mild bleaching agent, and its effervescent action gently penetrates and cleans the fabric. Ask a pharmacist for sodium perborate (you shouldn't need a prescription). Rinse the quilt by dunking it in clean water (in the bathtub), then dry it flat outside on a dry day.

The Wheres and Hows of Storage

❖ The best place to store a quilt is in a two- or four-ply acid-free rag box from an art supply store. Fold your quilt in thirds, with the top to the inside. Place acid-free tissue paper (also from the art supply store) between the folds and around the entire quilt, then place the quilt in the box. The quilt should never come in direct contact with the cardboard. The wrapping materials are important here. Some papers contain sulfur, which is acidic and over time will damage the quilt.

Pillow Fight(s) Mildew

❖ Another way to store quilts is in white cotton king-size pillowcases, which allow them to breathe. If you store textiles in plastic bags, they're more susceptible to mold, mildew and being mistaken for a sack of trash. Don't use colored pillowcases; the colors may rub off onto the quilts.

Offer It Protection

❖ If you have to keep a quilt in a wooden drawer, paint the inside of the drawer with polyurethane varnish and line it with acid-free paper, clean cotton sheets or unbleached muslin. Avoid letting the quilt come in direct contact with the wood. All woods contain sulfur, which will cause the fibers to deteriorate gradually. And don't store

PUZZLER

THIS LITTLE BIRD WAS WORTH more in the hand than in the bush—in fact, it kept things readily at hand.

ANSWER: Sewing bird. Clamped to a worktable, it held fabric in its beak.

The Safe That Wasn't

AROUND 1950, THE CONTRACTOR I was working for bought a safe at an auction in Boston. He arranged to have a locksmith open the safe in Boston, but he failed to tell the locksmith that he wanted to use the safe later. The locksmith simply cut a hole in the back of the safe with a torch.

When the safe was delivered to our New Hampshire office, my boss wasn't interested in it anymore. "Junk it!" he told me. But before I did, the superintendent volunteered that he could use the safe. I set the combination for him, and he put it against the wall in his office and kept his important papers locked up in it. Only a few of us knew that the safe had a hole in its back, and after a while everybody forgot about that hole but me.

EARL remembers...

A few years after that, I went to work for a competing contractor. One day I got a call from the superintendent with the safe. He had locked some special papers in it and couldn't get it open. He wanted me to help him open it.

I didn't remember the combination I had set, so I just pretended to "crack" the safe until the superintendent got bored and left the office. Then I closed the office door, pulled the safe away from the wall, and opened the safe door. When the superintendent returned to the room, I was resetting the combination for him.

He was very impressed that I had opened the safe and asked what he owed me. I charged him $15, which in those days was a tremendous amount of money for half an hour of work.

When I got back to my office, my new boss was on the phone with my old boss, who had called to express his outrage. I told my new boss what I had done, and that tickled him no end.

Sometimes if you can't solve a repair problem in the obvious way, it pays to go at it from another direction.

a quilt wrapped in plastic. This might contain polyvinyl chloride (PVC), which can cause yellowing.

How to Avoid Age Lines

❖ Every few months or so after placing a quilt in storage, bring it out and refold it along slightly different lines so that the creases won't become permanent.

❖ If you're storing a small quilt, such as a baby's quilt, here's a way to avoid creating crease lines: Get a six-inch-diameter tube from a carpet store and wrap it with acid-free tissue paper from an art supply store. Roll the small quilt gently around the tube and paper, then cover the whole thing with another layer of acid-free tissue.

Permanent Markings

❖ Don't pin any labels to your quilt before storing it. The pins will leave rust and holes in the fabric.

BOOKS

Sunshine, Go Away

❖ Set up your bookcases away from direct sunlight, which will fade bindings and dry them out.

Judge a Book by Its Cover

❖ To treat a leather binding that's become dry and brittle, rub it with a special preparation consisting of three parts neat's-foot oil and two parts lanolin. This preparation, made by a library supply house in New York, has no trade name but is available at most shops that sell used or rare books. (When treating old leather bindings, do not use leather treatments sold at shoe stores.) Oil will darken old leather, especially *dry* old leather, so test this first on a small, inconspicuous area to be sure it won't darken the surface more than you're willing to accept, or in such an uneven way that it will ruin the binding. If you're pleased with the result, apply the product to the rest of the binding, rubbing it in well. Wipe the book thoroughly, then stand it up with the pages fanned open and let it dry for

24 hours. When it's dry, lightly buff the surface. A very dry book may need a couple of applications.

Avoid Dirty Books

❖ To remove greasy finger marks from cloth book covers, rub them with stale bread.

Clean Bindings with Salt Soup

❖ Rid your cloth bookbindings (*not* the pages) of greasy spots by mixing up a few tablespoons of water with enough salt to form a soupy paste. Test the solution in an inconspicuous area to be sure the binding is colorfast. Then spread some of the paste on the spot. When it's thoroughly dry, just brush or wipe off the paste with a clean brush or soft white cloth.

Baby Your Books

❖ Another way to remove a greasy stain from a cloth bookbinding is to sprinkle the spot with an absorbent powder such as baking soda or cornstarch (cornstarch baby powder will work in a pinch, too) and let it sit overnight. In the morning, gently remove the powder with a soft brush. An unused clean cosmetics brush works well.

Afta You Clean It, You Can Read It

❖ For more stubborn oily stains on bookbindings, combine a few drops of cleaning fluid such as Energine or Afta (available at most hardware stores) with enough cornstarch to make a thin paste. Apply the mixture in a hidden area first to test the binding for colorfastness. Then spread the mixture in a thin coat over the spot, let it dry and brush the area clean.

PUZZLER

ONE OF THESE SHOULD COME with all TV purchases or fireplace installations. Short of sporting a beverage holder, it addresses all the couch potato's needs.

ANSWER: *Combination knee warmer and nutcracker. It conducted heat from the fire to the knee and held nuts to be cracked with the accompanying hammer.*

MAKE IT LAST

Mark These Words

❖ The best bookmark you can use is a sheet of thin acid-free paper, which you can find at better art supply stores. Avoid using any other paper, or even acid-free paper that's thicker than a single sheet, which can hurt the spine of your books.

❖ Avoid leaving newspaper clippings in a book. Eventually, the acid in the newsprint will harm the pages.

❖ Don't leave any paper clips in a book, either. They'll rust and leave a stain.

Aw, Dry Up!

❖ To treat a damp book on which mildew is starting to form, stand the book up and fan the pages. Let it dry in a warm, well-ventilated area. After it's dry, take the book outside and wipe off any mildew powder with a soft brush.

❖ To prevent mildew from forming again, sprinkle the pages with talcum powder or cornstarch until any excess moisture is absorbed, then brush or shake the powder off.

Must You?

❖ To eliminate the musty odor books acquire after being stored for long periods, sprinkle 3 to 4 cups of cat litter in a plastic kitchen trash bag and place the books inside. Seal the bag well and leave it in a dry place for a few days while the cat litter absorbs the odor. If the books still smell musty after three or four days, replace the kitty litter and repeat the process.

❖ If you don't own a cat (and therefore have no cat litter), put musty-smelling books in a bag. Leaving the top of the bag open, place the whole thing in a larger bag of charcoal briquettes. Like the kitty litter, the briquettes will absorb the odor—but you need to take care that the charcoal doesn't rub off on the books.

It's a Wilde, Wilde World

OSCAR WILDE, a man who was never without a throwaway line, once wrote that a cynic is a man who knows the price of everything and the value of nothing. But then, Wilde never dealt in antiques.

Shelve These Ideas

❖ To fill empty space at the ends of the shelves and keep your books upright, support them with hardwood blocks. Avoid using bookends, which can damage book covers.

Keep Them out of Close Quarters

❖ Arrange your books at the front of the bookshelves rather than pushing them to the back. This will let air circulate behind them and prevent mustiness or mold.

❖ Pack books relatively loosely on their shelves—not so tightly that it's hard to get them out.

A Helping Hand

❖ To remove a book from a bookshelf, reach in with your hand, if you can, and tip the book back toward you. (Avoid grabbing the book by the headband or the sides of the spine. You'll loosen the glue that holds the headband to the binding.) Then grip the book firmly by the front and back covers and pull it out. If you can't fit your hand in, push the books on either side a little way into the shelf. This will give you room to grab the book correctly.

CERAMICS

No-No's

❖ Never put any antique ceramic item in the dishwasher. The heat and the bleach in the soap will ruin the piece.

❖ Never soak unglazed earthenware or terra-cotta in water, which can seep into the piece, causing it to disintegrate before your eyes.

PENS

Empty Your Bladder

❖ If you collect antique fountain pens and use them infrequently, flush the ink out of each pen with clear lukewarm water, then dry the pen before you store it. It's common for an antique fountain pen to have a rubber bladder inside in which the ink is stored. If the residual ink dries, it can cause the bladder to crack.

❖ If your antique metal fountain pen gets clogged with ink, soak it in a solution of equal parts ammonia and warm water, then rinse and dry the pen. (This works for metal pens only.)

PIPES

A Little Nip for Your Pipe

❖ To keep your briar pipe's stem and bowl squeaky clean, dip a pipe cleaner in vodka and run it through the pipe. Vodka is odorless and cleans more gently than rubbing alcohol (which is around 70 percent alcohol and definitely *not* drinkable). Use this method on briar pipes only; liquor will ruin other kinds. (If you're not a drinker, you can buy small bottles called nips, containing only a couple of ounces, from the liquor store.)

If It Didn't Come from the Briar Patch

❖ Use a dry pipe cleaner to clean any kind of pipe except a briar one.

STAMPS

The Stamp of Approval

❖ If an item in your stamp collection tears, mount it in an album rather than trying to repair it. Stamps are worth more torn than restored.

Look at It This Way

❖ Consider spending a little extra money and buying albums made especially for stamp storage. They're constructed with polyvinyl chloride–free

PUZZLER

WITH THE SHARP BLADE ATTACHED to the handle, clearly this was used to cut something. But what?

ANSWER: *Tobacco. A device like this was standard equipment in an old country store. Fastened to the countertop, it was used to cut your nickel's worth from a plug of stiff tobacco.*

plastic. PVC is a chemical in some plastic products that causes paper to become brittle and deteriorate.

WATCHES

Like a 3,000-Mile Checkup

❖ Have your vintage watch professionally cleaned once a year (or once every year and a half) by a reputable jeweler. Virtually any watch produced in the fifties or earlier was designed and manufactured in the expectation that it would receive a major cleaning once a year, just as your car requires a 3,000-mile checkup.

Save Your Energy

❖ To extend the life of the battery in your watch, pull out the stem when you're not wearing it. Remember to push

---

COMMON MISTAKES

Avoid an Untimely Demise

SOMEWHERE ALONG the line, the rumor got started that if you dropped a vintage watch into water, you could save it by putting it in the refrigerator. That's not true. In fact, the movements of those watches were traditionally made of highly rust-prone metals, and putting a watch in the fridge can actually speed up the rusting process.

It *is* true that if you drop an old watch in the water—especially salt or chlorine water—you must act immediately, before rust starts to develop. Your best bet is to take the timepiece to a professional jewelry repair person right away, but if that's not possible, here's what to do: Remove the back of the watch and dry it gently with a hand-held hair dryer set on Low. Hold the dryer about eight inches from the watch. Don't touch any of the moving pieces inside. When the watch has dried, check to see if the dial is made of paper. If it's not, place a drop of oil—any oil, including cooking oil, will do in a pinch—into the back of the watch. There's no particular spot to aim for—just hit the center of the watch—then replace the back. (Forget the oil if the dial is made of paper, because the paper could be ruined by the oil.) And next time, stop watching the clock when you're poolside.

---

the stem back in before you put the watch back on, though. This is especially important if it's a waterproof watch, because the stem is where the main waterproof gasket is installed.

Rub-a-Dub-Dub

❖ The plastic crystals of many vintage watches can be cleaned with silver or brass polish. Rub it on with a clean soft cloth, polish and then rub it off. You'll need to apply a little elbow grease, but the results will be worth it.

Watch Your Step

❖ Take off your vintage watch (or any watch that's not waterproof) before you go into the bathroom to shower. The inner workings of most watches are made of extremely rust-prone metals, and the humidity in a steam-filled bathroom can cause rust to develop within a few hours.

OTHER COLLECTIBLES

Coin-al Knowledge

❖ If, while rummaging around the attic, you come upon an old coin collection and are tempted to clean it, dust it with a dry cloth or a feather duster. Coins can lose 50 percent of their value *immediately* if they're cleaned with any kind of liquid or polishing agent.

Comic Book Hero

❖ To preserve your precious Batman and Silver Surfer comics (as well as vintage postcards and sheet music), store them in three- or four-mil Mylar bags, which protect them from humidity and tearing. Make sure you ask for Mylar, a plastic product free of polyvinyl chloride (PVC). Ordinary plastic bags may contain PVC, a chemical that speeds up the rate at which paper deteriorates. You can buy the bags from a reputable comic book dealer or an archival supply catalog (ask your local librarian or museum curator for resources).

Movie (Poster) Magic

❖ Store a vintage movie poster rolled with the image facing in so that it doesn't get scratched. Lay the poster on a large sheet of acid-free paper (available at good art supply stores), which is designed for storing and conserving valuable paper products. Then roll it up and place it in a cardboard tube. Never seal a poster with rubber bands, which can damage the paper. Store the poster on its side in a cool, dry place.

Sports Cards: Safe at Home!

❖ Store and display your baseball cards in acid-free Mylar album sleeves, available at better art supply stores.

❖ Don't try to repair a torn or damaged sports card. It's worth more damaged than repaired.

New Approaches to Rubber-Stamp Decisions

❖ Store your rubber-stamp collection in a wooden spice rack. Look for the kind that has individual nooks for the spice bottles. That way you can display *and* protect your stamps.

❖ If your collection of rubber stamps is extensive, you might want to store the stamps in an old oak typesetter's case, the kind with lots of drawers. The cases are attractive and offer good protection for the stamps, but you may have to do some hunting to come up with one. Seek them out at antiques shops and flea markets.

OLD PHOTOGRAPHS

Watch the Company They Keep

❖ To avoid contact with acids that will eventually destroy your photos, store them in a metal cabinet with an enamel finish, or wrap them in acid-free tissue paper and put them in acid-free boxes (both the tissue and the boxes are available from art supply stores). Don't keep photos in or near wood (this includes wooden dresser drawers), and try to avoid cardboard boxes. Both wood and wood pulp give off harmful chemicals.

Save the Photos; Toss the Albums

❖ If your favorite family photos are saved in photo albums from the 1960s or 1970s, take your photos out of the old albums and mount them in new ones made with acid-free paper. (The paper and plastic in the old albums—especially the ones with self-stick pages—are often highly acidic. The cardboard gives off peroxides, while the polyvinyl chloride in the plastic emits gases that hurt the photo images. And if you wait too long, the adhesives on the cardboard tend to dry out, so that the prints can't be removed.) Use corner mounts or the little hinges that stamp collectors use.

❖ Don't use glue or rubber cement to stick your photos directly to the paper pages of any album. Both contain chemicals destructive to photos.

Something Smells Funny

❖ If you can smell the pages in a photo album, don't buy it. It's probably made of vinyl.

PUZZLER

BEFORE THERE WERE HOME entertainment centers, sermons and speeches helped fill leisure hours. When they ran on a bit too long, this device came in handy.

ANSWER: Armrest, used in church pews.

Forget about Rainy-Day Pleasures

❖ Ideally, store your photos in the main part of your house. A closet is fine as long as air can get in and circulate. The attic may seem like a great place to spend a rainy day looking at old photos, but it's a terrible place to store them. Temperatures up there can vary dramatically, causing the pictures to become either damp or brittle. And if the roof leaks, your pictures will be ruined.

❖ Avoid storing photos in the basement, where dampness is likely to encourage mildew and where you could get water damage in a flood. If you must keep photos in the cellar, make sure they're at least six inches off the floor.

A Flat Statement

❖ Stack your photos flat for storage rather than filing them vertically. But don't stack too many on top of each other; three-quarter-inch stacks are about right. If you stack them too deep, you put pressure on the photos at the bottom of the pile and limit air circulation. This can cause the photo paper to absorb moisture and the emulsion from one photo to stick to the back of the next.

The Whole Town Was Wound Up Tight

WHEN I WAS A SELECTMAN in my town in the early 1950s, I took it upon myself to try to unroll an old composite aerial photo of the village. The photo, which had been made years earlier to help figure out property boundaries, had been left rolled up for so long that the paper started to crumble when I tried to unroll it. But I didn't give up.

I laid the rolled photo on my workbench. Then I lifted up one edge and applied a damp rag to the surface of the photo, unrolling it a little bit as it absorbed the moisture. Every day I repeated this procedure until the photo was competely unrolled. Then I mounted it in a frame so that it would stay flat. We used that photo in the se-

EARL remembers...

lectmen's office for the next ten years—until a new aerial shot was taken.

Since photos are dipped in water as part of the developing process, a little moisture usually won't hurt them. But the key phrase is "a little." Apply the dampness very carefully, to the surface only, and test a corner first to be sure it won't harm the photo. As to unrolling any old document, I definitely advise that you take your time and open the roll slowly.

❖ When storing precious photos, place a sheet of acid-free tissue paper between each pair.

Keep Your Mitts Off!

❖ Never touch the surface of a photo. Fingerprints leave oil on the surface. If you have to handle it, pick it up by the edges.

Good, Clean Photos

❖ To clean oil stains, fingerprints or dust off an old photo, rub it gently with stale bread. The bread absorbs oil and acts as a very gentle abrasive.

Don't Let 'Er Rip!

❖ To repair a rip in an old photo, apply Japanese paper and rice or wheat starch paste, available from art supply stores. Don't use adhesive tape, which can stain the photo.

Who *Was* That Masked Man?

❖ To mark the back of an old photo, type or write out an adhesive label and stick it to the back of the print. Don't write on the back of a photo with a ballpoint or felt-tipped pen. The ink may bleed through to the front or rub off onto the surface of another photo with which it comes in contact.

❖ If you don't want to bother making a label for your photo, mark the back with pencil—but use one with soft lead and try to apply as little pressure as possible so that the impression won't come through to the front of the print. Or use an artist's grease pencil.

Framed!

❖ When mounting a valuable photograph for display, use an acid-free mat to keep the surface of the photo from directly touching the glass. When a photo comes in direct contact with glass, its image is transferred to the glass in a process called ferrotyping. Mount the photo and mat in a metal or acrylic frame, and back the frame with acid-free mat board to keep out dust and pollution. Don't seal it completely, though, by taping around the edges of the frame or by sealing it with a kraft paper backing. You don't want moisture to get trapped inside.

CAMERAS AND FILM

Contain the Action

❖ To avoid damage from high temperatures and humidity, always keep film in its canister until you're ready to use it.

For Cool Pictures

❖ At home, store your film in the refrigerator to avoid damage from extreme temperatures. Remove it from the fridge several hours before you want to use it, so that it has time to reach room temperature before you load it into the camera. That way, it will be less brittle and less likely to develop condensation when exposed to the air.

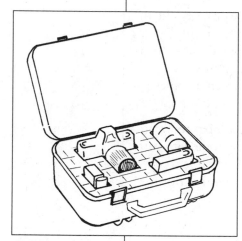

With the best kind of camera case, you custom-cut the foam block to provide a snug fit for your camera.

For the Roving Photographer

❖ When you're traveling with an expensive camera, consider transporting it in a metal or high-impact-plastic case for better protection. Choose a case that's strong, waterproof, dustproof, gasket sealed and lockable. The better kind contains a foam block that you custom-cut to fit your camera.

❖ On day trips, carry your camera in a water-resistant shoulder bag.

Proper Camera Care Is a Piece of Cake

❖ If you need to leave your camera in a hot car for any length of time during your vacation, put it in a plastic trash bag, seal the bag carefully and then place the whole thing in an insulated picnic cooler along with a piece of "blue" ice (available anywhere camping or picnic supplies are sold). It'll protect your camera from the heat, which can cause film to become cloudy.

❖ When traveling, keep film in an insulated container, such as a polystyrene-lined cool box.

Photo Safaris

❖ If you're taking your camera to a warm, humid climate, ward off rust and fungus by putting some silica gel desiccant (available from camera shops) in a porous bag and storing it with your camera equipment and film. Take time in the course of your travels to dry the desiccant periodically by warming it in an oven or over a gentle heat source.

❖ In a pinch, substitute uncooked rice for the silica gel desiccant. Though somewhat less effective, it works the same way, absorbing the moisture that would otherwise damage the camera and film.

Mail It In

❖ One way to avoid potential airport damage to undeveloped film is to carry with you the envelopes provided by mail-order film developers. Send the film in as you shoot it, and the prints will be waiting for you when you get back home.

Filter Out Lens Damage

❖ If you have a single-lens reflex camera, put an ultraviolet filter over the lens in addition to the normal lens cap. The filter won't affect your pictures, but it will keep dirt and grease from getting onto your lens—and it's a lot cheaper to replace a scratched filter than a scratched lens.

EYEGLASSES

Silky Smooth and Scratch-Free

❖ Most eyeglasses these days have plastic lenses. Keep from scratching those lenses by cleaning them with a dry, lint-free cloth (preferably silk) rather than with a paper towel or tissue, either of which may damage the coating on the lenses.

❖ If you want to use a liquid to wash your plastic-lens glasses, use a professional lens-cleaning solution (available from your optician). Do not use window cleaner, which will dissolve the coating on the lenses.

I Can See Clearly Now

❖ If you have glass lenses in your spectacles, use a solution of equal parts vinegar and water to clean them.

A Turn of the Screw

❖ After inserting a new screw (or tightening the old one) in your glasses, twist it tightly and seal it by applying a small drop of clear nail polish to the top of the screw with a toothpick. This will keep the screw from loosening again. Be careful not to get any of the polish on plastic lenses or frames, because the acetone in the polish will eat away at the plastic.

MUSICAL INSTRUMENTS

Pianos: A Little Light Music

❖ If you have a piano with ivory keys, place it near a window or another light source. Sunlight is bad for a lot of things, but not ivory. In fact, constant darkness will cause ivory to yellow.

Tickle Those Ivories

❖ Make it a point to clean out the inside of a piano every three to four months, brushing off dust with a soft paintbrush and holding the nozzle of a vacuum cleaner nearby to catch the loose dust before it falls down into the instrument.

A Slow Tune

❖ Older piano and organ keys can be faced with ivory, bone or celluloid. Clean them with a mild detergent on a little damp cotton. Figure on ¼ teaspoon of dishwashing liquid per 1 gallon of warm water. To keep the cleaner from getting down between the keys, clean one key at a time—lifting each key and depressing the two on either side.

Instant Ivory Cleaners from the Fridge

❖ To clean yellowing ivory, cut a lemon in half, dip it in salt and rub it over the surface. When the ivory dries, wipe it with a damp cloth and buff.

❖ If you don't have a lemon handy, clean your piano keys with plain yogurt. Just place a small amount on a clean white rag, wipe it on the keys and rub it off.

Fret Not!

❖ To prevent your fretted wooden instrument from drying out when you're not using it, you need to maintain the moisture content in the wood. One way to do that is to invest in what the pros call a green snake—a flexible rubber tube about eight inches long. The snake, which has a sponge inside it, has small holes in its sides. Just soak the snake in water, wring it out and wipe it off—there should be no water dripping from it. Then place one end of the snake in the sound hole of the instrument and hook the larger end on the edge of the sound hole. The sponge slowly releases moisture into the hollow of the instrument, maintaining the humidity inside the piece and keeping it from cracking. You can buy green snakes, also known as Dampits, at better musical instrument stores.

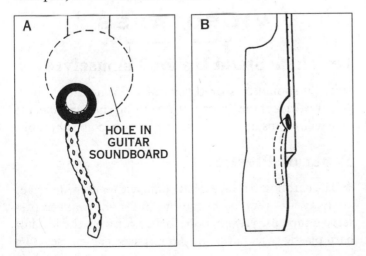

A green snake—seen through the front of a guitar (A), and viewed from the side (B)—can extend the life of a wooden instrument.

Lacquer Is Slicker

❖ Polish lacquered wooden instruments (such as clarinets) with a little household furniture polish (such as Pledge) sprayed on a clean, white cotton cloth. Use just a little, because too much will gum up the keys. And never spray the clarinet directly, for the same reason.

Brass, Inside and Out

❖ Swab out brass instruments occasionally to remove moisture. This is especially important right after you finish playing, in order to get rid of accumulated saliva.

❖ Your best bet for polishing brass and other metal instruments is a cloth impregnated with a gentle cleaner such as liquid Pledge. Don't use brass or other metal cleaners, because they tend to remove the protective lacquer coating on the instrument.

String Savers

❖ Before putting a stringed instrument away, slacken the tension on the strings so that they won't shrink during storage and warp the neck of the instrument.

❖ When storing a stringed instrument, be sure its weight is supported from underneath. Don't hang it by its neck, as this will put stress on the glued portions and, over time, stretch the wood.

VIDEOTAPES

Let Them Stand Up for Themselves

❖ Tapes should be stored vertically, not horizontally. If you lay a videotape on its side for a long enough time, the tape will sag inside the cassette and may become unusable.

Paper or Plastic?

❖ The cardboard sleeves that come with most videotapes are okay for everyday programs, but if you want to preserve a tape for years, you're better off with the kind of hard plastic case that professionals use. These cases do a better job of keeping out dust and offer more protection if a tape is dropped. You can buy them from your local video duplicator at a relatively low price. Or check with a video store, which may have used plastic cases it's willing to sell.

Instant Conditioner

❖ If you're going to store a videotape for a long time, fast-forward it to the end of the tape. This will make you rewind the tape the next time you play it, which will

---

BUY IT TO LAST

What to Look For in a VCR

REGARDLESS OF ALL the electronic bells and whistles you can get on a VCR these days, it's the durability of the mechanical parts that will determine how the unit stands the test of time. Every time you push in a tape, you start gears rotating, arms swinging and capstans engaging. That creates a lot of wear on the unit over time, so you need to be sure that the machine you buy will hold up. Here's how you can tell.

See what it's made of. Check to see whether the mechanical parts—the timing gear, for example—are metal or plastic. Plastic is less durable to begin with and can be further weakened by the heat the unit generates. In addition, plastic gear mechanisms, which are assembled in one piece, are virtually unrepairable. Particularly to be avoided are units that have controls hidden behind hinged plastic doors. The doors are notorious for breaking.

Check how it weighs in. Plastic, of course, weighs less than metal—which is part of the reason to choose a machine that is physically heavier and larger than some of the cheaper models. In VCRs, weight equals durability: the heavier the unit, the less mechanical trouble you're likely to have. Smaller, lighter machines may have lots of electronic features but are likely to have lower-quality mechanical parts.

Listen up. Load a cassette into the machine, but don't hit play. Turn down the volume on any televisions displayed nearby and put your ear next to the VCR. Do you hear a noise coming from the machine? If so, don't buy it. The noise indicates that the video heads are turning when a tape is inserted, which puts more wear on the heads, motor bearings and your videotape. (You may find this even in expensive machines. Avoid those as well.)

---

recondition it to a certain extent. Don't leave tapes in storage without touching them. They should be rewound and fast-forwarded from time to time.

The Untouchables

❖ Never touch the surface of a videotape. The oil from your skin can attract dirt and grease, which will end up inside your camcorder or VCR.

COMPACT DISCS

Slippin' and Slidin' Can Hurt

❖ Always store CDs in their cases, and be particularly careful not to stack two CDs out of their cases on top of each other. If they slide around, the silk-screened label on the bottom one can scratch the music-carrying underside of the other.

A Warped Idea

❖ Always keep CDs in a cool spot. Don't leave them in the sun or in a hot car, as they can warp or even melt.

❖ If you think a CD is warped, lay it on a piece of glass or a mirror and check for gaps. If it is warped, try warming the disc very slightly in the sun or with a hand-held hair dryer set on Low. Put it between two pieces of waxed paper and lay it on a flat surface with a few large books on top. Keep it there for a few hours, then repeat if necessary.

CD Does It

❖ Clean your compact discs as infrequently as possible. You should be able to tell when they need it by the way they sound when you play them. Any CD will last longer if you do as little as possible to its surface—which, contrary to popular belief, can be as delicate as that of a vinyl recording.

❖ To clean a CD, apply a little rubbing alcohol on a clean, white cotton cloth. Wipe straight across the CD. Never use a circular motion, which will scratch the surface.

Stay Away from the Shrink

❖ Keep your records in their slipcovers, but remove the outside plastic. Over time, the cellophane will shrink and bend the cardboard—and the record inside. Keep the record in the inner paper liner, not directly in contact with the cardboard sleeve. Because the paper doesn't create static electricity, the record will be less likely to attract dust.

A Pressing Concern

❖ Store records vertically in a cool, dry, clean space, out of the sun and away from heating vents. Build or find a

A Record-Setting Sandwich

D O YOU REMEMBER record albums? If you can think back to the days before compact disc players, you probably remember LPs—long-playing records. But I date back to the days of the old 78 rpm recordings, back before records were made of vinyl.

Believe it or not, I still listen to my collection of old 78s. (Bing Crosby is one of my favorites.) The records are made of Bakelite, and they warp horribly if they aren't kept upright in their covers, but it's not a big deal to fix this problem. I take the warped record and sandwich it between two pieces of plate glass. (Plate glass is heavier and thicker than today's window glass.) Then I place the record-and-glass sand-

EARL
remembers...

wich in the sun and check on its condition every hour or so. The sun warms the record, which takes the shape of the glass—flat!

I don't recommend this approach for vinyl records, but it's great if you still have a collection of 78s.

special cabinet with vertical dividers so that about ten records can be set loosely in each section. Don't allow too many records to lean against each other, and don't stack them on top of each other, or the weight will press dust into the grooves.

TELEVISIONS

Screen Out the Dirt

❖ Before you clean your TV screen, turn off the set and wait till it's cool. (If it's an instant-on set, unplug it.) If you don't, the act of wiping the screen can cause static buildup that will discharge back to your TV, resulting in severe damage. Even if the set is off, don't touch the controls immediately after cleaning your set. Instead, touch a grounded item first to release any static charge.

❖ To prevent dirt from building up on the glass and dimming the picture, clean your TV screen often with a soft cloth dipped in rubbing alcohol or a mild dishwashing liquid and warm water. Or use a sheet of fabric softener that's been through the dryer. Never use any other liquid cleaner or an aerosol product to clean your screen. Excess moisture can get inside and damage sensitive electronic parts.

AUDIO AND VIDEO EQUIPMENT

Don't Shake, Rattle or Roll

❖ Keep your CD player on a sturdy surface where it won't be subjected to a lot of jolting or vibration. If you keep it on a wobbly shelf, it will skip every time you walk across the room. (If you put a CD player on top of a speaker, you also may get skipping—in this case, from the vibration of the speaker.)

Buy Some Protection

❖ The best thing you can do to keep your VCR alive for a long time is to protect it from dust. Buy a dustcover at an electronics store or sew one yourself. Put it in place whenever the machine isn't being used.

Made for the Shade

❖ Keep your VCR out of direct sunlight, because heat will dry out the oil that lubricates the heads and other moving parts, and it will melt any nearby tapes. Don't pile books, magazines or videotapes on top of the machine. If they block the vents that are meant to keep the unit cool, it can overheat, causing serious damage.

Nothing Worse Than a Dirty Head

❖ It's a good idea to clean the heads in your VCR about once every 20 to 40 hours of operation. The easiest

Should You Buy an Extended Warranty?

WHEN YOU PURCHASE any piece of consumer electronic gear (such as a TV, camcorder or VCR), the salesperson will often try to sell you an extended warranty along with the machine. The temptation is to think, "I'm spending all this money, what's a few dollars more?" In fact, extended warranties are not a good investment. Here's why.

First, you can't make a claim against the extended warranty until the factory warranty runs its course. Unfortunately, most extended warranties begin the day of the purchase. So if you buy a five-year extended warranty and your machine has a one-year factory warranty, you're actually getting only four years of extended coverage.

Second, the factory warranty center usually won't do your repairs after the original warranty has run out. You'll have to take the machine to a local repair shop, pay for the work out-of-pocket and then submit a claim for reimbursement from the extended warranty company. This can be problematic. For instance, if the problem is mechanical (the most common kind) and the company claims you abused the machine, it can refuse to pay. And many warranties contain exceptions, such as damage caused by power surges, in fine print.

Statistics show that less than 20 percent of people who buy extended warranties use them, and of those less than 20 percent ever collect even partial repayment.

method is to use a cartridge-type head cleaner, but these can be abrasive. It's been estimated that running some head cleaner cassettes for 12 seconds is the equivalent of 1,200 hours of playing time. The best solution is to take your VCR and camcorder in for a professional cleaning once a year. The pro will take the unit apart and clean it with foam swabs and a liquid cleaner.

❖ Dirt is almost always the culprit in a malfunctioning VCR or camcorder. If the picture is snowy but the sound is fine, chances are your VCR heads are dirty. Take the machine to a pro for cleaning.

Head Games

❖ If you rent lots of video and electronic games, take a minute before you play a rented game and clean the cartridge contacts (the prongs that fit into the player) *three*

Sometimes It Pays to Procrastinate

IF YOU'RE GOOD AT repairing things, you'll always be hearing from people with things to repair. A long time ago, a friend asked me to fix his Super-8 movie projector. Since he told me there was no hurry, I took my time with it. But apparently he was either less patient or more forgetful than I thought. When I finished a few weeks later, he informed me that he'd already bought a new projector and that I could keep the one I'd repaired.

EARL
remembers...

Although I certainly don't plan it that way, the same thing has happened to me a number of times with other items I've repaired. I've found that when you repair an item as a favor, you could well end up its owner!

or four times with a cotton swab dipped in rubbing alcohol. Rental outlets don't always maintain and clean their cartridges thoroughly, and this preventive maintenance on your part will keep the rented cartridge from gumming up your player.

The Pause That Destroys

❖ Don't keep a VCR or camcorder in pause mode for long. In pause, the heads continue to spin against the tape, but the tape doesn't move. When that happens, the oxide wears off the tape in that one spot and ends up clogging the heads.

Reruns

❖ If you don't record or watch tapes very often, stick a tape in the player once a month or so and fast-forward and rewind it from beginning to end. Rotating the bearings this way spreads the oil around. If the machine is left to sit, the oil will eventually dry out.

A Strong Case for a Strong Case

❖ One of the easiest ways to make your camcorder last longer is to store it in a hard case when it's not in use or when you're traveling. Buy the kind that has inner foam you can cut to match the size and shape of the camera and accessories. Most of them have little precut squares that you tear out by hand to conform the lining to the shape of your camera.

Camcorders Shouldn't Fly Alone

❖ If you're traveling by air, carry the camcorder on board—don't check it through. It wasn't built to stand up to baggage handlers.

You're Not Jacques Cousteau

❖ If you're shooting at a beach or on a boat and your camcorder gets wet, dry it off with a soft cloth. If it gets soaked, remove the battery and don't operate the unit for 24 hours. If it doesn't work after that, take it into the shop and keep your fingers crossed (if it was salt water, prayer is more in order).

❖ If you're using your camcorder outside and you find it cumbersome to keep putting it back in its case, stuff it in a clean plastic bag to keep it dry and protected from dirt.

Don't Touch That Dial

❖ When a camcorder is in automatic focus mode, the focusing ring will rotate automatically. Don't hold on to the ring while it's moving, or you'll strip the mechanism.

Don't Let Your Camcorder Get Sunburned

❖ Avoid pointing your video camera lens at the sun or any other intense light source, even when you're not recording. This is a problem mainly with older tube cameras, but "shooting the sun" isn't good for any camcorder. Intense light can "burn" a spot on the main recording element, leaving a small spot on all subsequent recordings—an expensive problem to fix.

Record Only

❖ Use your camcorder only for recording, not for playing tapes—that's what a VCR is for. The components in a camera are much smaller than those in a VCR and will wear out faster.

COMPUTERS

Before Your PC Goes on Strike

❖ There's a saying that if you are comfortable in a room, your computer probably is, too. Set up your computer in a dry area of your house with a relatively moderate temperature—not, say, a damp basement or a spare room that's generally left unheated. If your house isn't air-conditioned and you absolutely can't avoid using the computer on hot days, at least run a fan in the room where you're running the PC.

Dust Off the Sewing Machine

❖ Inquire at your local kitchen supply store to see if the store sells cloth appliance covers that might fit your computer, monitor and keyboard. Or whip up a few simple fabric covers on the sewing machine. Dustcovers are an important part of maintaining your computer. Plastic versions look good in the computer catalogs, but they're likely to develop a static charge and attract dust. When you pull the cover off the computer, a lot of the dust falls onto the machine. Besides, when a cloth cover gets dirty, you can just toss it in the washing machine.

It's a Trap!

❖ When you shut off your computer, wait a few minutes before you cover it, or you'll trap the heat inside.

❖ If you live in a city where air pollution is a problem, lay a terry-cloth towel over your computer, on top of your regular dustcover. Terry has a dense weave that captures most airborne particles.

Avoid Dirty Pictures

❖ Once a week or so, unplug your computer and use a damp cloth to clean off any dust that has accumulated on the screen, keyboard, central processing unit and printer.

❖ To clean grime off any part of a computer, first unplug the machine. Then dampen a rag with a little ammonia in water and wipe the machine with the rag.

For a Clean Screen

❖ Alternative cleaners for computer monitors are a damp paper towel or a static-free product designed for the purpose and sold at computer stores. Or use a household glass cleaner. Be sure, of course, to unplug the machine first.

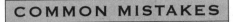

COMMON MISTAKES

Eat, Drink and Be Merry—Away from Your Computer

DON'T EAT OR DRINK around your computer. That cup of coffee may keep you awake, but a spill could put your keyboard to sleep—permanently. If you do spill liquid on the keyboard, don't try to clean it; just take it to a dealer. Since most keyboards cost as much to repair as to replace, you're probably looking at a new one if this happens.

❖ To clean the screen of a laptop, wipe it with a damp cloth. Avoid all commercial cleaners.

❖ To clean a monitor screen without water, which might spill into your keyboard and ruin it, wipe the screen with a sheet of static-free fabric softener that has been through the dryer. Don't use a *fresh* sheet of fabric softener, which might leave a film.

Ever Seen a Computer Charge?

❖ If the weather is cold and dry, you can build up a charge of static electricity just by walking around, especially on carpets. A good shot of static electricity to your computer can cause it to crash. So before you begin work, touch a doorknob or a metal cabinet—anything metal will release the charge.

❖ If static is a serious problem with your computer, consider investing in special desk or floor mats that control static. These are available from computer or electronics stores or from mail-order computer supply companies.

Before You Take Your Drive for a Drive

❖ Before moving your computer from one place to another, insert in the disk drive a special spacer available from your computer supply store. Or put in an old disk that you're not using anymore. This will prevent the disk drive's read/write head from bouncing up and down and causing damage to the drive.

A Hunger for Power

❖ When setting up your computer, be sure to plug it into a circuit that isn't used by other power-hungry appliances. A space heater or microwave, for example, can play tricks on your circuitry. A few lights or an electric clock, however, won't make much difference to the average computer.

PUZZLER

NOWADAYS, WE JUST TELL THE tire man what size we want. But when wheels were wood and tires were iron, the blacksmith needed one of these.

ANSWER: *Traveler, which the blacksmith would run around the rim of a wagon wheel to determine how much iron strapping he needed to make a tire.*

Avoid Bolts from the Blue

❖ When a thunderstorm starts, unplug your computer and the phone line to your modem until the shower's over. Like any powerful electrical appliance, a switched-on computer can attract lightning—a hazard for both you and your computer.

❖ Similarly, if a big snowfall threatens to interrupt the power, unplug your computer until the danger has passed. When the power comes back on, it can create almost as much surge as a lightning strike.

On Again, Off Again

❖ When you stop working on your computer for a few hours, go ahead and turn it off, even if you plan to return to it later in the day. The heat buildup from leaving it on will do more harm than the act of turning the machine off and then on again.

Fade to Black

❖ If you leave your monitor turned on over a long period of time, the phosphors on the screen can wear out, "burning in" the image that's normally on the screen. To prevent this, turn the screen brightness down when you're not using the computer, or install one of the many screen saver programs on the market.

Mouse-ke-cheer

❖ To clean an unresponsive computer mouse, first turn the mouse over. On the bottom of the mouse, you'll see a round plastic plate with a hole in the center. Through that hole, you'll see the tracking ball. Hold the mouse upside down in your right hand and unscrew the plate, turning it counterclockwise. Remove the plate and dump out the tracking ball. Wipe the ball with a soft, dry cloth (no liquid, please). Then use your vacuum cleaner or mini vacuum to clean out the inside of the mouse. Dampen a cotton swab with some rubbing alcohol and clean out the space where the ball fits into the mouse. Then reassemble the mouse.

COMPUTER KEYBOARDS

Keyboard Kleening

❖ Clean your computer keyboard once a month, using a cotton swab dipped in rubbing alcohol to clean dust from between the keys. Or use a pastry brush (available from kitchen supply stores), a good choice because it's made of soft, 100 percent natural bristles. Use a brisk, circular, upward motion to get the dust out.

❖ Another alternative for keyboard cleaning is a soft cosmetics brush (clean and unused, of course).

Nature Abhors a Vacuum, but Keyboards Don't

❖ If these approaches sound too laborious, try running a vacuum cleaner over your keyboard. Or spray it with a can of compressed air, available from camera shops.

❖ Another alternative is to use one of the special mini vacuums that lets you remove dirt from hard-to-reach places. These are available from computer supply stores.

A SECOND LIFE

We Knew Computers Were an Educational Aid

SOME PEOPLE can find a use for anything. One kindergarten teacher we know tears the edges off old tractor-feed computer paper and uses the holes to introduce her young pupils to the science of counting.

COMPUTER PRINTERS

Toward Cleaner Type

❖ Clean your printer regularly with a vacuum cleaner. The paper you run through the printer contains a lot of dust, which tends to get into your entire computer system and eventually damage it. Use the crevice tool on your vacuum to remove any loose paper particles.

❖ An alternative is to spray the printer with compressed air, available at camera shops. Cover your computer before cleaning the printer. Otherwise the dust will fly off the printer and into your computer. It's even better if you can take the printer outside, or at least out of the room, when you clean it.

All Papers Are Not Created Equal

❖ If you want your printer to last, be sure to use good-quality paper made for computers. Cheaper paper made for copy machines tends to shed more dust, which can shorten the printer's life. Finer papers with a high rag content also shed a lot of dust. Save them to use with your fountain pen.

FLOPPY DISKS

Avoid Naked Disks

❖ Store your disks in a closed box or file. This will keep them out of harm's way and prevent contamination by dust, smoke and pollutants. Store disks loosely, not packed in, to prevent damaging the disks and the data they contain. And keep them upright, not lying flat. Pressure can affect the data on the magnetic surface of the disk.

Buyer Beware

❖ When it comes to floppy disks, you get what you pay for. Buy the ones in the middle to low price range, not the cheapest ones, which tend to shed their coating. This puts dirt on the read/write heads of the floppy drive and can cause you to lose data.

Get Your Back Up

❖ If you already have cheaper disks on hand, use them for storing your backup files rather than for everyday use. That way, they won't be handled as much, and you won't be as dependent on them to hold up.

Dangerous Liaisons

❖ If you need to attach a 5¼-inch disk to hard copy, place the disk in a paper sleeve and place the sleeve loosely in a folder with the pages. Don't paper-clip the disk to the

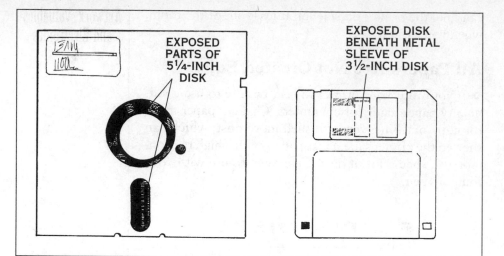

EXPOSED PARTS OF 5¼-INCH DISK

EXPOSED DISK BENEATH METAL SLEEVE OF 3½-INCH DISK

Hold a floppy disk by its protective covering. Avoid touching the exposed sections of the disks with your fingers, because the chemicals on your skin can damage them.

pages. Doing so is likely to scratch the disk and damage it permanently.

❖ Never touch the sensitive surface of a floppy disk with your fingers.

FAX MACHINES

Watch What You Feed Your Fax

❖ To prevent damage to your fax machine, make sure the documents you feed through it are clean and dry—no wet ink, grease or correction fluid. Also make sure there are no foreign objects such as staples, paper clips or loose adhesive tape, all of which can damage the rollers.

This Is No Time for a Jam Session

❖ If the document you need to fax is on coated or carbon-backed paper, make a photocopy of the original, then fax the copy. The same applies to papers that are particularly thick, like index card stock, or thin, like onionskin. Any of these papers is likely to jam the machine.

❖ Similarly, if a document is curled, wrinkled or torn, avoid jamming the machine by faxing a photocopy or by placing the original into a transparent plastic sleeve (available from office supply stores or mail-order catalogs) before transmitting it.

Dust It from the Inside Out

❖ To clean dust from inside a fax machine, spray the area with a can of compressed air, available at camera shops.

And Afterward, You Can Baste the Bird

❖ In a pinch, when you're fresh out of canned compressed air and need to blow dust out of your fax machine, use a turkey baster. Just make sure it's spotlessly clean.

Get the Message

❖ While you're cleaning a thermal fax machine, open it up and use a damp cloth to wipe down the narrow strip of glass that covers the scanner.

❖ Next, run a damp cloth over the recording (or thermal) head. This should easily remove the waxy crystalline substance that tends to build up on the head (the part of the machine that heats up to react with the heat-sensitive fax paper).

Roller Wrinkles

❖ Finally, wipe off the rubber rollers in the fax machine with a cloth dampened in a little water or alcohol. The rollers attract ink, graphite and dust, which can cause lines or spots on your fax image. Pay special attention to the separation rubber, which feeds documents into the machine.

Sports, Recreation and Hobbies

I'VE HAD A BUM FOOT since I was a kid, and it's never been easy for me to walk. So early on, my father outfitted me with a bicycle.

The first bike he got me was a used girl's model. One day I was coming down a hill at a good clip when the frame cracked, and I found myself sitting on the pavement holding only the handlebars. There was no repairing that bike, so next my father got me a used man's bike that was so big I couldn't reach the pedals from the seat. I had to ride with one foot through the frame.

When I was 12, my life as a bicycle owner took a definite turn for the better. My father invested in a bike that was not only brand-new but also exactly the right size for me. Now I had something worth tinkering with. I promptly set about building a sidecar for the bike so that I could carry my books to school and bring home groceries for my mother. For the base of the sidecar, I was able to use the frame of an old rotary lawn mower, to which I attached a wooden box and a rubber wheel.

I used that bike until I learned to drive, and it was still in good shape then. I like to make old things last more than most folks, but in this case what made all the difference was having something good to start with.

The same applies to sporting equipment. Start by buying the best quality you can afford and then follow the advice in this chapter to keep it in good shape just as long as possible.

Of course, we all could hold on to recreation equipment longer if we never used it. With every throw, hit, jump, dive and glide, we subject it to the toughest competition there is—Mother Nature, who always plays to win. Leather, cloth and even the toughest synthetics are no match for the sun's ultraviolet rays, which can cause rubber to crack (and eventually leak), metal to fade and wood to rot. Dirt and sand get ground into valuable equipment and increase its rate of wear. Water dissolves baseballs, turns leather to soup and rusts ferrous metals. Salt water also leaves harmful salts and corrosion.

But you can beat the elements at their own game and still enjoy yours. Try making your sporting goods last longer with these practical precautions and quick and easy maintenance tips.

TENNIS RACQUETS

Don't Spring a String

❖ If you own one of the new, large-size tennis racquets, store it in a dry closet or some other spot where temperature extremes are unlikely. Avoid leaving it in the car on a hot day. Because these modern racquets are larger, they're strung tighter, and the strings are subject to considerable shrinkage and expansion when the temperature fluctuates.

It's Good for the Wood

❖ Old-fashioned racquets also should be stored in a dry spot like a closet, where temperature fluctuations are unlikely, but for a different reason: laminated wooden frames are vulnerable to changes in temperature and humidity.

❖ When your wooden racquet frame gets chipped and worn, restore it by sanding the injured spots lightly, then applying a couple of coats of good polyurethane varnish. Use an artist's brush to avoid getting varnish on the strings; it may dissolve them.

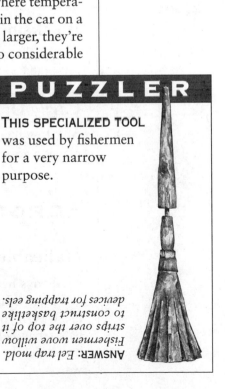

PUZZLER

THIS SPECIALIZED TOOL was used by fishermen for a very narrow purpose.

ANSWER: *Eel trap mold. Fishermen wove willow strips over the top of it to construct basketlike devices for trapping eels.*

GOLF CLUBS

Join the Clean-Play Club

❖ Since synthetics have replaced wooden club shafts and molded grips have replaced wound leather, routine maintenance has been reduced to just about nothing. However, you should wipe the club heads clean after each day's play and clean out the little grooves with the point of a tee. Or stop by a pro shop and pick up a brush that's made for this purpose.

Driver Dressing

❖ If you have drivers with boron or graphite shafts, make sure your club-head covers are long enough to protect the shafts as well as the heads. These high-tech composites are more vulnerable to denting than metal shafts.

HORSESHOES

Blacksmith Not Needed

❖ Remove burrs from the edges of horseshoes with a half-round file.

Carry On

❖ A bowling bag (available at most bowling centers) makes a good carrying case for horseshoes.

CROQUET EQUIPMENT

Malleable Mallets

❖ Always hang mallets in a cool, dry place, such as a garage, in their carrying case or between two wooden pegs in a wall. If you don't have a carrying case, store each mallet so that its head forms a T over two nails. Never leave the mallet leaning unsupported against a wall, as it might warp.

Protect the Heads

❖ Occasionally brush a thin coat of shellac on mallet heads to waterproof them and protect the wood.

Sticky Wickets

❖ Use a wooden hammer, called a smasher, to drive wickets into the ground. If your croquet set didn't come with a smasher—most inexpensive sets don't—place a piece of wood across the crown of the wicket before driving it into the lawn. Driving wickets with a metal-headed hammer will chip or bend them.

The Day the Lumberyard Became a Mini Mart

BACK IN THE 1940S, I used to frequent a particular lumberyard. One day I noticed the manager was in a sour mood, so in the course of our conversation, I asked him what was bothering him. He told me that his upstairs tenant had left —and, as partial payment for all his back rent, had left behind all his belongings, including a complete miniature golf course. The manager didn't know what to do with that golf course.

I volunteered to take it off his hands. It was an 18-hole course, complete with tunnels, windmills and a loop-the-loop. I discovered that it was built in two- by four-foot sections, so it was easy enough to move. Every time I visited the lumberyard, I took home a few sections of the course. I set it up on the vacant lot next to my house, where my neighbors and family had a great time playing with it.

EARL remembers...

Now I golf on a regular course every chance I get. But I got my start on the miniature course that I saved from an uncertain fate. It's amazing the fun you can have for free if you keep your eyes open.

ARCHERY EQUIPMENT

Sometimes It's Best to Come Unstrung

❖ Always unstring your bow before storing it. Leaving a bow strung eventually causes it to lose some of its tension, and it won't shoot as well.

Don't Stand Up Your Bow

❖ Hang the bow in a cool, dry place such as an inside closet. Never stand it on one tip, or it may warp.

Use the Rest on the Salad

❖ To prevent broad-head arrow tips from rusting, coat them with a thin film of oil before storing them. If you hunt with your arrows, use vegetable-based oil instead of petroleum products, or your prey may smell you coming.

BOWLING EQUIPMENT

A Clean Ball Is a True Ball

❖ Clean your ball frequently to maintain its designed roll and spin characteristics. Rub the ball with a clean cloth and Windex glass cleaner, 3M Finesse-It II (available from auto body shops), rubbing alcohol or one of the bowling-ball cleaners sold at any bowling center.

❖ If you're bowling competitively, be careful in your choice of cleaner. Some products are banned in competition because they may soften the surface of the ball, allowing it to "track" too easily. These substances include denatured alcohol, nail polish remover, gasoline and other fuels, and most solvents.

A Strong Finish

❖ If your ball gets scratched, restore the original finish by wet-sanding with extra-fine-grit (400 grit or finer) wet-or-dry sandpaper, then polishing with 3M Finesse-It II (available at auto body shops).

So Clean You Could Eat Off It

❖ To clean your bowling ball quickly, run it through the dishwasher. Empty the machine, put the ball in the lower rack, fill the soap dispenser with dishwasher detergent and run the machine through one cleaning cycle. The heat will draw oil and dirt out of the ball, and the soapy water will rinse it off.

TABLE TENNIS EQUIPMENT

Save the Drinks Till *after* the Tournament

❖ Avoid placing cold drinks on your Ping-Pong table. The condensation on the glasses will permanently mar the painted plywood top. If you absolutely must play "beer-pong," at least use coasters or place mats under the cups.

On the Face of It

❖ If you've invested in rubber-faced paddles, be sure to clean them gently with a damp sponge after each use, dry them thoroughly and store them in a case. Washing restores the "bounce" to the rubber face and also adds speed to your volleys. If properly cared for, these paddles can last for decades.

❖ An alternative way to care for rubber-faced paddles is to wipe them down with a rubber cleaner sold by the manufacturers of the best paddles. Get this cleaner at the same place you bought your equipment.

COMMON MISTAKES

The Law of Unintended Consequences

WHEN TABLE tennis balls dimple or split, discard them. Some people try to get the dimples out with the heat of a wooden match. Often what they get instead is a tiny blowtorch when the ball catches fire and lets out the compressed air. It's not a method that's recommended.

BILLIARD CUES

Don't Miss Your Cue

❖ Store your cue in a case that protects it from humidity, which can warp the cue. Hard cases offer more protection than soft ones. If you have a soft case, hang it upright in a closet.

BASEBALL EQUIPMENT

Cap Care

❖ To wash a baseball cap and thus hold on to it longer, you need a plastic device that protects the visor from water, which will ruin its cardboard stiffener. These cases—one brand is Cap Keep—are available from many general sporting goods stores or team-clothing companies for less than $10. Put the cap in its case and wash it in your dishwasher, along with the dishes.

Mighty Mitts

❖ Before breaking in a new baseball glove, rub into the leather several thin coats of neat's-foot oil, sold at shoe stores, or special glove oil, available where gloves are sold. Repeat this process whenever the glove leather appears stiff or dry.

PUZZLER

You might say that these were par for the horse. Dobbin wore them to improve your game.

ANSWER: *Sod shoes, to protect golf greens and fairways in the days of horse-drawn mowers.*

DIVING GEAR

No-Salt Diving

❖ After you scuba or snorkel, be sure to rinse all your gear gently (no high-pressure jets!) in clean, fresh water. This is especially important after use in salt water to prevent the salt from eating into your equipment.

Divers Should Be Softies

❖ Hand-wash suits, masks, gloves and fins regularly in warm water with a mild detergent. Rinse them thoroughly in lukewarm water. Then rinse them again, this time in a fabric softener like Downy. Sunlight tends to evaporate the oils from neoprene, but the fabric softener will prevent that.

Service Means Safety

❖ Be sure to have all breathing equipment serviced by a certified diving shop once a year. If you exceed 75 dives a year, get it serviced twice. This will prolong the life of the equipment—and the diver.

The Mask

❖ Store your diving mask in a tightly sealed box, especially when you travel to tropical dive sites. For some reason, cockroaches like to chew the silicone rubber sleeve that fits the mask to your face, and the box will keep the mask safe. Storing it this way also will keep the sleeve from yellowing.

❖ If your mask has a torn sleeve, don't toss it out! A good diving shop can replace torn sleeves on many kinds of masks.

SURFBOARDS

Bag It!

❖ Use a board bag to protect a surfboard from dirt and bumps. These terry-cloth sacks, which cost about $50 at surfing shops, have a plastic fitting at one end to protect the nose of your board. Without a board bag, the wax used to improve your footing on the board's slick fiberglass will attract dirt and grime.

SAILBOARDS

A Presail Checklist

❖ Before each use, check the attachments on your sailboard for corrosion. If you find any, scrub it off with a wire brush and wipe the part with a substance like WD-40. If the parts are deeply pitted, replace them. Replace the straps themselves when you notice significant wear.

❖ Also before each use, check the skeg for proper fit. Skegs are most often damaged or broken during transportation and storage.

❖ The universal joint is made of rubber, so it can become worn with repeated use. Inspect it carefully before each use, looking for cracks and checks. And make sure its connection to the board is secure and uncorroded.

And a Postsail Checkup

❖ Always check a sailboard for cracks or splits after each use—especially if you're using a composite board, because these have seams that can leak. If you find your board becoming heavier, it may not be because you're getting weaker. You probably have a leak somewhere that's allowing water to get inside the board. If the board didn't come with a breathing plug for draining it, buy one and install it yourself. Breathing plugs are available from any sailboard dealer.

❖ After each use, check the foot straps of your sailboard for worn or loose attachments. Check the skeg for cracks. If you find any problems, take the board to a repair shop.

The Proper Position for Resting on the Beach

❖ On the beach, lay the board on its side, with the top of the mast on the ground, or remove the mast and lay the board upside down. Never rest the weight of the board on the skeg.

Watch That Rinse Job

❖ After using a board in salt water, always rinse it completely in fresh water as soon as possible. When it evaporates, salt water leaves behind corrosive chemicals, especially in the nooks and crannies of the most highly stressed parts—centerboard and skeg, universal joint and sail grommets and fittings.

❖ Also pay special attention to your rinse job around the sleeve that holds the mast in the luff (vertical forward edge) of the sail. There's a lot of stress on the sail here, especially at the tack, or forward lower corner, and a little salt or sand in the sleeve can cause a terrific amount of abrasion.

Remember Your Seventh-Grade Science Class

❖ When rinsing your board of salt water, don't forget the metal fittings. Salt water promotes electrolysis of steel or stainless steel in contact with aluminum. In a very short time, this process can leave your board's metal fittings welded stiff and crusted like an old battery terminal.

Wax Carefully

❖ About once a month during the sailing season, wash the board of your sailboard with a mild detergent (taking special care to remove sticky tar balls). Then wax it with a product recommended by the manufacturer—preferably one that blocks ultraviolet light. Be sure not to make the board slippery underfoot by waxing it where you stand, especially when maneuvering.

Not for the Budget-Minded

A NY MAN WHO has to ask about the annual upkeep of a yacht," said J. P. Morgan, "can't afford one."

Sail Rot

❖ Take the sail off the mast whenever you're not using it, especially if the board is in the sunlight. Ultraviolet light will eventually rot the fabric.

Avoid Sunburned Sailboards

❖ Always store sailboards out of direct sunlight, which will eventually weaken them.

Don't Sail in the Fog

❖ Never store a sail wet for more than a couple of days, or its transparent plastic window may "fog" and become opaque.

The Waves Roll—So Should Your Sail

❖ When preparing a sail for storage, roll it with the line of the battens as the axis of the roll. The battens are the stiff plastic inserts that hold out the trailing edge, or leech, of the sail. You can leave them in their pockets during storage—if you loosen them to reduce the stress on the sail material.

❖ Don't fold a sail if you can avoid it. The sail material is laminated, and folding can cause delamination.

Keep the Board Upright

❖ Store the board vertically if possible. If it has a breathing plug, remove the plug before putting the board in storage and tape it to the board near the foot straps. That way, the stickum left behind when you remove the tape won't hurt your beautiful wax job.

BOATS, CANOES AND KAYAKS

Clean Boats Live Longer

❖ If your boat has a synthetic hull, clean it monthly—beginning the day you take delivery—with detergent. (Don't let the excess detergent run into the lake or river!) Rinse, dry and follow up by applying a furniture wax such as Pledge.

❖ Another approach is to wash the hull with a product called Cleaning Detail, a slightly abrasive marine cleaner that won't harm the surface of your craft. Rinse and thoroughly dry it, then treat the hull with 303 Protectant, a material that removes oxidized paint and protects against ultraviolet light. Follow the manufacturer's instructions.

Storage: Support Them, and They'll Reach a Ripe Old Age

❖ Proper storage is critical to helping small craft survive. The key requirements are keeping them dry, out of the sun, upside down and off the ground. Make sure your boat or canoe is resting on its opposite gunwales equally. Place your kayak in a sling or shaped support to prevent hull deformation.

Give Your Boat a Lift

❖ If you have no nice, dry barn or garage, you can store small craft outdoors—but always up on sawhorses or boat frames, with waterproof covers. Ideally, prevent the cover from touching the hull, as this causes filming and discoloration, often in unsightly patches.

When in Doubt, Pull It Out

❖ If you're not using your small wooden boat for an extended period of time, pull it out of the water. This applies to craft used on lakes and ponds as well as those used at sea. Fresh water encourages wood rot even more than salt water.

Always Remember to Test Your Work

EARL remembers...

A S A KID, I ASSISTED my father in his contracting business year-round. One of my jobs was to help maintain the summer cottages and small boats on a nearby lake.

In those days, it seemed that every cottage had a wooden rowboat, and many of them had canoes as well. I'd paint each rowboat—inside and out—as necessary, then varnish and paint the wood-and-canvas canoes. This was a time-consuming chore, but a wooden boat or canoe will dry out and leak if you don't keep it sealed.

While I didn't particularly enjoy opening and closing the cottages, it was pleasant to be outside in the summer. But the best part was that I got to work on some bigger, fancier boats as well as the rowboats and canoes. And, of course, I had to take them for an occasional test spin after I finished my work.

It was a tough job, but somebody had to do it.

A Little Rot Shouldn't Make You Distraught

❖ Sometimes it's possible to save small areas of wood that have gotten punky by injecting them with an epoxy resin designed for the job and available at most marine hardware stores.

But Don't Get Carried Away

❖ Where there is too much damage or where structural strength has been compromised, you'll need to go further and actually replace the rotten parts. Don't try to use shortcuts here; you could endanger both your craft and yourself.

BUY IT TO LAST

Canoe Paddles You Can't Destroy

INCREASINGLY these days, paddles and oars are constructed of synthetics and aluminum. Although many traditionalists consider these newcomers unsatisfying aesthetically, a hard plastic-and-aluminum paddle is virtually indestructible and an excellent choice for shallow, rocky water.

It Might Have Been That Rock You Paddled Over

❖ Check the exterior of a wood-and-canvas boat or canoe regularly for scratches, cuts and gouges. When you find any, either paint them with the touch-up paint supplied by the manufacturer or fill them with epoxy filler and then paint over the patch.

Trim Treatments

❖ Treat the wooden trim on your small boat frequently—either with oil, as is common today, or with the varnish found more frequently on older boats. You can spot varnish by its hard, shiny finish, which chips when it's injured. Oil has a lower luster, which it loses when it needs replenishing. In either case, treat the craft fairly frequently with the same material, especially if paddles, oars or docks frequently rub against any woodwork.

Help from the Fire Department

❖ Minimize the damage from rubbing against the dock by tacking chunks of old fire hose—the kind with the cotton fabric outside—to the edge of the dock. Use two-inch roofing nails to secure the hose in a wavy pattern, like ribbon candy, wherever the boat can rub against it.

Avoid Splitting Up

❖ If your oars or canoe paddles are made of wood, check them frequently for worn or pitted spots in the finish. These will permit the blade to soak up water—and that, in turn, will lead to splitting. To prevent this, lightly sand any worn spots, then apply a coat or two of polyurethane. Repeat the process as often as necessary.

INFLATABLE BOATS AND RAFTS

The Right Way to Clean

❖ Clean your inflatable boat or raft regularly, and be sure to do so before putting it into storage for the winter. After opening the self-bailer, hose down the boat to flush away sand and other debris. Wash the deck and keel with warm soapy water, rinse and let everything dry. Check to make sure the self-bailer isn't clogged, and remove the drain plugs to get out any water trapped between the hull and the deck.

Targeting Tar

❖ Tar is not friendly to any inflatable. Remove it with a product specifically recommended by your boat's manufacturer or dealer. Or try applying a mild oily substance such as mayonnaise or vegetable oil and letting it sit briefly. Be sure to rinse off the substance thoroughly, or you'll have a raccoon problem. Never use paint thinner, strong detergents or any silicone-based product.

Look for the Leak

❖ Check for suspected slow leaks in your buoyancy tube the same way the propane man checks for gas leaks: wipe on a foamy mixture of soap and water and watch carefully for bubbles that appear to be growing. Patch any leaks with a kit available from the raft's manufacturer. Be careful to observe the temperature, humidity and time recommendations in the instructions.

Inflatables Aren't Invincible

❖ If you must leave your inflatable craft in the sun for more than a few days, cover it with a breathable canvas. The sun's ultraviolet rays, which wear down so many materials, are enemies of even the hard plastics from which these inflatables are made.

BICYCLES

Chain Gang

❖ The most important regular maintenance for your bicycle is to clean and oil the chain every few rides. Use a rag to clean the worst gunk off the chain, then scrub it with an old toothbrush and a solvent such as kerosene.

❖ Here's another method for lubricating a bike: First, spin the crank while holding a wire brush to the chain and the jockey wheels of the derailleur. Then coat the parts you cleaned with a Teflon-based spray-on lubricant such as Tri-Flow. Finally, wipe off excess oil with a rag.

Time to Change the Chain

❖ Replace the chain of your bike every year or two, depending on how frequently you ride. An older chain tends to wear the chain ring and rear sprockets it touches. It's much smarter to replace the chain periodically than to replace those more expensive parts.

Lube Job

❖ Lube the brake and gear cables of your bike once a year or anytime they may have gotten water in them. Buy specialized cable lube at a bike shop. Usually it comes with a needle-nosed applicator. Put a couple of squirts into the upper cable housings, and while you're at it, squirt a little lubricant on the brake mounts and the pivot points of your derailleurs.

❖ Every six months or so, remove your bike's seat and wipe off the seat post. Use Tri-Flow to lubricate the seat post and quick-release levers on the seat and wheels.

If It Rained on Your Parade

❖ If you arrive home with a wet bike, dry it as carefully as possible with a soft rag and, if possible, spray it with a product like WD-40. Wipe off any excess spray to prevent dust from sticking to parts, then store the bike in a warm, dry place. This may be a garage in summer or a heated entryway or spare room in winter.

Scrub Your Bike

❖ After a dirty ride, wash your bike with a soft-bristled scrub brush and warm soapy water. Once it's dry, lube the chain and the jockey wheels on the derailleur with Tri-Flow.

Thar She Blows!

❖ If you're reasonably faithful in tending to the routine maintenance of your bike, the mishap you'll most likely experience is a flat tire—either a blowout or a puncture. Whenever you're bicycling more than a few miles from home, carry along spare tubes and a small, frame-mounted tire pump. It's a good idea to bring a patching kit as well.

How to Handle a Blowout

❖ To deal with a blowout on the road, you'll need to replace both the tire and the tube. Luckily, they're not hard to remove from the rim when they're flat. Take the wheel off the bike and, hooking a finger or screwdriver under the tire bead, lift it up and over the wheel rim all the way around. Reach in and pull out the tube, then finish removing the tire.

A SECOND LIFE

Foam Pads: Work from the Ground Up

DON'T THROW AWAY old closed-cell foam ground pads once they're torn or you're tired of sleeping on them. Scraps of closed-cell foam make great padding. Try duct-taping them to the gunwales of your boats or to the ends of a roof rack for your car. Or use the foam with rubber cement to fashion a foam sleeve for your water bottle that will help keep hot drinks hot and cold ones cold.

❖ The new tire and tube go on the same way, but in reverse. Be careful not to twist or crimp the delicate tube. And be sure that the valve stem sticks out straight through the hole in the rim. If it's crooked, the edge of the hole will saw it off. Seat the tire bead carefully all the way around on both sides and pump up the tire slowly, making sure that the fit is smooth. Then spin the wheel and watch the tire tread for "wiggles" as it goes around. If you find any, let out some air and straighten the tire before completing inflation.

Tubular Imperfections

❖ If your flat is caused by a puncture, you may want to patch the leak in the tube, too. Think of this as a short-term solution, however. In today's high-pressure tires, a patch makes quite a bump on the pavement each time the wheel goes around, so you'll need to replace the tube once you get home.

Baby That Tire

❖ Whenever you get a flat, sprinkle some talcum powder in the tire before putting in a new tube. The talc acts as a lubricant and helps the tube fit properly in the tire.

From the Battlefield to the Backwoods

BACKPACKS USED to be made of heavy-duty canvas and leather straps, and they lasted for generations. We know folks who still swear by World War I surplus haversacks that by current standards are abysmally primitive. For most people, though, the early models were replaced by the famous World War II "ski pack," an aluminum-frame rucksack that, when loaded, wore two strips of raw flesh across your lower back and, when you fell forward on your skis, came up over your head and pinned you facedown in the snow.

Today's packs, by contrast, are marvels of design and synthetic materials—though far less entertaining for your fellow hikers. Some of them seem a bit heavy on the sophisticated adjustment straps, but they are light, durable and pretty long lasting. If you treat them right, they too should last for generations.

BACKPACKS

Leave 'Em in Stitches

❖ When packing for a long trip outdoors, don't leave home without a Speedy Stitcher Sewing Awl, made by the Stewart Manufacturing Company in Northboro, Massachusetts. It uses waxed cobbler's thread and works very well for heavy-duty repairs to packs, tents and tarpaulins. In a pinch,

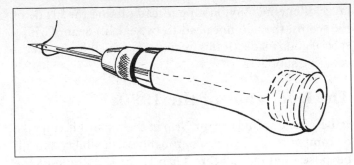

A Speedy Stitcher Sewing Awl is a worthy addition to any camper's emergency kit.

you can use it on clothes, too, but it'll leave you looking like Frankenstein's monster.

After the Bears Have Left the Campground

❖ For slashes or spark holes in synthetic pack fabric, a couple of pieces of Kenyon K Tape—one on the inside and one on the outside—are the best medicine in the field. Kenyon K is a self-adhesive nylon tape designed for this purpose. If you don't turn the edges of the tear, be sure to sear them as soon as possible with a hot knife blade; this prevents them from unraveling. After you get back home, have a patch stitched in by someone with a heavy-duty sewing machine.

TENTS

There's Such a Thing as Too Much Stick-to-itiveness

❖ At the start of each season, treat all tent zippers with silicone to prevent them from sticking. It's best not to use a spray, which is likely to damage the fabric along the zippers, but if that's the only silicone you have, spray it onto a small cloth and wipe the zippers with that.

It's Goo-goo-goo-good

❖ If the needle holes in the seams of your new tent, sleeping bag, parka or mittens were not protected by the manufacturer, seal them before use with a thin layer of Seam Grip, preferably on the inside of the seam. (If you see a layer of one-inch nylon tape already lining the inside of the seams, they do not need to be sealed.) Seam Grip, a special goop made for this purpose, is available from most camping suppliers.

The Duct Tape of the 1990s

❖ Be sure to include Seam Grip in the repair kit you take on camping trips. In terms of toughness, flexibility and all-purpose usefulness, Seam Grip is the duct tape of the 1990s. Apply just a few drops to penetrate and seal the problem area in your tent or sleeping bag. Or use it in the field as an emergency form of glue.

❖ Fill tears in mosquito netting by putting a strip of masking tape on one side of the hole and daubing some Seam Grip on the other side. Once the Seam Grip dries, pull off the tape.

Your Tent Should Breathe So You Can, Too

BACKPACKING TENTS have improved vastly since the days of lightweight canvas, when a finger touched to the inside of the roof during a rainstorm produced a very unpleasant leak. The new synthetic tent fabrics are not waterproof, nor should they be; waterproof fabrics sweat on cool nights with the moisture given off by your body while you sleep. Instead, a waterproof fly, pitched over the permeable roof and walls of your tent, provides weather protection, while the fabric beneath is free to breathe. And you can breathe more easily knowing that raindrops won't be falling on your head while you sleep.

Let Your Tent Hit the Sack

❖ When it's not in use or being dried, store your tent inside its sack in a cool, dry place. Light as they are, modern tents must be handled with a little more care than your father's army surplus pup tent.

They Really Wanted a Tree House Anyway

❖ Sunlight is a particular enemy of lightweight tents. Don't leave a really good one pitched all summer in the yard for the kids to play in.

Take Along a Tarp

❖ If weight isn't a big problem, as on a canoe trip, take along a lightweight waterproof tarp, about six by eight feet, and use it as a ground cloth under your tent. Rough ground, especially with stones or little stubs of cutoff

Fun Doesn't Have to Be Fancy

EARL remembers...

WHEN I WAS YOUNG, my whole family used to pile into the Model T and go camping for the weekend. We'd drive most of the day, then stop at what looked like a good spot and ask a farmer if we could camp in his field.

While we kids swam in the river or played in the field, my father would set up our tent. It was a large white tent with a big fly that overhung both sides. (My brother and I slept under the fly on either side of the tent, since there wasn't room for the whole family inside.) I think the tent came with long wooden poles as supports, but they were too big to fit in the car. Instead, my father fitted together short lengths of metal pipe to form the structure for the tent. He threaded all the pipes and fittings himself.

Even by the standards of those days, our camping gear was pretty crude. But you don't need state-of-the-art equipment to enjoy the great outdoors.

saplings sticking up, can easily tear tent fabric. If rain is threatening, be sure to tuck the edges of the tarp back under the edges of the tent so that it won't trap rainwater and drain it into the tent. The tarp can also be used as a temporary roof over your cooking area, as a windbreak or as a canoe sail.

Roll It Right

❖ If you arrive home from a camping trip with a tent that's still damp, hang it up in a shady place till it dries thoroughly. Then roll it up and put it away. Roll up the poles, fly and stakes inside it, lest someone move the bag carelessly and lose a few essential pieces. Never put a tent away while it's still wet or damp—that's an invitation to mold and mildew.

Be Gentle with It

❖ If your tent really needs washing, wipe it down with a mild soap (like Ivory Liquid or Woolite) and a sponge, then hose it down with water. Never use detergents, solvents or washing machines, which can remove irreplaceable coatings from the fabric.

The Tent Companies Have a Deal with the Mosquitoes

❖ Avoid spraying the fabric of your tent with hair sprays or bug killer, and don't spill fruit juice or insect repellent on it. Any of these may "melt" tent fabric.

SLEEPING BAGS

If a snagging zipper causes baffling problems (A), sew a piece of heavier fabric over the wind baffle (B) to keep it out of the way.

Long Live the Liner!

❖ To extend the period between cleanings for your sleeping bag, use a light flannel or nylon sleeping bag liner. You can get one of these from a mail-order outfitter or stitch one out of an old flannel sheet. Fold the sheet lengthwise and stitch across the bottom and halfway up the open side.

Don't Be Baffled

❖ Occasionally, the wind baffle inside the zipper of your sleeping bag will develop a maddening tendency to catch and bind. To eliminate this, use a sewing machine to stitch a strip of stiffer fabric over the baffle.

Next Time, Don't Sleep So Close to the Campfire

❖ Patch rips or burns in the field with duct tape or nylon mending tape. Even the smallest tear must be attended to, or you could wake up some morning feeling down in the mouth.

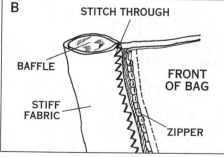

A INSIDE WIND BAFFLE

EXTERIOR FLAP

B STITCH THROUGH

BAFFLE

FRONT OF BAG

STIFF FABRIC

ZIPPER

AIR MATTRESSES

Let Them Breathe

❖ It's best to store an air mattress flat with the valve open. If you have to roll or fold it, do so very loosely.

❖ If your air mattress gets wet, let it dry naturally out of the sun. Never store an air mattress while it's still damp.

Avoid a Rocky Night's Sleep

❖ Keep solvents, insect repellent and stove fuel away from your mattress. Any of these can eat away at the fabric.

❖ On long trips, carry a repair kit provided by the mattress manufacturer. Before you start off, make sure any cement in the kit is still usable.

CAMPING STOVES

Am I Blue?

❖ Before each trip, make sure your stove is clean and rust-free, produces pressure and burns with a steady blue flame.

Stove Storage

❖ Store your stove over the winter in a dry place. You needn't drain it, but if it has an integral tank, store it right side up.

OTHER CAMPING EQUIPMENT

Lantern Talk

❖ Protect your lantern's mantle from breaking by transporting the lantern in a box, preferably the one it came in.

Need a Light?

NEVER TRY TO LIGHT a stove inside a tent or any enclosed area. With any stove, you're dealing with highly flammable liquids and gases under quite a bit of pressure. An exploding stove can make a fireball substantially larger than the average tent. Don't ask how we know.

Stuff newspaper in the cavities around the lantern to prevent it from moving, and stow the box securely and upright in your car or camper.

A Clear-Sighted Solution for Lanterns

❖ You'll get more light out of your lantern if you clean its glass globe when it becomes covered with soot. Use a glass cleaner with ammonia or a solution of ½ cup of ammonia and 1 gallon of water. Then wipe the globe dry with newspaper.

Flush Your Filter

❖ Clean your water purifier with mild bleach after every trip to kill any critters remaining in the filter. Make a solution of 1 to 2 teaspoons of household (5 percent) bleach and 1 quart of water. Pump the solution through the filter, then remove the filter from the solution and pump the purifier until all the solution is gone.

FISHING RODS

The Do-It-Yourself Fishing Rod Case

❖ Always store your fishing rod in a case when it's not being used. If your rod came without a case, make your own out of polyvinyl chloride (PVC) tubing, available from any plumbing or electrical supplier. Buy a piece of tubing long enough to accommodate your rod, along with one end cap, one screw cap and a can of PVC cement. Attach

A piece of PVC tubing makes an inexpensive storage case for a fishing rod.

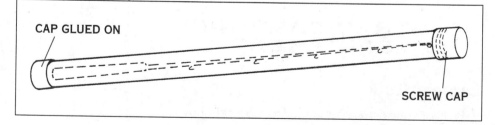

CAP GLUED ON

SCREW CAP

one of the caps on each end, and you'll have a good, solid rod case that will take almost any abuse, float quite visibly if your canoe gets overturned and do double duty as a walking stick. Never leave a good rod propped between a couple of studs out in the garage. And don't store it horizontally on two pegs that allow it to sag between them.

Don't Be Misguided

❖ Check the guides on your rod regularly and touch up any fraying or exposed windings with rod-winding lacquer.

❖ With extensive use, the guides themselves can become worn almost through, at which point they will fray the line. When they reach that stage, either replace them yourself or have the manufacturer do it.

The Stocking Check

❖ Check for rough spots on line guides by passing an old nylon stocking across each surface of the guides. If the stocking runs, it's time to replace the guides, so your line won't be cut next time you're playing a lunker. Don't wait for nicks you can see.

Spare the Rod, Save the Story

MOST DAMAGE to fishing rods occurs when they're not being used. The warranty rod-repair departments of most manufacturers will tell you that almost every broken rod comes back with a note explaining that it broke "while fighting a big fish." The repairmen can tell that almost all the fractures were caused by a slamming car or screen door or a heavy foot on a boat bottom. To save embarrassment and your rod, secure it carefully when you're on the go.

FISHING REELS

Watch Out for True Grit

❖ After each use, remove the spool and wipe off the surfaces where grit can collect.

Give Your Reel the Boot

❖ Store your reel in its original box, a leather bag or one of the new neoprene boots, which will cover it and keep it from hard knocks, too.

A Reel Rinse

❖ Immediately after each fishing trip, rinse your reel to clean out salt or dirt. Use a gentle stream of fresh water from a hose. Be careful not to use too strong a spray, which may force dirt deeper into the reel's components.

FISHING LINE

How to Manage Monofilament

❖ The most vulnerable type of fishing line is the monofilament used in spin fishing and as leader material in fly-fishing. Be sure to rinse salt water off such a line before putting it away. Neglecting that step will "set" its coils, and the next time you use it, you'll think you're casting a Slinky.

❖ Change a monofilament line each year or at least every two years.

❖ Keep your line away from gas, oil and solvents.

Watch Out for Heat Prostration

❖ Avoid extreme heat. Never set your reel and line on the back shelf of your car on a hot summer day.

How to Stay Afloat

❖ Most floating fly lines are sold with little packages of cleaner. Use the cleaner after every couple of outings to remove dirt and residue from a floating line.

Bug Off!

❖ After covering yourself with insect repellent, remove any residue from your fingers before making your next cast. Otherwise the insecticide will eat away at your line.

"Silent Cal" Strikes Again

CALVIN COOLIDGE, the wry, solemn president who hailed from Vermont, took a shine to fishing, although he wasn't very good at it. Coolidge wasn't an especially cheerful guy, but he knew how to poke fun at himself. One of his most famous lines was a response to the question of how many trout there were in his favorite fishing spot, the Brule River. Coolidge said that estimates put the trout population above 45,000. "I haven't caught them all yet," he said, "but I've intimidated them."

FLIES AND LURES

A Manicure Job Can Be A-Luring

❖ If you have a wooden plug that gets banged up in the course of a fishing season, coat the chips in the paint with a little clear fingernail polish. Or use red, to simulate wounds; predators prefer already-wounded prey. But don't put off treating the lure, or those chips will escalate quickly when the lure gets soaked next season.

Give Them Room to Spread Their Wings

❖ When storing flies for the winter, make sure they're dry and in a large enough storage container that their wings and tails don't bump against the inside of the box or against any other flies.

Fish Have Nothing against Mothballs

❖ If you're at all concerned about moths, sprinkle a tea-spoonful of moth flakes in each box of flies—or spread a larger amount right in the drawer where they're stored. Smelly as the flakes are, they don't seem to affect the flies' efficacy the following year.

WADERS

Up (on) a Tree

❖ Always rinse waders thoroughly with fresh water and allow them to dry before putting them away. Or instead of putting them away, hang them from an inexpensive wire boot tree designed for just that purpose.

To keep fishing waders hanging in there, use a wire boot tree.

CLIMBING GEAR

Clean Your Cord

❖ Wash your rope every few months to remove the accumulated dirt and oil that can hamper the rope's performance and shorten its life. Hand-wash ropes in a bathtub or in a washing machine set on the gentle cycle. Add a little fabric softener, such as Downy, to improve the rope's handling, but don't use any detergent, or the rope will stiffen when it dries. Hang the rope in loose coils to dry.

Keep It Moving

❖ Lubricate moving parts on climbing equipment, such as carabiner gates and spring-loaded protection devices, with a Teflon-based lubricant such as Tri-Flow, available at bike shops. Don't use oil or WD-40, which will capture more dirt.

❖ If moving parts jam up, try cleaning your gear in a bath of kerosene or white gas (such as Coleman fuel). However, be careful not to get the fuel on nylon slings; it might weaken them. And be sure to allow plenty of ventilation for this process.

These Boots Were Made for Huntin'

IN THE FALL OF 1911, Leon Leonwood Bean knew two things. He knew that his dry goods business was just barely hanging on, and he knew that his feet hurt. And why shouldn't they? He was on them all day, running errands and waiting on customers. But his feet really suffered during hunting season. They'd get soggy and blistered in those leather hunting boots—especially after the first wet snow of the season. Bean loved to go on long hunting vacations (one of the reasons his business suffered), but his feet couldn't take it. He tried wearing galoshes to keep them dry, but they were too big. He tried padding the galoshes with several pairs of socks, but they were loose around the ankle, which kept him from getting good footing.

One day Bean was standing in his store, worrying about his feet, when he noticed a display of low-cut galoshes in the corner. He took a pair to a cobbler and told him to sew on some leather tops. To someone with less vision, they might have looked like duck's feet, but to Bean they looked perfect. They were snug where they ought to be and waterproof everywhere else. He called these boots the Maine Hunting Shoe, and he founded his mail-order business—one of the most successful in history—on the sure knowledge that hunters need dry feet.

IN-LINE SKATES AND ROLLER SKIS

Hot Wheels

❖ Before each use, check all the wheels on your skates or skis for wear, damage or looseness. The wheels are usually mounted on nylon hubs, which can get quite hot during high-speed skating. Never use a skate with a damaged or loose wheel. Repair or replace the wheels as necessary.

Keep Your Bearings

❖ Protect your skate's bearings by frequently wiping them clean with a soft cloth.

❖ Never skate through water, grease, oil, gravel or sand—all of which are likely to damage the bearings.

ICE SKATES

Keep Your Edge

❖ To keep your figure skates looking their best, touch up the worn edges of the soles with a little Sno-Seal, then polish the boots with white liquid polish before competitions.

Skaters Should Feel Secure

❖ In recreational and figure skates—unlike hockey skates—the supports that hold the blades are screwed and pegged into the leather sole of the boot. Check these screws frequently for any loosening and tighten them if necessary. Eventually, when your efforts at tightening don't seem to work, you'll probably have to squirt a little epoxy into the screw holes, then thread the screws back into place. This should keep the blades secure.

Cut a Fine Figure

❖ Be sure to get your skates sharpened regularly, especially if you're a figure skater or hockey player. And don't hand the job to just anyone. Ask around to locate someone with a reputation for knowing what he's doing. Any high school or college hockey coach can give you the name of a good skate sharpener. Or see if you can still find a cobbler in your area. Cobblers often sharpen skate blades, too.

HOCKEY STICKS

It's a Wrap!

❖ Protect the blade of your hockey stick—the area that's most vulnerable and also gets the most wear—by wrapping it tightly in friction tape. This tape is sticky on both sides but stickier on one side than the other. Place the stickier side in contact with the stick. Then rub on a substance called Snap Wax. The wax will prevent moisture from seeping into the friction tape and provide a temporary, slippery surface on the bottom of the stick. Both the tape and the wax are available from the same stores that sell sticks.

It Must Have Been That Blow to the Head . . .

❖ To repair a crack in the handle of a hockey stick, wedge the crack open far enough to inject a little epoxy into it. Clamp the repair as the directions on the epoxy recommend. When you remove the clamp, wrap several collars of stout adhesive tape around the joint. This will prevent splinters from jabbing out should the stick split again at the same place.

PUZZLER

ON A DIFFERENT NOTE, THIS AD-justable apparatus helped set the right tone for hymn and her alike.

ANSWER: *Pitch pipe.*

SKIS

Start the Season Right

❖ At the start of each season, get your skis tuned up at your local ski shop. They'll hone the edges on your down-hill or cross-country skis, apply a running wax to the base and furniture wax to the tops, and adjust the safety release on your bindings. (Manufacturers recommend a shop tune-up every ten ski days. This is more than most people ski in a year, so if you take care of the job at the beginning of the season, you should be all set.)

The P-Tex Solution

❖ Fix small grooves or dents on the bottoms of your skis with P-Tex plastic. You can buy P-Tex "candles," about the size of licorice sticks, from any good ski shop. Put the damaged ski flat, bottom side up, on some old newspapers on a work surface. Hold a flame to one end of the candle until it begins to burn—this will take 10 to 15 seconds. Once it's ignited, the candle will steadily drip melted plastic. Aim the candle so that it drips into the groove or hole in your ski bottom and the plastic fills every crevice. Carefully put out the candle and save what's left for future use. Wait until the P-Tex on your ski is cool to the touch, then use a metal scraper to remove the excess plastic and smooth the surface until it is even.

❖ P-Tex is good for minor fixes, but if your skis have large gashes or holes—anything deeper than about one-eighth inch—take them to a ski shop for professional repair.

Protect Your Investment

❖ Always transport your skis in a ski bag, using the inexpensive plastic or rubber clips available at any ski shop to keep them from sliding against each other. It's especially important to cover your skis when they're on the car roof while you're traveling over salted roads. If you don't want to bother with ski bags, at least cover the bindings with simple slipcovers (available at ski shops) when you're traveling on freshly salted highways.

Separation Is Good for the Sole(s)

❖ When storing synthetic skis, place them upright and separate. The separation ensures that the skis will not pull against each other's camber. Camber is the curve of the ski from end to end, designed to keep the tips and tails tight against the snow when your weight is pressing down on the middle. It's extremely important for control, especially in icy and rough skiing conditions.

PEG   PEG

For off-season storage, drive pegs into a garage wall and mount your skis on them horizontally.

❖ Another way to preserve camber during storage periods is to lay each ski, binding down, across a couple of pegs that are far enough apart to support the ski near the ends.

If You Would Choose Wood

❖ If you're lucky enough to have a pair of old-fashioned wooden cross-country skis, clean the bottoms at least once a year with a wax solvent (kerosene, paint remover or gasoline). Then recoat them with pine tar, "cooked" into the surface with an iron, a blowtorch or a torch fitted with a metal smoothing blade.

❖ If you scrape wax off your wooden cross-country skis often during the ski season, you may need to replace the tar several times as well.

Top-Notch Treatments

❖ Whenever your wooden cross-country skis sustain damage that might admit moisture to the unprotected wood, you'll need to treat the tops of the skis. Cover any chips or scrapes with the same finish used on the originals. It may be Danish oil, polyurethane or high-gloss enamel paint.

For Storage, Positioning Is Everything

❖ When storing wooden skis, place them upright. Strap them together, bottom to bottom, with a block of wood—about an inch larger than the skis' natural camber—placed between them at the midpoint. Coolness and dryness are the keys to selecting the right spot to store wooden skis. Hanging them from the overhead joists in the cellar is ideal. If you leave them in the attic, heat and sun over the summer may make them brittle.

Don't Be a Basket Case

❖ If you lose a basket on a ski pole, don't throw the pole away. Ski shops sell spare baskets for many poles. Just push the new basket onto the pole tip until it locks into place.

❖ If your old basket splits but does not come off the pole, try tugging it off with pliers, or carefully cut through the plastic with a sharp knife until the split in the basket reaches the pole.

Even the Memories Were Made to Last

WHEN MY BOY WAS LITTLE, I bought him a toy fire engine. This was back before so many toys were plastic. The fire engine was made of metal and had battery-operated lights and a siren. My son loved it.

EARL
remembers...

He wasn't too hard on the toy, but it needed constant repair just the same. It seemed I was always gluing on a lens that had fallen off a light or soldering some part back onto the body of the truck.

Years later, I still had the engine in my house when my son had his own son. So I sent it to him to give to his boy. My son called to thank me when he received it, but he told me he had hidden the fire engine away. He was too fond of the old toy to let his son play with it and possibly damage it.

That was fine with me. Sentiment is reason enough to make something last.

Always Pack a Spare Basket

❖ If you're a cross-country skier, carry a spare ski-pole basket whenever you go into the backcountry. A basket-less pole makes for a long trek home!

Long-Distance Splinters

❖ When skiing in the backcountry, always carry spare ski tips in your pack as well as metal splints for poles. These simply screw or snap onto the broken ski or pole, enabling you to make it home.

❖ If you forgot the spare, you can "splint" a broken pole with a green stick and duct tape or hose clamps. For a broken ski tip, try taping or clamping a metal wax scraper across the break. It won't be pretty, but it'll get you out of the woods.

SKI BINDINGS

Don't Become a Human Snow Cone

❖ Apply a light coat of silicone spray to your Nordic or downhill bindings before you ski. This protects the bindings and prevents the buildup of snow and ice under your boots. Silicone spray is sold at hardware and automotive supply stores.

Ever Try Looking for a Lost Screw on a Mountain of Fresh Snow?

❖ Check ski bindings for looseness before each use. If they're loose, be sure to use the appropriate screwdriver to tighten them. Most ski-binding screws call for either a large-bladed regular screwdriver or a #3 Phillips head. Anything smaller may strip out the slots.

PUZZLER

SEE IF YOU CAN SMOKE OUT THE answer to this one, which caused quite a buzz when it was first introduced.

ANSWER: Bee bellows, used by apiarists to calm bees with smoke.

❖ If a binding screw keeps coming loose, take the screw out and push a gob of epoxy cement into the hole. Replace the screw, being careful to stop screwing as soon as it hits bottom. Let the epoxy set for the recommended time before using the ski.

SNOWSHOES

After Tramping through the Snow

❖ Brush a thin coat of varnish on the frame and rawhide webbing of traditional wooden snowshoes at the end of the winter to protect both parts from drying and cracking.

Patch Perfect

❖ Patch a puncture in the synthetic foot platforms of modern aluminum snowshoes with Aquaseal, a rubber cement sold at many sporting goods stores. Put a layer of masking tape under the hole and fill the puncture with Aquaseal. Remove the tape once the glue has cured. (This will take up to 48 hours.)

Defray Your Strapping Expenses

❖ If the synthetic foot beds or straps on your snowshoes fray, trim the loose ends to about one inch long, then carefully burn them back with a butane lighter. The melted fabric should prevent future fraying.

EXERCISE BIKES

No Sweat!

❖ Place plastic drip mats under your bike and all other stationary fitness equipment, and be sure to wipe down each piece with a barely damp rag after every strenuous use. One feature common to virtually all such machines is that since you aren't moving, you sweat all in one place, and that place is indoors. Perspiration is injurious to carpets or hardwood floors, and it will rust your machines if you don't wipe them down regularly.

Give Your Bike a Brake

❖ The least expensive exercise bikes provide resistance with an adjustable caliper brake, just like those on a ten-speed bike. Check the brake pads frequently for wear and replace them before they reach the point at which the calipers are rubbing on the wheel rim. Although the tension on the brake pads is adjusted with a rotating knob, the resistance is roughly the same no matter how fast you pedal. As you would expect if you drove your car with the parking brake on, this will cause fairly rapid wear on the pads.

Not-So-Safe Deposits

❖ Also check frequently for melted brake pad material that may have been deposited on the rim of the wheel. Remove it with a mild solvent designed to remove bugs from automobile grilles.

Avoid Anything Kinky

❖ Keep the chain of your exercise bike lubricated with a light penetrating machine oil. Wipe off any excess to prevent dripping or dust accumulation. If you see an occasional kink in the "unloaded" side of the chain (the lower side, running toward the rear sprocket), you've neglected it for far too long.

ROWING MACHINES

Ride the Rail

❖ Keep a rag and a mild household cleaner near your machine. After each use, rub down the top of the I beam–type monorail to which the machine is attached.

Keep Rolling for the Shore

❖ Roughness or sticking in the rollers means either that dirt has built up on the wheels or rail or that the wheels are worn. If the former, clean the rail; if the latter, replace the wheels. You can do either job yourself. See your dealer for the necessary parts.

Housing Check

❖ After every couple of hundred hours of use, shine a flashlight through the guard screen of your rowing machine's flywheel, with its spinning vanes and air intake, and check the housing around the fan. If it's dusty, simply remove the screen and clean out the housing with the crevice tool on your vacuum cleaner.

Either Oar

❖ The handle that acts as your rowing machine's oar drives the flywheel by means of a bicycle chain. Be careful not to twist this chain, and be sure to lubricate it after every 50 hours or so of use. (The flywheel axle sprocket is rather small, and the chain must be well lubricated to straighten out smoothly after bending around the sprocket. You'll know if you've put off the lubrication too long, because the chain will start skipping or running rough.) Just dampen a small rag with a teaspoonful of 20-weight oil, pull the chain all the way out and wipe it thoroughly with the oil. Use a clean rag to wipe it dry, then test the chain for flexibility by running a thumb and forefinger along it, bending it as you go. If there are still stiff spots, oil it again.

PUZZLER

NOT FOUND IN MANY TACKLE boxes today, this device threw some light on a shaddy business.

ANSWER: Fishing cresset. The toothed end held flaming pine knots, which were held out over the side of a boat so that the light would attract fish—especially shad.

❖ If you still feel roughness during your workout after oiling the chain as best you can, check the sprocket. If the sprocket is worn, replace it.

STAIR CLIMBERS

Antiperspirants

❖ Before you use a stair climber for the first time, give it a coat of car wax to protect its finish from dripping sweat.

❖ Wipe the machine down after each use with a household cleaner on a rag.

TREADMILLS

Give Your Treadmill the Treatment

❖ Each day before using a treadmill, wipe down the deck (the two metal strips on each side of the belt) with a rag dampened with water and thoroughly wrung out. Every other day, do the same thing with the belt and control panel, and then dry them thoroughly. (Don't use any cleaning agents.)

It Needs a Lift

❖ Every week or so, raise the treadmill and vacuum up the dirt and dust under it. Every month, move the machine aside and wash the floor under it. Because you're walking on your machine, you're automatically using it as a doormat, and the dirt will either adhere to the track or get dumped beneath it.

COMMON MISTAKES

A Go, No-Go Decision

WHEN INSTALLING a treadmill, you can't afford to be careless about the electrical connections. Be sure to connect the machine to a dedicated and grounded electrical circuit into which nothing else can be plugged. The reason for the ground is obvious: you can get a very serious shock from an ungrounded machine, especially one with a belt moving rapidly and continuously over a broad surface. As for making sure you have a dedicated circuit, consider what might happen if you were jogging briskly along on your treadmill and another machine plugged into the same circuit tripped the circuit breaker, instantly bringing your running surface to a stop. It could be the epitome of the expression "shuddering halt."

SKI-TYPE EXERCISE MACHINES

Rough It Up a Bit

❖ If the drum on your machine—the part around which the cord wraps—is not turning smoothly, it may be that the leather brake pad has dried out. Remove the knob and spring that control the drum, then slide it off its shaft to expose the brake pad. The pad will be shiny from friction. Rough it up with sandpaper or a file and apply just a few drops of light machine oil. Let it dry for a day, wipe off any excess and reassemble the unit. Be sure you've gotten rid of the excess oil, or the first time you give one of the cords a good yank, you'll spray oil all over everything on the same plane as the drum.

Avoid Black Strap

❖ The skis on these machines provide resistance by means of a drag strap wrapped around a cast-iron flywheel located between your feet. From time to time, remove the strap and clean the grooved flywheel rim with a rag dampened with rubbing alcohol. In normal use at home, the strap should last at least five years.

❖ If the strap is becoming blackened or frayed, you can extend its life by reversing it. When you do, take a minute to check for any ground-in dirt particles and wipe them off.

PET ACCESSORIES

Birdcages: Twick or Tweet!

❖ If you keep a pet bird in a knock-down birdcage (a cage that's shipped flat and unassembled), be sure to tighten the nuts and bolts frequently. Curious birds can loosen the bolts with their beaks, and if the cage eventually collapses, your pet may escape or be injured.

Litter Lessons

❖ Clean and disinfect cat litter boxes once a month or so with a mild solution of household (5 percent) bleach (½ cup of bleach diluted in 1 gallon of warm water). Rinse very thoroughly before filling with fresh litter.

❖ Never use pine-oil cleaners on a litter box. These can be toxic to cats.

Plumbing, Heating and Cooling

P LUMBING DISASTERS NEVER STRIKE when it's convenient.

My dog woke me up one night, barking loudly and running from my bed to the kitchen and back again. When I got up and went into the kitchen, I could hear rushing water in the cellar. Checking further, I found to my dismay that a plug had blown out of a three-quarter-inch pipe at just about head height. Water was gushing out of the pipe under 60 pounds of pressure, and the pump was running full tilt.

As luck would have it, the pump switch was around behind the water tank. The only way to get to it was to run through the cascade, so in I went—in my shorts—for the coldest shower of my life. I shut off the pump, but there were still 80 gallons of water left in the tank to run out onto the floor. So I went for another shower and opened the basement sink faucet to help divert some of the water from the tank. By the time the tank was drained, I had another inch of water on the floor. If my dog hadn't warned me, however, my cellar could have been filled with water, as the pump would have run until it was shut off.

All of which suggests that your first step in dealing with potential plumbing and heating problems—and thereby making your equipment last longer—should be to get yourself a dog. It's not a bad idea, but in this chapter we'll give you lots of other ideas for prolonging the life of everything from toilet tanks to hot-water heaters. And we'll start by recognizing that routine—and some not-so-routine—repair and maintenance tasks are the keys to making your utility equipment and materials live a long and useful life.

298

The Milk-Carton Test for Your Shower

❖ The best way to make your hot-water system last is to reduce the amount of hot water you use. If an empty half-gallon milk carton placed under your shower spray fills up in less than ten seconds, you're wasting water and your heater is working too hard to keep up. Install low-flow showerheads and faucet aerators to reduce wear on the heater as well as energy use. Removing the old heads and installing the new heads take less than a minute and save a lot. Showerheads and aerators are available at most hardware and plumbing supply stores. If you can't find them there, call your utility company for the names of local retailers.

Improve Your Shower's Power

❖ The way to cure a clogged showerhead is to soak it in warm white vinegar. You can do this without removing the showerhead. Just locate a heavy plastic bag big enough to cover the showerhead. Heat enough vinegar in a pan to fill the bag. Pour the warm vinegar into the bag and tie the bag over the showerhead so that the head is immersed in the vinegar. Allow the whole thing to sit for eight to ten hours, then remove the bag. The showerhead should be unclogged and ready to use.

Handle with Care

❖ Whenever you use a screwdriver blade to lever a faucet handle or locking pliers to unscrew a faucet stem (the piece that the faucet handle turns), place a piece of cloth or adhesive bandage between the tool and the metal to avoid scratching the finish (and possibly ruining the part). In some cases, a smooth-jawed adjustable wrench will do the job just fine.

COMMON MISTAKES

Don't Polish Off the Bathroom Fixtures

WHEN CLEANING your bathroom, do not use abrasives on any fixtures or on cast-iron, enameled-steel, fiberglass or acrylic surfaces. Most powder cleansers contain abrasives that will dull and damage the shiny finish. Use liquid cleaners instead.

TOILETS

It Just Keeps on Running

❖ The tank ball is the plastic suction device that drops onto the hole—called the valve seat—at the bottom of the tank. A common toilet tank problem occurs when the tank ball doesn't sit properly on the valve seat. This causes the toilet to run continuously. Usually you can fix the problem by adjusting the lever arm above the tank ball (moving it up or down, or even bending the arm so that it drops down more accurately).

You Don't Have to Go with the Flow

❖ Another possible reason for a constantly running toilet could be a leak in the overflow tube. Look down into the overflow tube. If you can see water draining out of the tank and into the tube, you should replace the tube.

❖ To replace a leaky overflow tube, cut the new tube to the same height as the one being replaced. Remove any brackets on the old tube and gently turn it counterclockwise to unscrew it. Old overflow tubes have a tendency to break off at the bottom, leaving the threaded section still in the base. If this happens, insert an ice pick or a long, sharp knife between the threaded section and the base, forcing the threaded section to bend into the middle of the opening. Then remove it with pliers and install the new tube.

Make It Fit for Action

❖ If all else fails to stop a toilet from running and you have an older toilet with a metal valve seat, it may be that the valve seat is coated with mineral deposits or sediment. Extend the life of your tank by turning off the water, flushing the tank empty and using fine-grade steel wool to scour the edges of the valve seat until the tank ball fits better. Test the result by turning on the water and flushing the toilet. (Do *not* try this on modern plastic valve seats, as it may damage the plastic.)

Leaky Tank Bottom?

❖ If the tank is leaking from the bottom, don't panic. Unless there's a crack in the tank enamel, chances are the washers that seal the valve and valve seat are worn. Just pick up new washers at any hardware store. When installing them, go easy with the wrench. Too much pressure can crack the tank, and your small problem will have suddenly become much bigger.

Eek! A Leak!

❖ If you notice water on the floor around the toilet bowl and the tank and porcelain seem to be fine, don't rush to buy a new toilet. The wax gasket at the bottom of the toilet seat is probably leaking. You can replace the gasket yourself. Just set aside a few hours and get someone to help you with the heavy lifting. Begin by shutting off the water-supply valve to the toilet. Remove as much water from the bowl as you can by first emptying the tank, then using a sponge to remove the rest of the water. Unscrew the base of the toilet, then have a friend help you lift it up and lay it to one side. Scrape off the old wax gasket with a putty knife before replacing it with the new gasket. When you finish, check the seal by pouring water into the bowl.

Cold Sweats

❖ To correct a sweating toilet tank, some people recommend draining the tank, gluing one-half-inch-thick Styrofoam to the inside as an insulator and caulking the cracks between the Styrofoam panels. Kits for this procedure are available at plumbing supply stores. Because it's relatively inexpen-

PUZZLER

THIS DUAL-PURPOSE INSTRUMENT, hinged in the middle, came in handy before the invention of pot holders.

ANSWER: *Lid lifter.* Closed, it was used to lift a stove lid on a woodstove; opened, to lift the covers from pots and kettles.

sive, this approach might be for you if you're watching your pennies. However, before you try it, you should know that it's not totally reliable and sometimes affects flushing performance.

A Dose of Historic Preservation

ABOUT 1953, I WAS BUILDING an office at a new sand and gravel plant. Since it was in the country, I needed a well dug to get water. I had a backhoe dig 20 feet down, and we found plenty of water, so I figured that problem was just about solved.

I was plumbing the office toilets, putting in a heating system, finishing the inside woodwork and working 72 hours a week to do it all. So I was a little slow writing to the state for a sample kit to test the well. They were slow getting one to me, too.

EARL remembers...

Meanwhile, I tasted the water, and it tasted and smelled fine. The weather was hot, so I drank a lot.

Finally, I filled the test jug and sent it back to the state. The results indicated that the water was too salty for drinking. I hunted up the road agent and asked whether he salted the dirt road that went by the plant. When he said that it was never salted, I wrote the state for another test jug.

The state wrote back that if the road had no salt on it, there must be an old cemetery nearby, as the test showed formaldehyde in the water. Sure enough, there was an old cemetery right across the road. When I checked with the road agent again, he admitted that they had been forced to fill in the well in the cemetery years ago because of the same problem.

I stopped drinking the water after that. But I think the reason *I've* lasted so long is that I'm remarkably well preserved.

❖ If you're willing to pay more for a more reliable way to stop a toilet tank from sweating, hire a plumber to install a mixing valve. The valve mixes a little warm water into the line to the tank, bringing the water in the tank closer to room temperature. With less disparity between water and room temperatures, you won't have to worry about condensation and dripping.

DRAINS

Get the System Moving

❖ For an inexpensive, environmentally safe way to keep your drains clean and the system working longer, mix together 1 cup of baking soda, 1 cup of salt and ¼ cup of cream of tartar. Once a week, pour ½ cup of this mixture down the drain, followed by 1 quart of boiling water.

❖ If you didn't take preventive steps in time and your drain is already clogged, pour in ¼ cup of baking soda, followed by ½ cup of vinegar. Cover the drain until the fizzing stops, then flush with 1 quart of boiling water.

❖ If you don't have baking soda handy, try this alternative cure for a clogged drain. Boil 3 cups of vinegar, pour it down the drain and wait ten minutes for it to take effect. The drain should be ready to use.

Air to the Throne

❖ If all the fixtures in a bathroom drain slowly or a basin or tub drains very noisily, the vent (a three-inch pipe sticking out of the roof directly above the bathroom) may be blocked. This sometimes happens when leaves from an overhanging tree branch fall into the vent and become packed in tightly enough to block it. One way to clean it out is to take the garden hose up on the roof and run a strong stream of water into the vent to dislodge the plug. If the water backs up, you'll know it's still plugged and you need to try again.

❖ Another way to clear a clogged vent is to use the hose as a snake and try to push the clog down.

WATER PIPES

Rust Busters

❖ If your old house has galvanized pipes and you start to notice a decrease in water pressure, try to find a plumbing service that will ream out the pipes and flush the rust from the system once a year. Although galvanized piping is a perfectly good material, the zinc coating (galvanization) on the pipes often starts to wear out after about 20 years or so. This is when rust forms, gradually filling in the pipe's original diameter and reducing water flow to your tub or shower. Cleaning the pipes on an annual basis will help you hold on to them longer.

Learn to Love Lukewarm

❖ To slow rust formation in galvanized pipe, turn down the water heater's temperature. Set the gauge at 80° to 85°F. The hotter the water, the faster rust will develop again. By taking action to extend the life of your pipes, you'll also save money on heating your water.

Avoid the Deep Freeze

❖ If you have continuing problems with frozen pipes, try insulating any pipes that are in cold places (under a crawl space or the kitchen sink or in other vulnerable locations). Pipe insulation is available in polyurethane foam, polyethylene foam, expanded rubber and fiberglass. The salesperson at your plumbing supply store can help you determine what's best for your needs.

Leave the Light On for Them

❖ Here's another way to avoid frozen pipes: keep a light on under the sink

PUZZLER

THIS WAS AN OLD-TIME BAKER'S tool, placed over hot ashes. But what did it bake?

ANSWER: Long-stemmed clay pipes, also known as churchwardens. (We'd love to know how they got that name!) The pipes were placed in the rack, then left over hot ashes to bake out any impurities in the clay.

all the time in the winter. This will provide warmth for pipes that tend to freeze. Make sure, however, that no flammable items are left close to the bulb.

Run from the Cold

❖ If you're expecting a really cold spell, keep the water running—just barely dripping. Moving water doesn't freeze.

Well-Thawed Ideas

❖ The most popular method of thawing frozen pipes is to blow hot air on them from a hand-held hair dryer. If the pipe is 8 inches or more from a wall or ceiling, you can improve on this method by using a board at least 6 inches wide and about 18 inches long. While applying the heat from the hair dryer, hold the board over the pipe (opposite the side where you're holding the dryer) and slide it along as you move the dryer. This concentrates the heat around the pipe.

Be Careful with High-Powered Solutions

❖ When thawing a pipe with a hand-held hair dryer, always observe appropriate safety precautions. By using any electrically powered device near metal plumbing, you run the risk of electrocution. Use a relatively low level of heat and be sure all devices are grounded and in good working order.

Pour On the Heat

❖ Another way to thaw a frozen pipe is to wrap a big towel around it, place a pot underneath it and pour boiling water over the pipe and towel. The hot water will thaw the pipe without creating a fire in the plumbing space. This technique works best in areas where you have plenty of room to maneuver.

Switch It Off

BEFORE ATTEMPTING to clean or repair any electrical or mechanical appliance, be sure to turn off power both at the unit and at the service panel or fuse box. A furnace or air conditioner may also have a separate disconnect switch, located either on the wall near the furnace or outside near the central air unit. It should be turned off as well. In a gas water heater, turn the knob to Off. Also be sure to turn off any other incoming substance, such as gas, oil or water.

BATHTUBS

When Your Tub Cracks Up

❖ To repair a hairline crack in a porcelain tub, apply bath-tub caulk. Work the caulk well into the crack, then use a damp cloth to wipe off any excess around the crack. Don't touch any of it that's directly over the crack. Let the caulk sit overnight or until it's dry, then use a single-edge razor blade to remove any excess caulk and leave a smooth surface.

No More Ring-around-the-Bathtub

❖ You can keep a bathtub longer if you keep it clean. To prevent that annoying bathtub ring from forming when you drain the tub after a bath, add a squirt of dishwashing liquid to your bathwater.

WELLS, PUMPS AND SEPTIC TANKS

Get the Grease Out

❖ Scrape all grease from dirty dishes into a tin can and dispose of it in the trash. Or at least make sure drain water from the kitchen sink and dishwasher runs through a grease trap. Position the trap (or have a pro do it) in a cool area that will not freeze and where it's easily accessible for cleaning. Grease cannot be digested by the anaerobic bacteria in septic tanks. Instead, it rises and forms a scum that combines with detergents to clog the leach field. Ultimately, it will cause failure of the field.

Well, Well

❖ Consider installing a dry well near your house for "gray" water—water that does not go through the toilet. This will reduce the demand on your

---

COMMON MISTAKES

Septic Tanks and Disposals Don't Mix

IF YOU HAVE a septic tank, it is usually not a good idea to install a garbage disposal. The stuff from the disposal may create an excess load on the tank filtration system, allowing some of it to pass through to the leach field. This can cause your septic tank to plug up prematurely.

---

septic tank, which normally runs all waste from your house into a leach field, and will increase the life span of both the tank and the leach field. (A dry well can reduce required septic tank capacity by as much as 50 percent.) In addition, you can design the dry well to provide the water for basic lawn- and tree-watering needs—as long as it does not come into contact with the edible parts of plants. Plan the dry well so that water slowly leaks out of the bottom and into the soil, with plenty of room for the soil's bacteria to work on the water before it reaches any plants or grass.

Don't Park over the Septic Tank

❖ Do not drive anything heavier than a riding lawn mower over the leach field of your septic tank. The field needs oxygen to operate properly. Compacting the soil will damage the field and shorten its effective life.

WOOD-BURNING STOVES AND FIREPLACES

Go for Body Warmth

❖ Be sure to temper your new cast-iron stove. While a cast-iron stove can last you a lifetime (and possibly your children's as well), these stoves also are brittle. They can crack in the process of shipping or assembly or when warming after lying idle in frigid weather for some time. If you have a new stove or you haven't been to your cabin after several months of cold winter weather, break in the stove gradually with a small fire, adding fuel after the stove body has warmed up.

Disposable Liners

❖ Your firebox liner (usually cast iron, refractory cement or firebrick) helps the stove or fireplace last longer. The

Baby, It's Cold Inside!

OPEN-HEARTH fireplaces can be very pretty to look at, but they cool the house as they burn. Such a fireplace can take less than six to seven hours to use up all a small house's air for combustion. You won't suffocate, though, because all that air will be replaced by air coming in from the outside through cracks in the walls, basement and attic. If that air is 20°F, think of how you're cooling your house. The fireplace itself releases only about 10 percent of the heat it generates back into the house.

Stoves of Steel (or Cast Iron)

IF YOU'RE IN the market for a woodstove, look for one made of steel or cast iron; these materials conduct heat better than firebrick, glass or any other commonly used stove material. If you need a stove for, say, a garage or an outbuilding, consider light sheet steel; it will heat quickly and lose the heat just as quickly after the fire goes out. For heating your home, the cast-iron stove is probably a better bet; it will warm more slowly and radiate longer. Here are the features to look for in each.

STEEL

- Steel plates at the side and bottom that are at least one-quarter inch thick
- A steel plate on top that's at least five-sixteenths inch thick
- A minimum of welded seams. Some of the best stoves wrap a single sheet of steel into the back, sides and front.
- No hollows, tiny air bubbles, holes or bumps in the welded top joints
- Firebrick sheathing the entire interior

CAST IRON

- Joints that are tight and caulked
- No pockmarks, ripples, cracks or uncalled-for ridges in cast surfaces
- At least three-sixteenths inch of uniform thickness (including the cast inner liner)
- Paint or enamel that's smooth, even and free of blemishes
- Legs, hinges and door handles that are built to take punishment

Whichever kind of stove you buy, it shouldn't hurt to touch its handle. Open the door of a woodstove you're considering, and see if you can easily keep your hand from brushing the hot firebox walls. All handles should be made of wood, wire coil or even high-quality plastic to keep your hand cool.

---

firebox walls take a beating from both large logs banging against them and high heat. At the end of each heating season, check the liner for cracks, breakage and wear. Most liners should last for five to ten years. Replacing or (in the case of refractory cement) repairing the liner helps preserve the integrity of the outer shell.

How Dry I Am

❖ Be sure to use wood that has been seasoned—that is, allowed to dry after cutting—for at least one year, preferably two. Never burn wood that's freshly cut, as it gives off

a lot of third-degree creosote—which can ultimately lead
to a chimney fire.

Keep It High and Dry

❖ While firewood is drying, it's important to keep it outdoors but away from the ground and from moisture. It
also needs to be kept covered. If you don't have a wood-
shed, try stacking your cordwood on old shipping pallets
to raise the bottom logs off the wet ground. Then cover
the stack with a tarp or a sheet of plastic at least four mils
thick. Leave an air space between the covering and the
wood and along the bottom so that moisture can escape
as the sun warms the wood. Never store firewood in the
basement or another indoor spot. Green wood gives off a
lot of moisture, which will only exacerbate any problems
with a damp basement.

Life Is Hard—Your Wood Should Be, Too

❖ Extend the life of your chimney flue by burning hardwood such as maple or oak. Never burn softwood such
as pine. Hardwood burns longer and produces less creosote. Besides affecting the fire's draw, excessive creosote
buildup can ultimately degrade the
chimney's flue or cause a chimney fire.

CHIMNEYS

Santa Doesn't Have Time for This

❖ Have your chimney inspected every
year for creosote and possible structural damage. Many chimney-cleaning
companies offer free inspections and
estimates.

Only You Can Prevent Chimney Fires

❖ If you're a frequent fireplace or
woodstove user, clean your chimney

Watch Out for Third-Degree Burns

EXPERTS CLASSIFY creosote as
one of three "degrees." First-
degree creosote is sooty and
fairly easy to clean. Second-degree
creosote is flakier and harder to remove. Third-degree creosote is the
worst case—a tarry substance that
sticks to the flue walls and is the
most difficult to remove. While the
frequency of your fires and flue
cleanings can affect the type of creosote buildup, the choice of wood
you burn also has a big effect.

often. The rule of thumb is to do this once a year if you burn a fire three times a week or more, every other year if you average twice a week and every third year if you're a very occasional user.

One Time to Let Fresh-Cut Wood Near Your Chimney

❖ An inexpensive way to clean a chimney is to lower a rope from the top and tie the end hanging down the chimney to the trunk of a small, cut fir tree. From the roof, haul the tree up through the flue. Then drop the free end of the rope down the flue and pull the tree back down. (Like most techniques for cleaning chimneys, this is a messy operation. Be sure to cover the hearth and all adjacent areas before beginning it.)

Chimney Sweeps Aren't Lightweights

❖ Another way to clean a chimney is to dump into an old pillowcase or feed sack some rough, heavy material such as old tire chains. Fill the bag so that it's wide enough to scrape the sides of the flue, and weight it so that it will drop down the flue. Proceed as with the tree in the previous hint. If you can get someone to help you, use two ropes. Attach one to either end of the sack and take turns pulling it up and down. This method will swab the flue as well as scrape it.

Don't Let the Flue Get the Better of You

Protect the inside of your chimney with a chimney cap.

❖ Even if you routinely clean your chimney yourself, it's a good idea to hire a professional every third year or so to be sure that your flue is in the safest and most effective shape.

To Cap or Not to Cap?

❖ If your chimney shows signs of water or moisture problems, consider installing a chimney cap to direct the water away from the chimney. When water gets into your flue, it may combine with creosote and soot to form acids that can corrode a galvanized flue or weaken the mortar in a masonry flue. The moisture can also seep into mortar cracks, then freeze and expand, breaking apart the mortar.

Seal the Deal

❖ If the bricks in your chimney are not the best or are starting to crumble from age, seal the outsides with a clear masonry sealer. (Be sure it's a masonry sealer made specifically for brick and concrete and not a general masonry product.) This will prevent the bricks from absorbing rainwater, which can ultimately freeze and crack them.

Tight Straps Squeeze Loose Bricks

❖ If you have an unused antenna strapped to your chimney, take it down as soon as possible. The strapping for the antenna can place stress on the mortar, causing the bricks to loosen before their time.

HEAT-DELIVERY SYSTEMS

An Annual Checkup

❖ Whatever type of heat-delivery system you use, be sure to have it checked once a year for the first few years—and as often as experience dictates thereafter—by a qualified technician. Have the service tech lubricate any motors and/or pump parts (unless your new furnace uses a permanently lubricated motor).

Dirty Boilers

❖ Dirty boilers don't last as long as clean boilers. If your steam-heating system has never been cleaned, hire a con-

Heating Systems: Defining the Terms

I T'S IMPORTANT to know what kind of heating system you're dealing with if you want to make it last longer. Heat-delivery systems generate heat from boilers, furnaces or heat pumps. Boilers heat water, and either steam or water then travels through the house via radiators or coils. Furnaces and heat pumps heat air, which is delivered through duct systems. Heating appliances use one of four types of fuel to supply the heat: oil, gas (either natural gas from a pipeline or propane gas from a tank), electricity or solar energy (often using one of the other fuels as an auxiliary source). The kind of heating appliance you have and the type of fuel it uses determine what system-preserving measures you should take.

tractor to do the job. It should take about a day. There are no shortcuts.

❖ If your boiler does not have a drain valve, ask your contractor to install one. That way, once a year you can drain out the sediment that accumulates in the bottom of the boiler. This will make the equipment last longer.

COMMON MISTAKES

Your Heating System Needs a Breath of Air

WHEN WORKING with heating systems, never plug any intake pipes. Oil and gas systems require combustion air—air that is necessary for complete combustion of the fuel when it is burned in the appliance. Lack of sufficient combustion air will lead to the accumulation of carbon monoxide in gas-fired units and soot in oil units. In old homes, owners used to rely on natural drafts through cracks around doors and windows to provide combustion air for fireplaces, water heaters and furnaces. But today's tighter new homes (and older homes that have been well weather-stripped) must vent in outside air through metal duct pipes that run right to the appliance's burner. Sometimes homeowners try to reduce cold-air intake or drafts by stuffing or plugging such outlets. That is *extremely dangerous* and risks carbon monoxide poisoning for you and your family.

Antifreeze Antidote

❖ Contractors sometimes recommend filling the pipes of hot-water heating systems with antifreeze instead of water. This is a worthwhile approach to making your pipes last, but only if you use antifreeze designed for boilers, not car antifreeze. Auto antifreeze won't hold up under boiler heat. Also make sure that you change the antifreeze every year. Old antifreeze is corrosive to metal.

Easy on the Oil

❖ Yes, there is such a thing as too much maintenance. Do not put more than two drops of oil per year into each oil hole in your burner motor assembly. More than that will collect dirt, which will damage the bearings.

FORCED-AIR HEATING SYSTEMS

Fiberglass Filters: Let There Be Light

❖ Fiberglass filters in hot-air heating systems are usually encased in either wire mesh hammock or cardboard framing. In the space between the furnace body and the ductwork, you

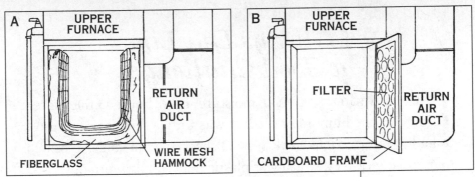

A | UPPER FURNACE | RETURN AIR DUCT | FIBERGLASS | WIRE MESH HAMMOCK

B | UPPER FURNACE | FILTER | RETURN AIR DUCT | CARDBOARD FRAME

should find a slot with a tight-fitting cover. Once a month, take off the cover and remove the filter it contains. Hold the filter up to a flashlight or light bulb. If the light is at least partially blocked, replace the filter (they are inexpensive). Vacuuming the fiberglass particles in an attempt to extend the filter's life is not recommended, as it will pull all the fiberglass out of the filter.

Dustcover

❖ If the cover on the filter slot is loose, bend the sides to tighten it, then cover the edges with duct tape to prevent dust from entering through the cracks.

All It Needs Is a Vacuum Job

❖ Consider buying a foam rubber or steel mesh filter from your heating contractor. If you vacuum it monthly during the heating season, a single unit will last for years.

Other Filters, Other Fixes

❖ When a foam rubber or steel mesh filter gets especially greasy, remove it from the furnace, squirt a liquid spray degreaser such as Fantastik on it and let it sit for an hour or so. Then rinse it outside with a garden hose or inside in the bathtub. Finally, before putting the filter back in place, spray it with a "filter coat"—a light oil coating that helps the filter work better. The spray is available from heating contractors.

❖ If you have an electronic filter (the panel over the filter will have a switch that turns the filter on and off), simply clean the filter once a month with Fantastik, then rinse it. Make sure the filter is absolutely dry before putting it back

Before you can inspect the fiberglass filter in a hot-air heating system, you'll need to find it. Remove the cover from the space between the furnace body and the ductwork, and look for either a wire mesh hammock (A) or a cardboard frame (B) containing the filter.

I Always Did Like
a Good Challenge

USE A HUMIDIFIER TO KEEP moisture in my house in the winter. One day the humidifier died. It was only a few years old, so I hadn't expected it to break down. I checked it out, and it appeared that the drive pulley, which was plastic, had simply worn out.

I went back to the store where I'd bought it and complained. The salesman laughed and said, "I've got half a dozen humidifiers in here in the same fix." He claimed that there was no way to fix the machine; no replacement parts were available from the manufacturer. Then he had the nerve to ask me if I wanted to buy a new humidifier. I told him I planned to fix my existing machine.

EARL remembers...

I couldn't stand the idea of discarding an entire appliance because a single part had worn out. So I studied the drive pulley and concluded that it would be pretty easy to fashion a replacement out of wood using my lathe. It took me less than an hour to get the humidifier back in action.

Sometimes it takes extraordinary effort to keep a machine going. But the most challenging cases can be the most rewarding.

in place. Replacing it while it's still wet would be roughly equivalent to taking a shower with a hand-held hair dryer. Do not apply the oil filter coat to this kind of filter.

Drum Up the Right Cleaner

❖ If your furnace humidifier has a drum filter (characterized by a tube-shaped evaporator pad to filter liquids, held in place by a plastic drum shaft above the water tray), you can extend the life of the filter (and the humidifier) by cleaning it. First, be sure to turn off the power and the water-line valve. Then remove the filter and soak it in a solution of three parts vinegar and one part water. Keep it immersed until it softens, then squeeze away the excess solution. If the pad does not soften, replace it with an identical new one.

WATER-DISTRIBUTION HEATING SYSTEMS

Help! Homeowner Boiled Alive in Shower!

❖ Combination water-heating and boiler systems use an antiscald valve (sometimes called a mixing valve) to insert cold water in the hot-water pipe at a selectable temperature setting. This moderates the water temperature for household use. After several years, the valve can stick, allowing either too much or not enough cold water to enter. If it starts to leak or you notice your showers getting hotter, hire a contractor to replace the valve immediately. The antiscald valve is the weakest link in the boiler system. Replacing one will help the entire system last longer, prevent injuries and keep your energy bill down.

HEAT PUMPS AND CENTRAL AIR-CONDITIONING

It's as Easy as Washing the Car

❖ Help extend the life of an air conditioner or heat pump by cleaning the coil fins of the unit's outdoor con-

COMMON MISTAKES

Heavy Metal

FOR MANY YEARS, people thought you could make radiators more efficient by painting them with metallic paint. This turns out not to be the case; metallic paint actually reduces heat transmission by 7.4 to 9.2 percent. If your radiators are currently covered with many layers of paint, you can make them more efficient by removing the paint altogether. First, tap the metal gently with a ball-peen hammer. The vibration will make most of the paint drop off. Then use a wire brush to get the last of it. You don't have to disconnect the radiator or call a plumber. Once the radiators are stripped, brush them with mineral oil to give them a sheen.

If you must paint a radiator, use a flat black, nonmetallic paint such as stove black. Or if you want the look of a bronze or silver radiator, use a heat-tolerant light gray or brown paint. Auto body primer works well, too, and holds up under radiant heat.

denser with a garden hose. When you look at the outside unit of an air conditioner or heat pump, you'll spot the coil fins: the radiator-like grilles just inside the outer panels. Don't use a knife, stick or screwdriver blade to scrape away dirt. Such treatment can damage the unit.

WINDOW AIR CONDITIONERS

They Just Don't Go with the Christmas Decorations

❖ Window air conditioners last longer if you remove them and store them for the winter in a dry space. The windowsills will last longer, too, without the air conditioners sitting on them.

❖ Before putting an air-conditioning unit back in place at the beginning of the cooling season, oil the motor and blower unit. Check for rusting metal parts and repaint as necessary.

Avoid Cover-Ups

❖ To make the outdoor portions of your central air conditioner last longer, don't cover them during the winter. The units are designed to be weather resistant. A watertight cover can trap moisture within the unit.

Cleanup: It Doesn't Take Much

❖ At least once a month during the cooling season, remove the filter (the foamlike substance just inside the plastic front) from your air conditioner and wash it in the sink with any mild dishwashing liquid and water. Then rinse and wring it dry. While the filter is drying, wash the front panel and vacuum the coil fins (the aluminum grille).

Aw, It's Just an Awning

YOU CAN'T FIND a much more basic method of cooling your home than awnings. They've been added to houses ever since man first squinted into the sun from a permanently built home. Awnings built from man-made materials such as cloth will eventually break down from the sun's ultraviolet rays, requiring repair or replacement. Make your awning from natural materials, such as wood, and it will last much longer. After the initial coat of paint or polyurethane varnish, it also will require less maintenance.

WATER HEATERS

Improved Performance on Tap

❖ Once or twice a year, draw at least a bucket of water from the tap at the bottom of the tank of your oil- or gas-fired hot-water heater. (Do this more often if your water is hard.) In the course of normal use, sediment (mostly calcium carbonate) accumulates at the bottom of these heaters, insulating the water from the burners and wasting energy. Worse, it can cause overheating, eventually rusting and weakening the bottom of the tank. Draining water from the tank should take out most of the sediment.

Deposits and Withdrawals

❖ Every year or two, you may want to have a technician check the water heater's lining for deposits that can reduce capacity, inhibit heat exchange and shorten the tank's life.

Give Your Water Heater a Jacket

❖ Water heaters have insulation built into them, but if you want to make your water heater more efficient, buy an insulating jacket (available from hardware stores) and wrap it around the unit.

PUZZLER

IN THE DAYS BEFORE POP-TARTS and instant waffles, this offered a surefire way to cook your breakfast.

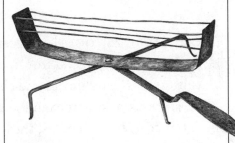

ANSWER: *Fireplace toaster. The bread was placed in the tines, then rotated in front of the fire for toasting.*

The Home Workshop

OR AS LONG AS TOOLS have been used, they've been abused.

I have an old metal froe, a cutting tool used in the early days for splitting shakes, shingles and clapboards by hand. All you have to do is take one look at my froe, and you can tell that it really took a beating. The top is covered with dents, showing where it was struck repeatedly by a metal hammer.

It used to be understood that you never hit a metal tool with a metal tool. Instead, you hit metal with wood and vice versa. A person would drive a froe with a wooden mallet and use a metal hammer to drive a chisel that had a wooden handle. (Going that advice one step better, my father taught me to drive a chisel with the *side* of my hammer's head. That way, it's easier to hit the butt of the chisel while you're concentrating on its cutting edge.)

The metal in today's hand tools is much better than it was back when my froe was forged. But to make my hand tools last longer, I still follow the old advice whenever I can. In this chapter, we'll recall those old rules and introduce a few new ones as well. Did you know that there's a place for suede brushes, tennis shoes, baking soda and lard in your workshop? Or that the time may come when you'll want to put your paintbrush in the freezer or store paint upside down? Read on and learn how you can keep your tools as long as I've held on to my old froe—and keep them in better shape, too.

THE BASICS

No More Mr. Nice Guy

❖ If you must lend tools, first paint your initials on them using Day-Glo paint. Or paint a bright stripe around the handle of your favorite tool. The color will stand out like a sore thumb on your neighbor's workbench and will help you spot a rake or hammer that you've left outside.

Do You Know Where Your Tools Are?

❖ Hang your tools on a large piece of Peg-Board, then draw an outline around each piece. If a tool is ever missing, you'll know it right away.

WORKSHOP STORAGE

Stick 'Em Up

❖ Store drill bits, router bits, screwdrivers, nail sets and other small tools in a wooden block that has several holes bored into it. Just stick the tools into the holes, and you'll know exactly where to find them when you need them. If you put a couple of eye hooks on one end of the wooden block, you can hang it from the Peg-Board where you keep your larger tools.

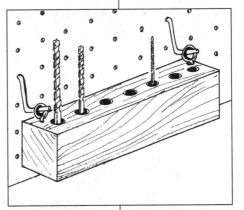

To store bits and small tools, bore holes in a block of scrap wood and insert the small pieces in the holes.

Just a Little Bit

❖ Protect your expensive router bits by lining a workshop drawer with rigid foam or foam rubber and storing the bits on this cushion. For added protection, cut recesses in the foam for individual bits.

Help from the Kitchen Cupboard

❖ To protect nails stored in coffee cans from rusting, put a teaspoon of baking soda in with them.

No Rust for the Weary

❖ To keep hand tools from rusting, use a rag to apply a thin coat of oil on the metal parts after each use. Then wipe the oil off before using the tool again. (If you don't wipe the oil off and start fresh periodically, the oily film will collect dirt and dust.)

❖ To create your own rust-preventive coating, combine ¼ cup of lanolin (available at pharmacies) and 1 cup of petroleum jelly in a double boiler over low heat. Stir until the mixture is well blended, then pour it into a clean jar. While it's still warm, apply a thick coating to your tools, outdoor furniture or other metal objects. When you're done, cover the mixture tightly. Rewarm it a bit before the next use.

Rustproof Toolboxes

❖ To keep your tools from getting rusty, put them in a plastic toolbox and glue some weather strip (or apply self-sticking weather strip) around the lid of the box to keep out the moisture that promotes rust.

❖ Another way to prevent rust is to toss a few mothballs in the toolbox. Or store the tools in wooden bins that contain a mixture of camphor (available from pharmacies) and sawdust.

Tool-to-Tool Carpeting

❖ Here's another way to keep your hand tools from rusting: spray a small piece of old carpet with a product like WD-40, then line your tool drawer or toolbox with the carpet. This is an easy way to coat the tools with a thin layer of oil, as the oil transfers from carpet to tools. When the carpet gets too dirty, just throw it away and put in a fresh piece.

A Rust Stop for Glass Cutters

❖ To store a glass cutter so that it will last longer, leave it standing in a small jar with half an inch or so of lubricat-

---

A SECOND LIFE

A Great Way to Do Your Nails

WHEN YOU use up a jar of hand cream, don't toss the jar. Use it to store nails. The film left in the jar will keep rust from forming on the nails.

---

ing oil in the bottom. The oil will protect the tip of the cutter from rusting. Wipe off the oil with an old rag before using the cutter again. It will stay rust-free and will last for years.

SUBSTITUTIONS

Just Scratching the Surface

❖ When you're smoothing dried joint compound on drywall, the plaster can clog your sandpaper in a hurry. Try

Ten Steps to a Better Toolbox

KEEPING THE CONTENTS of your toolbox in good shape is one of the best ways to make tools last longer. Here's a ten-step program to get you started:

1. Put a clean cloth or tarp on the floor and dump everything in your toolbox out onto the tarp.

2. Clean the outside of the box with some household cleaner.

3. Clean the inside of the box with a cloth soaked with paint thinner.

4. Clean all the oil and dirt off your tools using a rag soaked with paint thinner. Pay special attention to wrenches and screwdrivers.

5. Throw away all the rusted screws, bent nails and other junk that has accumulated in the toolbox over the years and that you'll never use.

6. Cut a piece of cardboard the size of the toolbox and lay it in the bottom of the box. It will soak up excess oil and protect your tools.

7. If you have a lot of loose wrenches, lay them on a cloth in order of size, then roll them up and tie the bundle with a piece of string.

8. Put the tools back in the box in order of reverse popularity, with the least used tools on the bottom of the box. Then you won't have to dig to the bottom to find a handy pair of pliers or a favorite screwdriver. Or buy a second toolbox just to store tools you hardly ever use (you know the ones), and buy an open tote box for the tools you carry around all the time to various projects.

9. Keep a flashlight in your toolbox, but keep the batteries separate till you need them. Leaving them in the flashlight for a long time can cause them to leak or go dead if the light gets switched on by mistake in the box.

10. Throw a few pieces of chalk into the box to absorb moisture and prevent rust from forming on the tools.

stapling a piece of aluminum window screening to a two-by-four block and using that instead of sandpaper.

Wrenching Decisions

❖ If you have to tighten or loosen a nut, use an open, socket or box-end wrench of the right size. Or use an adjustable wrench. But don't try to substitute pliers for a wrench. Pliers are intended for bending, grabbing and cutting, not for turning nuts and bolts. If you try to use them as a wrench, you're likely to strip the nut or round off the edges of the nut, making it harder to grip later.

❖ Don't cut wire with tin snips. The wire will nick the blade.

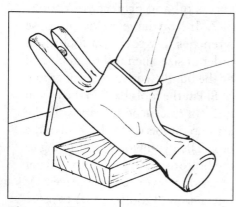

Place a small block of wood under your hammer's head before pulling nails with it.

HAMMERS

Science in Action

❖ When pulling nails with a hammer, always insert a small piece of wood under the head to act as a fulcrum. It will protect the wood holding the nail and, because it requires less force, will keep the hammer head from snapping off.

No More Battered Thumbs

❖ A little maintenance on your hammer will help keep it in shape for years. If the claws have worn down, sharpen them with a flat metal file. If the face of the hammer has become dirty or rusty, clean it with fine-grit sandpaper. This will keep the hammer head from slipping off the nail head when you strike it.

How to Pull a Difficult Nail

❖ A claw hammer is made to pull a nail safely by rocking it from side to side. Once you've cinched the nail, try pushing the handle to the left. Then regrab the nail and push to the right. You'll find this gives you a surprising amount of leverage without straining the hammer or your arm.

❖ Here's another way to pull a nail—especially an old nail—without breaking it. Work a pry bar beneath the head of the nail, then grasp the head tightly with a pair of locking pliers. Pry the nail out very slowly. Works like a charm.

CHISELS

On the Cutting Edge

❖ Protect the fine edge of your chisels with an old leather work glove. Cut off the fingers and thumb of the glove at the base and slip one "finger" over the end of each chisel. Punch a few holes around the opening and thread a leather thong through the holes to hold the piece in place.

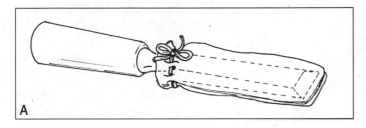

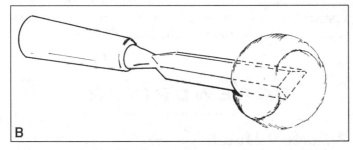

To protect the cutting end of a chisel, cover it with a finger from an old leather work glove (A) or a tennis ball (B).

Stay on the Ball

❖ You can protect the sharpened tip of a fine wood chisel with an old tennis ball. Just cut a slit the width of the chisel in the ball and insert the tip of the chisel in the slit.

WRENCHES

No Cheating Allowed

❖ Never extend a wrench handle with a pipe or another "cheater." Not only do you run the risk of putting more stress on the tool than it's designed for—and probably breaking it and some knuckles—but you'll probably also void the tool's warranty.

Wrenching Decisions

❖ Depending on how much room you have to maneuver in a particular situation, you may not have much choice about which wrench to use. But when you do have some leeway in tightening or loosening nuts on machinery, make an effort to use wrenches in this order of preference: box-end wrench, socket wrench, open-end wrench and adjustable wrench. The reason is that the more wrench you can get around the nut—as in a box-end wrench—the less opportunity there is for the wrench metal to flex and slip on the nut. A six-point box-end wrench (versus the 12-point version most commonly seen) provides the most grip of all. And the better the grip you can get on the work at hand, the longer you're likely to be able to maintain the machine.

PUZZLER

THIS ISN'T A FANCY gavel, but it was used by a "spokesman" of sorts.

ANSWER: *Wheelwright's hammer, made so that it could fit between wheel spokes when the craftsman was at work.*

SCREWDRIVERS

A Perfect Match

❖ Always be careful to match your screwdriver to the screw. Don't use a small screwdriver in a big screw and vice versa. If you do, you're likely to ruin the screwdriver, the screw or both.

Retirees Still Pack a Punch

❖ When an old screwdriver wears out, hold on to it—it's perfect for jobs such as opening paint cans and punching holes in cans. Don't use a new screwdriver or chisel to pry the lid off a paint can, as you can ruin the tip of the tool in the process.

Emergency Relief for Frozen Screws

❖ If you encounter a frozen pan-head screw that is nearly impossible to remove because the head is stripped from previous removal attempts, don't risk damaging your screwdriver with another try. Instead, grasp the head with a pair of locking pliers, such as the Vise-Grip brand. Not only will the pliers avoid the damaged part of the head, but they'll also give you more leverage to free the screw.

Where There's Smoke, There's a Fire Sale

ONCE WHEN I WAS A YOUNG MAN, I worked for an entire year salvaging goods from a burned-out hardware store, then rebuilding the store.

It took me months to get everything ready for the fire sale. Much of my time was spent showing items to a representative of the insurance company. If the insurance company decided to cover the expense of an item, I had to destroy it. The other items I cleaned up as best as I could and organized for the sale.

I still have some of the items I bought at that sale. Although the miter box I purchased was pitted from the fire and rusted from the water that put it out, after I cleaned up the box and painted it, it looked like new. I've been even happier with the 100-pound keg of screws that I bought for 50 cents. The screws had all rusted—but, sur-

EARL
remembers...

prisingly, I found that they held all the more for being rusty. They were *better* than new.

Fire sales are still a great place to find salvaged goods today. Sometimes the sales are unadvertised, so if you hear about a fire in a commercial building, it's smart to inquire whether there will be a sale of damaged items.

❖ Another trick for freeing frozen screws and nuts is to douse the hardware with a carbonated liquid such as cola or club soda. The carbonic acid in the soda may loosen up some of the rust and corrosion enough to make the nut or screw yield.

FILES

Get a Grip!

❖ Before using a file for the first time, attach a wooden handle to it. Handles, which are sold at most hardware stores, always make files work more easily.

Batter Up!

USE THE TAPERED sections of old, turned table legs to create nice file handles. Just cut them down to the right size and attach them to the files. And if you're good at carving, you won't find a better wood for hammer handles than ash from a discarded baseball bat.

Go All the Way

❖ Be sure you use the whole length of the file, not just a few inches of it, or it will wear prematurely in one spot.

Elvis Would Like This One

❖ If a file gets clogged with metal shavings, you can clean it out with a special file-cleaning brush or card from a hardware store. If you don't have one on hand, use a brush made for suede shoes—it'll work fine.

A Genuine File Cabinet

❖ Files that are stored away can become damaged if they bang into one another. Don't throw them into a toolbox. Instead, put them into a drawer lined with an old piece of scrap carpet. This will help keep the little teeth on your files intact.

File In

❖ If you're ready to throw away an old, dull file, here's an old-timers' trick to try before kissing it good-bye. Set it out on a windowsill for a while so that it gets a full range of sun, rain, heat and cold. That may sound like cruel and unusual tool treatment, but likely as not, the exposure will rust and corrode away just enough of the metal to put some bite back in the teeth.

A Little Dental Work

❖ To clean out individual teeth of a file, use a sharp nail.

LEVELS AND PLANES

On the Level

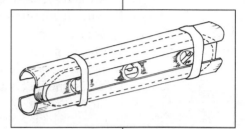

❖ A small torpedo level that gets thrown in the toolbox can easily be damaged. Protect the level with a short piece of old garden hose. Just cut two pieces of hose, each the length of the level. Then slit them down the side and fit them over the length of the level at the top and bottom. A couple of rubber bands will hold the guards in place. This will not only protect the bubble vials, but it also will keep the soft metal edges of the level from getting banged up.

To protect a torpedo level, cover top and bottom with pieces of garden hose. Rubber bands will secure the hose in place.

The Plane Truth

❖ Always store a plane on its side with the blade retracted. This will prevent the blade from getting nicked in your toolbox.

Keep the Plane Off the Paint

❖ If you want to keep your planes sharp as long as possible, never plane painted wood. Always remove the paint first by rasping or stripping it off.

Bright Is Bad

❖ If you see a thin, bright line on the edge of a plane iron—or any wood- or metal-cutting tool—it's a sign the blade is getting dull. Stop working and get sharpening.

Sock 'Em!

❖ If you're a collector of antique wood molding planes, you'll find that they'll last longer if you store them in protective cases. Old woolen socks make perfect inexpensive covers.

METAL RULES

Remedial Reading

❖ If your steel rule is starting to wear out and the numbers are getting hard to read, try this trick: rub the ruler lightly with fine-grade steel wool, then brush or spray on a thin coat of white oil-based paint so that the paint fills in all the numbers and markings. Before the paint dries, lightly wipe off the excess, leaving only the portion that's filling the indentations. The indentations should now be easy to read.

More Than a Floor

WHEN I RAN THE MAINTENANCE department at Yankee, I converted an outbuilding into a workshop. The structure required a lot of rebuilding, and when it came time to lay a new floor, I decided to use five-inch spruce planks. Folks who dropped by while I was laying the floor asked, "Why don't you use plywood?" That certainly would have been easier. But sometimes I use my workshop floor as a work space, and occasionally I need to drive nails into it. (I once assembled 40 large picture frames using a jig I nailed to the floor.) Driving a nail into a plywood floor is not a problem, but the plywood is likely to splinter when you try to pull the nail later. Nails come out of spruce planks easily.

EARL
remembers...

I've driven many a nail into that floor over the years, and the planks have lasted beautifully.

Measure for Measure

❖ Keep a steel tape measure working smoothly by applying a coat of paste wax along both sides of the tape, then rubbing the wax in lightly with a cloth. This will help the tape retract smoothly and will keep dirt from sticking to the blade.

HANDSAWS

Can You Hack It?

❖ When you mount the blade of a hacksaw, make sure the points of the saw's teeth are pointing away from you. Like files, hacksaws are designed to cut on the downstroke, so it's important that the blade be positioned correctly if you want the tool to last.

❖ When sawing with a hacksaw, use as much of the length of the saw as possible. This will prevent the teeth from getting dull in one place.

Guardin' Hose

❖ Protect the teeth on regular handsaws with an old piece of rubber hose. Cut a piece of hose the length of the saw blade, then cut a slit down the hose and place it over the teeth of the blade. The "hose trick" works on hatchets and drawknives as well.

Easy Off

❖ If your saw blade gets gummed up from sawing through wood that still has sap in it, clean it with spray-on oven cleaner. Or put a little paint thinner in a spray bottle and spray the blade in between saw strokes.

Don't Get Nailed

❖ Always carefully inspect the wood you are about to saw, taking care to look for any nails or other pieces of metal

The Square Root of Trouble

I⊤ SEEMS LIKE a good idea to apply a protective coat of oil to squares you use for marking and measuring—but avoid the temptation. The oil may transfer to the wood you're working on and leave a stain. If you keep the squares clean and dry, they'll be fine.

Give It a C-Plus

WHEN YOU BREAK a hacksaw blade, put the short pieces into a C-clamp and use the clamp as your new saw handle.

Give a hacksaw blade another chance.

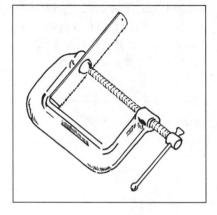

embedded in the wood. A couple of strokes with a handsaw against a hidden nail will dull it to the point of uselessness, and circular saw blades won't fare much better.

Try a Little Candle Power

❖ To protect and lubricate a handsaw, rub a candle stub over the blade. The wax won't stain your work the way oil can.

POWER TOOLS IN GENERAL

Keep Your Cool

❖ Make sure the air vents on your power tools are unobstructed so that cool air can circulate. This is especially important for woodworking tools, where sawdust can clog air vents and cause overheating. If a motor overheats, it will go to an early grave.

❖ Clean out the vents of your power tools with an old paintbrush, stick or cotton swab after each use. This will help prevent the motor from overheating.

Your Battery Will Remember If You Don't

❖ Battery-powered cordless drills and other power tools are now a standard part of the home workshop. The batteries themselves pack more power than ever on a single charge, but it still pays to observe some simple practices to get maximum use and life out of them. Make it a routine to run the battery down as much as you can before you put it back on charge. If, for example, you repeatedly discharge the battery only halfway, it will develop a "memory" for that level—that is, the battery will act as though it's exhausted at the halfway mark, and the rest of the potential will become inactive. Although battery and charger manufacturers have taken steps to address memory problems in recent years, most batteries can still succumb to this phenomenon.

Electric Drills: Check the Chuck

❖ Electric drills are probably the most popular power tools in any shop, and the chuck is probably the part of any drill that sees the most use and wear. When the jaws of a Jacobs chuck start to get old and ground down to the point it doesn't grip bits reliably anymore, don't kill the whole drill, just chuck the chuck. For only a few dollars, you can buy replacement chucks for common drills at a good hardware store or at the service center for the tool manufacturer.

To Change the Chuck

❖ To change the average chuck, first make sure the drill is unplugged. Then open the chuck as wide as possible and look into the jaws to find the screw that connects the chuck to the driveshaft. Remove this screw—it should turn clockwise, and it may be in tight. Once the screw is out, place the key in the chuck and unthread the chuck from the shaft—turning counterclockwise. (You may have to give the key a rap with a hammer to start the chuck moving.) Reverse the process to install the new chuck.

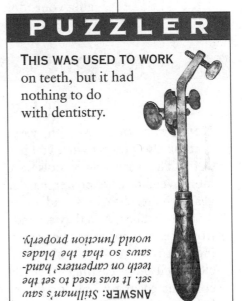

PUZZLER

THIS WAS USED TO WORK on teeth, but it had nothing to do with dentistry.

ANSWER: *Stillman's saw set. It was used to set the teeth on carpenters' hand-saws so that the blades would function properly.*

Watch How You Wear Your Belts

❖ If you have a belt-driven power tool, such as a table saw, band saw or jointer, and you have to remove the drive belt for some reason, make a note of its position and rotation on the machine before you take it off. The belt will last much longer if you reinstall it the same way. Reversing the direction, for example, means that the belt is forced to run opposite to the way its materials have set, and it will tend to fatigue rapidly.

Don't Force It

❖ Whenever possible, make a couple of passes at a job instead of forcing the tool beyond its capabilities and thus putting extra wear on it. For example, don't use a three-eighths-inch drill to do heavy-duty sanding with a six-inch sanding disk. And don't force a saw through material too quickly or bear down on a belt sander. Whenever a tool slows down, sounds as if the motor is laboring, overheats or starts to vibrate, back off—you're on the way to damaging your tool. The work may take a little longer this way, but your tools will last longer.

BUY IT TO LAST

The Power Shopper

IN POWER TOOLS, as with everything else, you get what you pay for. The better power tools have more weight, more power, harder gears, better bearings and more motor windings. And they're made from precision-machined body castings. Lower-quality tools have clamshell body castings—usually constructed of two plastic pieces held together with screws on one side. The power cord is often a good clue to the quality of the rest of the machine. If a tool has a long, heavy-duty cord, chances are the tool itself is of high quality.

The average life of most consumer power tools is between 7 and 12 hours, depending on use. (That doesn't sound like a lot, but a drill, for example, can make about 20,000 holes in that amount of time.) If that's not enough for your needs and if you want a better power tool, check out machines with the "light duty industrial" designation. These are better than the average homeowner variety but not as expensive as "heavy duty industrial." Light industrial tools can last 20 times longer than lower-priced homeowner tools, and they also have parts that can be replaced. Homeowner tools usually cost more to fix than to buy. Prices vary greatly, but as a rule of thumb, expect to pay roughly twice as much for a light industrial tool as for an average homeowner's version. So if a homeowner's drill costs $25, a light industrial version is likely to run between $50 and $75.

POWER SAWS

Clean Housing Promotes Long Life

❖ Dirt and sawdust can build up inside the motor housing of a table saw. If you use a shop vacuum to clean it out once in a while, the motor will last a lot longer.

High Pressure Will Blow It

❖ If you use compressed air to clean sawdust off your woodworking tools, make sure the pressure is set no higher than 40 pounds per square inch (psi). At higher pressures, you're likely to blow the dust into other components.

SAW BLADES

Separate your saw blades with pieces of cardboard, then secure them with a washer and wing nut to a plywood base. Now you're ready to travel.

Long-Playing Saw Blades

❖ To protect circular saw blades when they're not in use, slip them into the cardboard sleeves of old record albums. What to do with the albums? An old record rack makes a convenient place to store them.

Blade Runner

❖ Here's a handy way to protect your saw blades and make them easier to transport to your job: Cut a piece of plywood about a foot square. Cut a carrying handle in the plywood, then drill a three-eighths-inch hole in the center of it. Put a three-inch carriage bolt through that hole and through the center hole of the saw blades, then secure the blades in place with a washer and wing nut. Put sheets of cardboard between the blades for added protection.

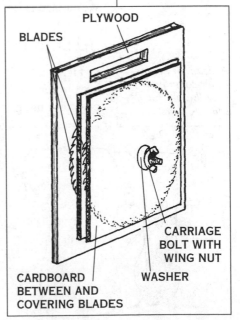

PLYWOOD

BLADES

CARRIAGE BOLT WITH WING NUT

WASHER

CARDBOARD BETWEEN AND COVERING BLADES

Don't Let Them Stay in Touch

❖ When you hang blades up on hooks, put heavy cardboard or some other material between them. Try to avoid letting them touch each other. If they do rub against each other, they are more likely to rust, and the blades may become dented or worn.

Keep 'Em Running in Circles

❖ After using a circular saw, remove the blade, soak it in warm water and mild dishwashing liquid and then wash it. The blade will cut better and last longer if it's kept clean.

SANDERS

Avoid Cloggers

❖ When buying sanding belts, look for those that are "open coat." This means that the grit/sand particles are spaced farther apart, allowing sawdust to escape more easily. "Closed-coat" belts have the particles spaced more closely together. They are more likely to clog and thus won't last as long.

Stick to the Beltway

A clean, dry paint-roller cover makes a great holder for sanding belts.

❖ Here's a handy way to store your sanding belts so they'll last: mount a couple of clean, dry paint-roller covers on pegs and hang the belts around the soft rollers. Or use a short piece of polyvinyl chloride (PVC) pipe as a hanger. Don't store sanding belts in a box or drawer where they can get creased.

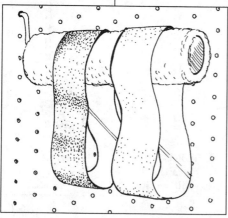

Run Faster, Jump Higher, Sand Longer

❖ You can revive clogged sanding belts by cleaning them with an old tennis shoe. Clamp the sander upside down and turn it on. Then rub the rubber sole of the tennis shoe over the belt.

Wood particles trapped in the belt will stick to the sole, and in a few minutes your belt will be ready to sand once again.

SANDPAPER

Keep Your Paper Dry

❖ Store your sandpaper and sanding belts in zipper-locked freezer bags. This will extend the life of the paper by keeping it dry.

The Sands of Time

❖ If you want sandpaper that will hold up, get the kind made with aluminum oxide. It lasts longer.

Make Contact to Save Your Sandpaper

❖ When you sand with fine-grit sandpaper, the paper often wears out before the grit. To prevent this, apply some self-adhesive contact paper to the back of the sandpaper before you use it. You'll get the full use of the sandpaper and won't have to throw it away too soon.

A SECOND LIFE

Old Sandpaper Never Dies

Don't immediately throw away medium- or fine-grit sandpaper after it's spent from a sanding project. Even though it's lost most of its bite, once you clap out the excess dust, it will be just right for knocking down the glaze between coats on varnishing or enamel paint projects.

DRILLS

But What about the Cholesterol?

❖ You can help your drill bits last longer by lubricating them with a little lard before each use. Lard costs less than lubricating oil, and it sticks to the bits better.

Bent out of Shape

❖ Sometimes it's best not to try to make things last too long. Check your drill bits for straightness by rolling them with your palm across a flat surface like a piece of glass. If the bit wobbles, it's not straight and should be replaced

immediately. Bent bits tend to break during use, which can
be dangerous.

Off with Their Heads!

❖ The very smallest bits are delicate and tend to break
easily. If you're doing a rough job like boring pilot holes
in molding, try using a finish nail in your drill instead. Cut
the nail head off with a side cutter and insert the remaining nail into the chuck just like a drill bit. Then save your
real bits for more precise work.

SHOP VACUUMS

This Is a Job for Super-Vac

❖ To clean up plaster dust—especially the kind left from
interior construction—always use a shop vacuum made
for this purpose. Never use a household vacuum cleaner
to get up plaster dust. The powder is so fine that it will
pass through the paper or cloth bag inside and make its
way to the motor, where it will destroy the brushes and
bearings. Besides heavier motors and a different design,
shop vacuums have replaceable filters made to stop such
particles. Newer models even have a shaker mechanism
to keep the filter clear.

Don't Cry Over Spilt Water

❖ If you need to clean up wet surfaces in the shop, use a
wet-dry shop vacuum made for heavy-duty work. Never
suck up water with a regular household vacuum, as you'll
risk destroying the motor and giving yourself an electrical shock.

SHARPENING TOOLS

Give More Than an Inch

❖ When working with a sharpening stone, use its full
length, not just a few inches in the middle. Otherwise
you'll hollow out the stone in that one place, and the stone
will become useless for larger, flat-bladed tools.

Temper Fugit

❖ Use your electric grinding wheel for metalworking tools and for garden tools like axes and hatchets. Don't try to sharpen woodworking tools on it; it's not nearly smooth or accurate enough.

Cool Off
before Returning to the Old Grind

❖ Go easy when using an electric grinding wheel. Overdoing it can overheat the metal and cause it to lose its temper. When using a grindstone, pause every now and then and dip the tool you are sharpening into a bucket of water. This will keep the tool from getting too hot. After rough shaping with the grindstone, do your final sharpening with a mill file or whetstone.

Another Bad Scrape

❖ Hand-held scrapers with removable blades become dull with use. Rather than throw away a blade, just pass a file over the dull edge, and you'll be ready to go. A good scraper blade can last for years.

Rapier-Like Wit

Washington Irving, author of "Rip Van Winkle," observed that "a sharp tongue is the only edged tool that grows keener with constant use."

LADDERS

What's Rung with This Picture?

❖ Before you use an old wooden straight ladder, set it on the ground and walk on the rungs. If they break, you'll know the ladder is no longer any good. Better to find out on the ground than 20 feet up!

In Good Standing

❖ If you have an aluminum ladder, you can strengthen the hollow rungs to make the ladder safer and longer-lasting. Measure the diameter of the rungs, then get some doweling that will fit snugly inside. Cut the doweling to the proper length and tamp it into the rungs. The rungs will then be less likely to buckle under pressure.

My Ladder Isn't for Lightweights

I STILL HAVE THE WOODEN extension ladder I bought in 1940. It's a heavy-duty ladder, suitable for things like carrying bundles of asphalt shingles up to roofs. The main thing I've done to make the ladder last all these years has been always to keep it bone-dry.

EARL remembers...

My old ladder has seen me through a lot of jobs, but it's extremely heavy because it's made of wood. If I had to get a new ladder today, I'd buy an aluminum builder's ladder. If you're in the market for a ladder, look for heavier metal and rungs that are welded on both the inside and the outside of the upright supports. Consider a heavy-duty model, which will stand up better to any abuse it might encounter. And, of course, make the ladder last even longer by keeping that abuse to a minimum.

Don't Finish the Job

❖ Always leave a wooden ladder unfinished. Don't paint it. Paint will obscure any hairline cracks that may develop as the ladder ages—telltale signs that a rung or leg is about to fail.

PAINT

Do You Have a Thick Skin?

❖ If you're tired of opening old cans of paint only to find a thick skin on the surface, try turning the can over before you store it away. Hammer the lid down to form a good seal, then invert the can. When you go to use the paint, the skin will be on the bottom, where it won't get in your way.

❖ To prevent a skin from forming on a partially used can of paint, cut a circle of waxed paper the size of the can and drop it on top of the paint surface. Then seal the can.

The waxed paper will keep the air from forming a skin on the paint.

A Not-So-Good Buildup

❖ If you're painting directly from the can, paint may build up on the can's rim, making it difficult to seal the can when you're done. The paint will then harden, and you'll have to throw it away. Avoid this problem by punching holes an inch apart inside the rim, using a hammer and nail. When you wipe your brush, the paint will drip right back into the can.

❖ Another way to avoid paint buildup on the rim of your paint can is to dump some paint into a plastic bucket or an old coffee can and paint from that instead of directly from the original can.

The Olden Glove Award

❖ If you have a pair of rubber gloves with a hole or two in them, don't throw them away. Use them when painting to keep (most of) the paint off your hands.

PAINTBRUSHES

It's Only Water

❖ When applying latex paint, use a brush with synthetic bristles. Save the natural brushes for oil paint. Latex paint contains water, which can break down a natural-bristle brush.

Don't Be a Big Dipper

❖ Dip your brush only about a quarter of the way into the paint. You want to paint with the tip of the brush, not the side of it. If you put too much paint on the brush, it'll be difficult to clean and may harden.

Bag It

❖ If you have to break for a few hours or even overnight, put a roller or paintbrush into a plastic bag and seal it with a twist tie. This will let you use a roller or brush for days without cleaning it and still make the painting implement last.

Chill Out

❖ If you want to break for even longer (as much as several days) when painting with latex paint, take your plastic bag with the wet brush or roller and place it in the freezer. When you're ready to paint again, take the bag out and let it thaw at room temperature.

Soft and Silky

❖ After cleaning latex paint out of a brush, do a final rinse in water that has a little fabric softener in it. It will leave the bristles soft and easy to use.

The Solvent Solution

❖ After you clean paintbrushes with paint thinner, you may be able to use the solvent again. Pour the dirty solvent into a clean, sturdy plastic bottle (such as an empty bleach bottle) and stuff some steel wool into the opening. Let the sediment settle for a few days, then pour the clear paint thinner, through the steel wool, into a clean container. The steel wool will catch any impurities, and the purified solvent will be nearly as good as new. Let the dirty solvent dry to a solid, then throw it away.

Start with a wide-mouthed gallon jar. Glue a block of wood onto the cover, then screw a cup hook through the cover and into the block of wood. Pour solvent into the jar, hang a dirty paintbrush from the hook, and the brush can soak without losing its shape.

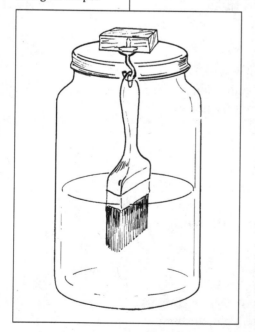

Let Your Dirty Brush Hang In There

❖ Paint solvent tends to evaporate quickly, so here's a way to get your brushes clean and prolong the life of the solvent. Get a wide-mouthed gallon jar and glue a small block of wood onto the top of the jar cover. Then screw a cup hook into the underside of the lid, with the threads going through the lid and into the wood. Pour solvent into the jar, hang your dirty brush from the cup hook and screw on the lid. You'll have clean brushes and no more evaporated solvent!

All Gummed Up

❖ Old, gummed-up paintbrushes often can be cleaned by boiling them in vinegar. Heat the vinegar in an old pan. When it starts to boil, work the brush back and forth against the bottom of the pan.

Is Your Brush out of Shape?

❖ If the bristles of a nylon brush are out of shape, soak the clean brush in very hot water for five minutes. Then place the brush on a flat surface and lay the bottom of a flat, heavy pan on top of it. When dry, the brush should be back to its original shape.

Do Double Duty

❖ If you do a big job with a paintbrush, it's likely to get stiff from the paint that accumulates near the handle. To avoid this, use two brushes at a time. While the first is in use, let the second one soak in water or paint thinner. When the first gets stiff, start working with the second and let the first soak. If you go back and forth, both brushes will remain free of excess paint.

PAINT ROLLERS

Luxury Liner

❖ If you keep dumping paint into a roller tray, eventually the layers will build up, and you'll have to throw away the tray. Instead, line the tray with aluminum foil or a plastic dry-cleaning or supermarket bag, then pour in the paint. When you're done, gather the corners, collect the excess paint and throw the mess in the trash.

On a Roll

❖ To clean a roller soaked with oil-based paint, roll the paint left in the roller onto dry newspaper. Then put about an inch of paint thinner in a clean roller tray. Roll the roller through the thinner, then roll it on more dry newspaper. Repeat, replacing the newspaper as necessary, until the paint is gone. Then wash the roller in warm soapy water, rinse, allow it to dry and wrap it in brown wrapping paper or place it in a plastic bag for storage.

Hang 'Em Dry

❖ When storing a used paint roller, put a little hook in the end and hang it up by the hook. Or put the roller back on the metal roller shaft and hang it so that the roller itself doesn't touch anything. Don't let a paint roller rest on its surface, or it will become deformed.

PUZZLER

THIS LONG-HANDLED English tool has a step, so that a farmer could put his foot down, and a sharp blade at the base. Animals were happy to see it used.

ANSWER: *Hay cutter, used to remove hay from a stack. It was also used to cut turnips, pumpkins and other vegetables for animal feed.*

ROPE

Tell Your Knots to Take a Powder

❖ If you have a length of rope with knots in it, don't throw it away. Try dusting it with some talcum powder. The offending knots may become much easier to undo.

Don't Come Unraveled

❖ Ropes that unravel often have to be thrown away. You can seal the ends of a nylon rope by holding it over an open flame and allowing the heat to melt the nylon into a solid stub that can't be unraveled. (Be careful it doesn't drip on your hand.)

❖ Seal the ends of a hemp rope by dipping them in shellac.

ODDS AND ENDS

Collar Your Flashlight

❖ Round flashlights tend to roll off work surfaces and onto the floor. To prevent this, cut a circle the size of the flashlight out of the top of a plastic coffee can lid and slide the neck of the light through the hole. Then cut a slice off the lid so that it's flat on one side. Now the flashlight won't roll, and the lid can help you position the light where you want it.

There's a Hole in the Bucket

❖ If your plastic bucket has a crack in it, don't throw it away. Light a candle and hold the blade of an old knife in the flame. When the blade is good and hot, run it slowly over the crack. The hot blade will melt the plastic. When it dries, the crack will be sealed.

It's Dust in the Wind

❖ When not using electrical outlets in your workshop, cover them with the special plastic caps designed to protect toddlers. Workshops create a lot of dust, and if the dust gets into electrical receptacles, it can cause a short circuit and possibly a fire.

Now *That's* Tacky

❖ If your tools get covered with oil or sawdust, clean them with a homemade tack cloth. Dampen a piece of cloth with a little turpentine and shellac, then wipe down the tool after use. The rag will pick up all the loose dirt. When you're done, store the rag in a closed plastic bag or large sealed jar until you're ready to use it again.

Cars and Other Motor Vehicles

WHEN I FIRST STARTED working for myself laying linoleum flooring, all I could afford was a little Cushman motor scooter. I bought it with money I'd saved from making birdhouses and lawn ornaments. The scooter had small wheels and not much power. Whenever I came to a steep hill, I'd have to get off and walk alongside it.

One day I dropped by my local garage to see if I could find an inexpensive used car. When I walked in, the manager was in a rage because one of his mechanics had just crashed the three-wheeled motorcycle they used to pick up parts. It seemed the mechanics were always getting into accidents because they drove the three-wheeler too fast, and it would tip over on curves.

I knew the manager of the garage fairly well. So when he finished cursing the day he'd bought the three-wheeler, I proposed a swap. I'd take the three-wheeler, and his mechanics could use my scooter. They couldn't get hurt on it, because the scooter didn't have enough power for them to speed. And I'd have a vehicle with power enough to get up hills. The manager was delighted with my proposal.

I drove that three-wheeler for years, winter and summer. I kept to the speed limit and maintained it well, so I never had any problem with it.

I've owned a good many motor vehicles since the day I traded two wheels for three, and as the years have gone by, the complexity of automobiles and other internal-combustion conveyances has increased more than I could have imagined. But a couple of things have stayed the same.

First, like my Cushman scooter, the most elaborately engineered automobile of today is made for the sole purpose of getting from one place to another, and it won't do that job very well if you don't keep it in good working order. Second, the keys to economical vehicle maintenance are still common sense and early diagnosis. Anyone with an unlimited bank account can keep a car running just about forever. The trick is to stay on the road without taking the next exit to the poorhouse.

In this chapter, we'll take a system-by-system look at what makes cars and smaller motor vehicles tick and discuss how to keep the repairman away for as long as possible. We'll see why long trips are better for your car than short ones, find out what your lawn sprinkler has to do with keeping corrosion at bay and discover automotive uses for kitty litter and baking soda.

ENGINES

Break In to Avoid Breaking Down

❖ When you break in a new car, keep idling time to an absolute minimum during the first 500 miles or so. When an engine is idling, very little oil circulates to the initially tight-fitting parts, causing extremely rapid wear. A new—or newly rebuilt—engine that is broken in properly will last far longer than one that is treated harshly during the break-in period.

❖ Don't exceed 50 miles per hour for the first 500 miles or so.

❖ During those first 500 miles, vary your speed often as you drive, but avoid rapid acceleration and deceleration.

Show Off That New Car to Your Friends in Kalamazoo

❖ You can also make your engine last by taking your new car on a sustained road trip to break it in, rather than starting off with a series of short hops around town. If a new engine is run briefly and shut off while still cold, the bare metal surfaces of some moving parts—which lack the protective glaze they will acquire with use—are extremely vulnerable to damage from condensation and other combustion by-products. Running the engine for a sustained period of time will prevent this.

The Road to Ruin Is Paved with . . . Well, It's Not Paved

❖ When you have a choice, take the highway instead of the back road. Dirt or gravel roads can be picturesque, but they're very hard on your engine. Tiny particles of dust that pass through the air filter dramatically increase engine wear. Moreover, the increased rolling resistance encountered by the tires means that your engine must work harder—which is why fuel mileage decreases by one-third on dirt roads.

On the Road to Ruin?

AT THE HEIGHT of the Great Depression, there were nearly 30 million cars on the road, a fact that caused Will Rogers to quip, "We're the first nation in the history of the world to go to the poorhouse in an automobile."

Don't Be a Lug

❖ When in doubt, downshift. "Lugging" your car's engine—accelerating to coax it up a hill in high gear, rather than shifting the manual transmission into a lower gear—puts it under heavy strain, reduces the flow of oil and causes rapid wear. If you think ahead and downshift early, you'll add thousands of miles to the life of your engine.

It's Tough to Start Out Cold

❖ Whenever possible, combine trips to avoid numerous short hops with a cold engine. Most engine wear—up to 95 percent of it, in fact—occurs within the first ten seconds of starting a cold engine, when its moving surfaces are poorly protected by oil. And when you do drive, start the engine and put the car in motion with as little delay as possible. Relatively little oil is supplied to its moving parts when the engine is turning over slowly, so you should never idle a car to warm it up.

It's All Downhill from Here

❖ If possible, leave your vehicle facing downhill when you park on a slope. That will ease the load on the cold, newly started engine when you are ready to leave.

Reddy Kilowatt to the Rescue

❖ If you live in an area with severe winters, you can greatly reduce wear on your engine—and make for much easier starting—by installing an inexpensive engine-block heater and plugging it into a garage or outdoor electrical socket during cold weather. Immersion heaters—which are inserted in place of the oil dipstick—are effective but less convenient than heaters that are installed in the lower radiator hose. In most cases, installation is a simple do-it-yourself job, with easy instructions provided with the heater.

Blanket Coverage

❖ On a cold winter night, try putting your vehicle to bed with a blanket. If the car lacks a block heater, simply placing an old blanket over the hood immediately after shut-

Emergency Tools and Supplies

N O MATTER HOW WELL maintained your car is and how careful a driver you may be, chances are good you'll probably find yourself standing next to your broken-down vehicle at the side of the road someday. Your car will last longer—and so will your temper—if you've prepared for that inevitable day by equipping your vehicle with a basic emergency kit. Pack the following items in your car's trunk, and you'll be ready for many common emergencies:

- Troubleshooting guide and owner's manual for your vehicle
- Lug wrench, jack and spare tire
- Flashlight
- Phillips-head screwdriver
- Slotted screwdriver
- Locking pliers
- Basic set of socket wrenches and open-end wrenches (cheap discount-store tools are adequate for such standby use)
- Tow rope or chain
- Jumper cables
- Old blanket
- Extra drive belts
- Two quarts of motor oil
- Spare electrical fuses (ask your mechanic or the dealer from whom you bought the car to put together a kit of replacement fuses for you)
- Hose clamps
- Duct tape or electrical tape
- Dry chemical fire extinguisher
- Small shovel and bag of dry sand or kitty litter (winter only)

ting off the engine may help retain enough heat to permit a fast start in the morning. And if the car is equipped with a block heater, the blanket trick will help it do its job more efficiently.

It's As Easy As Falling Off a Log

❖ How can you tell when your ignition system is due for a tune-up? One simple method is to calculate your average fuel mileage over the course of two tanks of fuel immediately after a tune-up, when your engine is running at maximum efficiency. (Record your mileage when you fill the tank and again when you refill it. Subtract one from the other, then divide by the number of gallons it took for the second fill-up.) Recheck your mileage periodically, and keep a written log. When the log reveals that your mileage has fallen off by 10 percent or thereabouts, you're due for a visit to your mechanic.

Lubrication and Filters

❖ One of the most basic keys to keeping a car in service is changing the oil on a regular basis. How often? Every 3,000 miles or so is a good rule of thumb. If in doubt, follow the manufacturer's recommendation (in the owner's manual) for "severe service." The "severe service" heading includes frequent short trips, stop-and-go driving, high-speed driving in hot weather and other common practices, so this approach should keep you from waiting too long.

❖ It's a good idea to replace the oil filter every time you change the oil. The old filter contains up to a quart of used oil, which will immediately contaminate the fresh oil you just added. The small added cost of the filter will more than pay for itself in increased engine life.

What's Up, Doc?

❖ If you decide to change your car's oil and filter yourself rather than taking it to a mechanic, you'll inevitably end up with oil on your hands. If that bothers you—and perhaps tempts you to postpone regular oil changes—buy a box of disposable surgical gloves at a pharmacy and slip into a pair before you lift the hood. When you're done with the operation, just peel off the gloves and throw them away.

Some Folk Wisdom Really Is

❖ About once a month, take your car out for an hour or two on the main roads. The long-standing belief that an engine can benefit from a periodic run at highway speeds has a solid basis in fact. If a car is driven primarily on short trips at low speeds, its engine oil will tend to accumulate moisture, unburned fuel and other impurities that accelerate engine wear. These can be harmlessly "boiled off" during a stint of highway driving that heats the oil to its optimum operating temperature for an hour or two.

Please Regrease Me

❖ It's a good idea to have your vehicle's suspension and steering professionally greased (sometimes described as a "chassis lube" or "grease job") at least once a year—or

Oil in the Carpet

I RECENTLY HAD TO GET an oil stain out of the carpet of my car. I still can't figure out where the stain came from. Maybe I stepped on an oil drip in a parking lot and brought it in on my boot.

In any case, the oil stain was easy enough to remove. I applied some paint thinner on a paper towel and dabbed at it until it dissipated.

Stains in the carpet of your car are no different from stains in your living room carpet, really. You should treat the stain in your car with the same urgency you would a stain in your house. Try to get it out as soon as you can after the spill. Once stains have set, they are much harder to remove.

E A R L
remembers...

every 6,000 miles if you travel on rough or dusty roads. That's more often than many automakers recommend, but while the car is on the lift, your mechanic will have an opportunity to spot any emerging problems with the exhaust system, steering linkage, brake pads, springs, shocks or struts and other components—before they lead to a costly (and possibly dangerous) mechanical failure.

Shed Light on the Air Filter

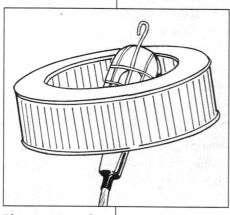

❖ Check your vehicle's air filter each time you change the oil. Look for a doughnut-shaped or oblong paper element located in a metal or plastic housing under the hood, remove it and hold it up to see whether light shines through the paper element. If not, replace the filter. The job requires no tools and takes less than a minute. A clogged air filter can lead to hard starts, rough idling and poor fuel economy.

If you can't see the light when you inspect your car's air filter, replace the filter.

❖ Another way to check for a clogged air filter is to warm up the engine, raise the hood and listen to the sound of the engine idling. Remove the air-filter cover and listen again. If the idle speeds up noticeably, the filter needs replacing.

BELTS

A Stiff Belt (But Not Too Stiff)

❖ Every time you check the oil, also take a minute to inspect the drive belts for cracking, fraying and proper tension (a belt should give about one-half inch when pressed in the center). Most vehicles have two or three drive belts, which ride on pulleys to power accessories such as the engine cooling fan, power steering pump, air conditioner and alternator. A broken belt can leave you stranded—and in some cases, lead to overheating and engine damage—so it's smart to do all you can to avoid that situation.

What the Well-Dressed Belts Are Wearing

❖ To make your drive belts work more efficiently and last longer, treat them every six months or so with a commercial belt-dressing spray, available at auto parts stores.

Play the Odds

❖ If your drive belts are 4 years old or older, it's a good idea to replace all of them, even if they appear to be in good condition. Once a belt approaches the 4-year mark, it's likely to fail within the next 12 months.

❖ When you replace a drive belt before it wears out completely, save the old one in the trunk in case the new belt breaks unexpectedly. It's not a difficult process to change the belt yourself, and even if you lack the tools or know-how, another motorist may be able to help you. You're also one step ahead if you go to a garage, which may or may not have the belt you need in stock.

❖ Another hedge against drive-belt failure is to carry an emergency drive-belt kit. This kit, available at most auto parts stores, lets you install a new belt without tools.

DRIVE TRAINS

Clutch Play

❖ Keep your foot entirely off the clutch pedal except when actually shifting gears, or you may cause the clutch to slip and wear out prematurely. It costs several hundred dollars to replace a clutch, but with reasonable care, the original clutch can last the life of the vehicle.

And Away We Go

❖ When you first start your engine, it will run at a high speed for a few moments, then drop down to a normal

PUZZLER

THIS LOOKS LIKE THE framework for a lyre, but we'd be liars to tell you that. Once upon a time, this was what you used when somebody said "Hop in."

ANSWER: Buggy step, to help passengers enter and exit a horse-drawn wagon or carriage.

Pickups That Plow Snow Perish Prematurely

I HAVE A 1979 JEEP pickup that I use for plowing my driveway, which is long and steep. It's a good vehicle, but it has been rough to maintain. It has an electric hoist for the plow, which used to run down my battery until I bought a new battery with a higher amp output. And the Jeep goes through tires faster than it should.

I don't blame the Jeep. Plowing puts a substantial amount of wear on any pickup. So if you want to make your pickup last, pay someone else to plow your driveway.

EARL remembers...

idling speed as the automatic choke disengages. Always wait for the engine to slow down before shifting an automatic transmission from Park into Drive, or it will slam into gear, putting a heavy strain on the transmission components.

❖ When shifting an automatic transmission from Drive to Reverse, or vice versa, make sure the vehicle comes to a complete stop first. Otherwise you'll gradually damage the driveshafts, constant velocity joints and other drive train parts.

Forgotten Fluid

❖ It's wise to check your automatic transmission fluid whenever you change your engine oil. For an accurate reading, be sure the engine is warmed up and running, with the transmission in neutral, when you check the transmission fluid dipstick—which is similar in appearance to the oil dipstick but is ordinarily located nearer to the back of the engine. If the dipstick registers low, add transmission fluid—of the type specified in your owner's manual—a pint at a time until the level reaches the "full" mark.

On a Different Note . . .

❖ A change in the sound of your vehicle's exhaust or the smell of exhaust inside the car usually indicates an exhaust system leak. Check it out immediately. Not only is the leaking exhaust gas a potential hazard, but should an exhaust pipe actually break while the car is moving, it's likely to tear off and destroy otherwise serviceable exhaust system parts in the process.

Watch Your Tailpipe

❖ To check the exhaust system yourself, cover the tailpipe with a rag to keep the exhaust from getting out. If you feel strong pressure and the engine starts to bog down, the exhaust system is probably okay. If you don't feel much pressure and the engine runs fine, the exhaust is escaping somewhere else, through a hole. Get the car to a repair shop.

BATTERIES AND STARTERS

Now Is the Time to Assault the Battery

❖ Remove any corrosive deposits from battery terminals by disconnecting the cable clamps from the terminals and using an old toothbrush to scrub the clamps and terminals with a solution of ¼ cup of baking soda and 1 pint of water. Rinse with clear water, then polish the clamps and terminals with emery paper or steel wool. After reattaching the clamps to the terminals, apply a protective coating of petroleum jelly to the clamp and terminal surfaces to prevent the corrosion from returning. Corroded battery terminals will prevent a battery from

---

The Tale of the Tailpipe

THE CONDITION of your vehicle's tailpipe—where the exhaust fumes exit at the rear—can offer some important clues about what's going on inside the engine. Fine deposits of light brown or gray powder are normal. Dry, black, sooty deposits suggest a problem with the air-fuel mixture, while wet, oily deposits probably mean that the engine is badly worn. A white, glazed appearance may mean that the engine is running too hot. Spotting such signs of trouble early and following up with a visit to your mechanic can prolong the life of your vehicle.

delivering its full output and may keep your vehicle from starting.

With This Ring I Thee Protect

❖ You can also prevent battery corrosion by slipping a pair of anticorrosion rings—inexpensive chemically treated felt rings, available at auto parts stores—over the battery terminals before bolting the cable clamps in place.

Pass the Bicarbonate

❖ Once or twice a year, or whenever the outside of the battery case begins to look dirty or grimy, clean it with an old toothbrush dipped in a solution of ¼ cup of baking soda and 1 pint of water. Deposits of dirt and corrosion can conduct current between the terminals, slowly draining the battery. Before cleaning, plug the vent holes in the

Play It by Ear: What Automotive Noises Mean

YOU CAN RECOGNIZE many expensive automotive problems-in-the-making before they advance too far if you actively listen for them rather than waiting until they become so loud that you can't fail to notice. Make a habit of occasionally turning off the radio and the heater or air conditioner, rolling down the windows and listening for suspicious noises. Some of the more common sounds you can hope *not* to hear include the following:

• **A grinding noise from under the hood whenever the engine is running.** This often points to a damaged water pump, alternator or power steering pump. To decide which, open the hood with the engine still running and hold one end of a three-foot length of hose to each of these components in turn. Hold the other end to your ear. You'll readily be able to tell which component is the source of the noise.

• **A grinding or rumbling noise that appears to come from one of the four corners of the car.** This warning signal probably means that a wheel bearing is going bad. If the sound appears to be coming from the right or left side of the vehicle, it may get louder as you steer in that direction and temporarily increase the load on the bad wheel. Conversely, the noise may diminish as you steer away from its apparent source. See a mechanic right away, or your wheel may fall off—a costly and unpleasant nui-

battery caps with toothpicks, or temporarily cover them with bits of duct tape, to ensure that none of the soda solution leaks into the interior.

It's a Gas, but It's No Fun

❖ Never smoke around a battery, and take care to avoid shorting the positive and negative terminals with a wrench or similar conductor, which will create an intense spark. All lead-acid batteries—like the one in your car—produce small amounts of potentially explosive hydrogen gas when in use.

Jump-in-a-Bucket

❖ To protect jumper cables from damage in the trunk of your car—and to prevent them from damaging the trunk—coil them neatly in a clean plastic bucket with a

sance, and a deadly one if you're in traffic or traveling at a high speed.

• **A loud squealing sound noticeable immediately after starting.** This is almost always caused by a loose or worn-out drive belt. In most cases, adjusting or replacing one or more belts—a simple and inexpensive procedure—will solve the problem.

• **In a front-wheel-drive car, a rapid clicking sound from one of the front wheels upon cornering.** This probably means that a constant velocity (CV) joint on that side of the car is worn. If the rubber boots that protect the joints are intact and the noise can be heard only during tight turns, you can put off the repair for a while. If the noise is continuous or audible during gentle turns, or if the rubber boots are torn, quickly make

an appointment with your mechanic.

• **A knocking or "pinging" sound from the engine during acceleration,** often accompanied by a tendency for the engine to run on momentarily after the ignition has been turned off. This suggests that you may be using gasoline with too low an octane rating. Try a tankful of higher-octane fuel and see if the problem goes away. If it doesn't, see your mechanic.

• **A ticking, thumping or banging sound from the engine that becomes louder and faster as the engine speed increases.** Such variable engine noises may be caused by problems with the valve lifters, pistons, connecting rods or a number of other things, all of which demand immediate attention if you hope to avoid major engine damage. See your mechanic immediately.

snap-on lid, such as an empty drywall joint compound bucket.

One Warmed-Over Battery to Go

❖ If your battery fails to start your vehicle in cold winter weather and no jump start is available, try disconnecting the battery and bringing it indoors for an hour or so. (Wear old clothes, since battery acid eats holes in fabric.)

A Real *Energy Crisis*

EVERYONE REMEMBERS the energy crisis of the early 1970s as a time when gasoline was expensive and sometimes hard to get. But in my opinion, the energy crisis was not even an inconvenience compared to gas rationing during World War II.

During the war, I worked for a contractor who was mining the mica needed to insulate electric motors. I think the ration for business use of a car during the war was 12 gallons of gasoline per week. For the gas-guzzlers of those days, that wasn't much.

EARL remembers...

I was still getting around on my motorcycle with a sidecar until one day I spotted a beautiful Plymouth coupe for sale near the mica-processing plant. A soldier had bought the car right before the war and then asked his father to sell it for him when he went overseas. I decided to buy the car for $765, which was a lot of money back then. But smaller cars were highly prized and hard to come by because of their gas efficiency.

The first day I drove the car to work, my boss complimented me on my purchase and offered to buy the car for $1,000. He owned a big black Buick sedan, a real gas hog. Then the plant foreman approached me about buying the car. But I told them both that I had what I wanted. I had already learned that making your gas last is more important than having a fancy car.

The warmed-up battery may have enough power to crank the engine to life.

Don't Be a Crank

❖ Avoid cranking your engine for more than a few seconds when trying to start it, or you'll overheat the starter motor and greatly shorten its life. A hard-starting engine indicates some sort of malfunction that will need attention from a mechanic sooner or later. Make it sooner, and you can save $200 or more on a starter replacement somewhere down the road.

COOLING SYSTEMS

A Fluid for All Seasons

❖ Make sure your radiator contains a mixture of equal parts antifreeze and water all year long. Despite its name, antifreeze does far more than prevent your cooling system from freezing. Because it also has a higher boiling point than water, it's able to dissipate heat more efficiently. That allows your engine to run cooler in hot weather, extending its life.

❖ Be sure to have the antifreeze (or coolant, as it is properly called) in your radiator replaced once a year, even if an antifreeze tester shows that the old coolant still offers adequate freeze protection. Coolant contains additives that protect your radiator and heater from rust and corrosion. Those additives lose their effectiveness over time, and replacing the coolant is a good way to make sure the additives are fresh.

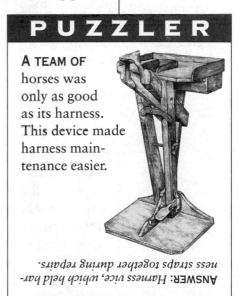

PUZZLER

A TEAM OF horses was only as good as its harness. This device made harness maintenance easier.

ANSWER: *Harness vice, which held harness straps together during repairs.*

Follow Your Nose

❖ If you detect the characteristic sweet smell of coolant after stopping the car, investigate immediately. You probably have a minor leak in a radiator or heater hose, or perhaps a leaky radiator. Leaky hoses are easily and inexpensively replaced, but if ignored, they will eventually fail and leave you stranded—perhaps causing severe engine damage from overheating.

A Thorough Debugging

❖ Whenever you wash your car, take a few moments to open the hood and give your radiator a thorough washing, directing the spray from the back of the radiator through the front. That will get rid of bugs and other debris clogging the cooling fins, allow the radiator to work more efficiently and help protect your engine.

A 100 Percent Solution Isn't the Solution

NEVER SUBSTITUTE straight antifreeze for a mixture of antifreeze and water. If a blend of equal parts water and antifreeze provides freeze protection down to −40°F, you might think that pure antifreeze will provide even greater protection. Not so. Straight antifreeze actually solidifies at a mere −4°F. To do its job, antifreeze must be diluted with water as specified by the manufacturer.

Another Job for Duct Tape

❖ If you need a temporary fix for a leaky radiator or heater hose, try a little duct tape. Turn off the engine, clean and dry the hose with a rag and wrap the area with several layers of tape. Loosen the radiator cap to ease pressure on the system, then drive slowly to get help.

To Keep Cool, Turn Up the Heat

❖ If your vehicle threatens to overheat when you're stuck in traffic on a hot day, turn off the air conditioner to reduce the load on the engine, roll down the windows and turn the heater to High. Your heater is actually a small auxiliary radiator located inside the passenger compartment and will draw considerable heat from the engine. You may be uncomfortable, but it beats damaging your engine by overheating it.

A Good Time to Be Neutral

❖ If your car is an automatic, try this trick when it threatens to overheat while you're stuck in traffic: rather than leaving it in Drive and holding your foot on the brake, shift into Neutral and rev the engine slightly. This causes the water pump (and the fan, in vehicles not equipped with an electric fan) to run faster and dissipate more heat.

HEATING AND AIR-CONDITIONING

Stuck without a Heater

❖ If your heater begins blowing air that's lukewarm instead of hot, the culprit may be a stuck thermostat. (This is especially likely if the engine also seems slow to warm up.) First try having the thermostat replaced—it's a relatively easy and inexpensive task. If that doesn't solve the problem, the heater core is probably clogged. Take the car to a mechanic to have the core replaced.

When It's 30 Below, Turn On the AC

❖ If you have an older car with an air conditioner, be sure to run the air conditioner occasionally, even during the winter. When an air conditioner goes unused for more than a few weeks at a time, its seals may begin to dry out and leak refrigerant. And that means you need an expensive recharge. To avoid that problem, most new cars have heater controls that cause the air conditioner to run whenever the setting is on "defrost," but that's not true of older models. (If you notice clear, odorless water dripping from beneath the hood after the air conditioner has been running on a hot, humid day, there's no need to worry. It's simply condensed humidity dripping from the air conditioner's evaporator fins, as it is supposed to do.)

Patience, Patience

❖ To avoid placing a burden on your car's engine before it is warmed up, don't turn on the air conditioner until you've started the car and driven a mile or two.

❖ If the car has been sitting in the heat with the windows rolled up, leave them down for a few minutes before turning on the air conditioner. This will exhaust the hot air and further ease the load on the air conditioner.

Cooling-Off Period

❖ Try to get into the habit of turning off your air conditioner a few miles before you reach your destination and shut off the car. That will allow the heat generated by the air conditioner to dissipate before you stop and protect your engine from absorbing the excess heat.

BRAKES

Brake Break-In

❖ To get maximum life from a new pair of brake pads, treat them gently for the first thousand miles. Try to avoid prolonged braking, sudden stops and high-speed driving during that period. Any of these may overheat the brakes, damaging both pads and rotors.

Used Cars

NEW CARS ARE FUN to drive, but the privilege is one you pay for dearly. From the standpoint of dollars and cents, the best buy you can make is often a three-year-old used car, which typically sells for about half the cost of a new one—while retaining far more than half of its life expectancy.

All bets are off, though, if the used car you select hasn't been well cared for by its previous owner(s). Here are some ways to make a wise decision on a potential used-car investment:

• **Do some homework beforehand.** Decide what type of vehicle you want—sport sedan, pickup truck, station wagon or whatever—then check consumer magazines and ask a knowledgeable mechanic which specific makes and models have proven most reliable and which have turned out to be dogs.

• **Shop for a used car at a new-car dealer's lot.** The new-car dealer keeps the best used cars taken in trade for resale and wholesales less desirable cars to dealers who sell used cars only. For that reason, the used-car lot can be a risky place to shop. You may also do well buying from a private owner, but unless state laws are on your side, you'll be on your own if problems develop later.

• **Find out who owned the car previously.** If you're buying from a dealer, ask to see the title, which will list the name(s) of the former owner(s). If the car has already been through several owners, was once owned by a commercial fleet or rental

Those Aren't Crickets You Hear

❖ Have a mechanic replace the pads on your front disc brakes when two-thirds of their original three-sixteenth-inch thickness has been worn away. Depending on how you drive, that should be every 30,000 to 50,000 miles.

❖ Some brakes have built-in wear indicators, which emit a chirping or squeaking sound when the pads need replacing. Pay attention to those sounds! If you hear a rasping, grating or grinding sound when you apply the brakes, get to a repair shop quickly, before you do expensive damage to the brake rotors. Those sounds mean you've waited too long and the pads are probably worn away to nothing. You're hearing metal-on-metal contact between the base of the pads and the steel rotor, which the pads grasp to stop the wheels.

---

company or was repossessed by a bank or finance company, you should think twice about buying: all of these circumstances suggest hard use and possible abuse. If the vehicle was owned by an individual who lives locally, consider looking the person up in the phone book, calling her up and asking how often she changed the oil.

• **Don't worry too much about mileage.** A well-maintained four-year-old car that has been driven 85,000 highway miles may go another 100,000 miles without serious problems. A similar vehicle with only 19,000 miles, driven only to church and to the grocery store by the proverbial little old lady, will probably show far more engine wear as a result of logging most of its mileage with a cold engine.

• **Check out the car to the best of your ability.** Look for rust, of course. Also bring along a magnet to check for signs of repaired collision damage; the magnet won't stick to damaged areas that have been repaired with plastic body filler. Inspect underneath for leaking oil or other fluids. Take the vehicle for a half-hour test drive and pay careful attention to how it sounds and performs. Make a mental note of any possible problems.

• **Finally, pay your own mechanic to give it a thorough going-over.** If the current owner won't agree to let you do so, walk away. If you decide to buy the car, the $50 or so you pay for an expert opinion is cheap enough. And if you decide not to buy it, the checkup will save you much more than $50 worth of grief.

How to Decelerate Decently

❖ When driving on the highway, you can spare your brakes by slowly letting up on the gas pedal to decelerate—avoiding braking entirely. Don't let up on the gas quickly and completely when moving at highway speeds, however, or you'll place a heavy load on the differential gears that transmit power to the wheels. Plan ahead and decelerate gradually and smoothly.

Make It a Habit to Brake

❖ Make a habit of engaging your vehicle's parking brake every time you park. If the brake is left unused for too long, the housings on the control cables—which activate the rear brakes when you pull the brake lever—may rust and seize up, leaving you without the brake when you really need it.

TIRES AND WHEELS

Tire Togetherness

❖ Tires should always be replaced in front or rear pairs. If you buy a brand-new tire for the front left and continue to use a half-worn tire on the front right, you'll get a pulling action that will place a heavy strain on the new tire and—in the case of front tires—make steering more difficult.

Be Gentle

❖ Avoid rough roads, sudden stops and acceleration, and speeds of over 50 miles per hour for the first 50 miles or so after installing new tires. New tires should be broken in gently to ensure that they seat properly on the wheel rims.

One-Way Tires

❖ Check the direction of the tread on your newly mounted tires. Most radial

PUZZLER

NO TRANSMISSION, NO DISC brakes—how did you keep from "freewheeling" when you and your team of horses drove a heavy wagon down a steep hill in the old days?

ANSWER: Drag shoe, slung under wagon wheels to slow the descent on steep roads.

tires have a symmetrical tread pattern, meaning that they turn equally well in either direction. Some tires, however—particularly snow tires with an aggressive tread—feature a tread pattern designed to turn in one direction only, as indicated by a directional arrow on the sidewall of the tire. Be sure that such tires are mounted correctly, or they will not perform as they should and will wear very rapidly.

Keep Up the Pressure

❖ To ensure that your new tires last as long as they should, make a habit of checking their pressure once a month with an inexpensive pressure gauge. The tires must be cold if you are to obtain an accurate reading. Let them cool down for at least three hours after driving before checking the pressure. Then unscrew the dust cap from the valve on the tire and press the fitting on the pressure gauge against the valve stem for a moment. The air in the tire will force out the indicator on the gauge, allowing you to read the pressure at the base of the indicator. If it's low, add some air and check again. When you're done, be sure to replace the dust cap on the valve.

Sometimes High Inflation Is Good

❖ For maximum wear, inflate your tires to the maximum pressure printed on the sidewalls of the tires themselves, rather than the pressure specified by the manufacturer of your vehicle. The automaker's suggested pressure is often several pounds lower—providing a softer ride at the expense of handling, fuel mileage and tire wear.

❖ If you're going on a long trip at highway speeds—especially if your vehicle will be heavily loaded or towing a trailer—it's a good idea to inflate your tires to a cold pressure that is a pound or two higher than normal in order to decrease rolling resistance.

The Tales Tires Tell

❖ When you perform your monthly tire pressure check, take a few moments to examine the treads for signs of unusual wear, which can indicate a variety of other problems. Tires that show signs of wear on one edge, for example, often indicate that the front end is misaligned. Cupped or scalloped wear may mean that the tire is out of balance, the wheel bearing is bad or the suspension needs work. If you find any of these warning signs, you should have your mechanic investigate as soon as possible. This will prevent further damage to the tires and possibly prevent more expensive mechanical problems from developing.

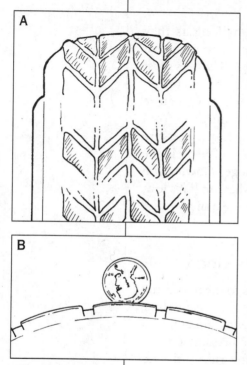

When the wear bars on a car's tires show as smooth bands (A), it's time to replace the tire. If you're in doubt, let Abe Lincoln give the tire the heads up (B).

Time to Re-Tire?

❖ When the tire tread has worn to a depth of less than one-sixteenth inch—the minimum safe depth—its built-in wear indicators appear as smooth bands running across the width of the tread. When the bands appear between more than two adjacent grooves, the tire should be replaced.

Ask Abe

❖ Another way to check tread depth is to insert a penny in a groove. If the top of Abraham Lincoln's head extends into the groove, the tire still has some wear remaining. If all of the head shows, the tire has less than one-sixteenth inch of tread left and should be replaced.

A Spring Thing to Do

❖ Don't delay removing your snow tires and replacing them with summer tires when warm weather arrives in the spring. Because of their blocky tread design, snow tires tend to overheat when driven on warm, dry roads, causing rapid wear and leaving them vulnerable to blowouts.

Do Not Pass Go

❖ Should you get a flat, stop and change it immediately (provided, of course, that you're in a spot where it's safe to do so). The original cause of the flat is probably repairable, but if you drive on it for even a short distance—to a nearby service station, for example—you'll probably cause irreparable damage and end up paying for a new tire or rim.

Spare the Spare

❖ To cut costs and save trunk space, automakers now equip most new cars with compact spares rather than traditional full-size spares. If you have a flat and replace it with a compact spare, keep your speed under 50 miles per hour and drive directly to a service station or tire shop to have the flat repaired. Because the smaller spare heats up more rapidly than a full-size tire, it can be damaged by sustained high-speed travel, particularly during hot weather.

Maybe You're Going the Wrong Way

❖ If, when changing a flat, you're having difficulty unscrewing the lug nuts that hold the wheel in place, stop

Take It to the Jam Back

WHEN THE WHEEL WELLS of the pickup I use for snowplowing rusted out, I took it to the jam back in my town. The fellow who runs the jam back is real handy, and he was able to patch the metal well enough for the pickup to pass inspection. As the truck is getting on in years, I suspect I'll have to return to the jam back again soon.

Some folks refer to a jam back as a body shop, but I still like the older term. Once when I advised a *Yankee* reader to go to a jam back for help with his car, he wrote back and asked, "Why do you call it a jam back?" I don't know how the term originated, but it seems like a good one. After all, that's what they do all day: take the car parts and jam them back together.

EARL
remembers...

for a moment and look at the end of the threaded stud. If you see the letter *L* stamped on the stud, the nuts on that side of the car (the left, or driver's side) have a reverse thread, meaning that you need to turn them clockwise to loosen them. That momentary pause can prevent delay, frustration and broken studs.

Cracking a Nut Problem

❖ If you find yourself missing a number of lug nuts when changing a tire, you can temporarily remove one nut each from as many of the remaining wheels as necessary and use them to make up the shortfall. Drive directly to a service station or auto parts store and buy replacements for the missing nuts.

BODY

Pull the Plug on Rust

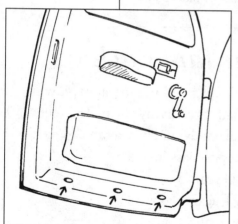

❖ Car doors often rust out from the bottom when water seeps past the rubber weather strip below the windows and collects inside the doors. To prevent that from happening, make sure that the drain holes in the undersides of the doors—which serve to give trapped water a way out—do not become blocked with dirt or surface rust. Inspect the undersides of the doors carefully and use a nail or a piece of stiff wire to clear away any dirt or debris that may be blocking the holes.

Keep the drain holes in the bottom of your car's doors unclogged to help prevent rust from forming.

Have Some Nice Cocoa

❖ When selecting floor mats for your car, choose ones made from cocoa fiber or some other similar material. Don't succumb to the temptation to protect your vehicle's carpeting from tracked-in mud and slush with oversize rubber mats. Because rubber mats don't breathe, they can trap moisture in the carpeting and give rust an opportunity to attack the floorboards.

How to Keep a Car Rust-Free

I RECENTLY TRADED IN my 1979 Oldsmobile and bought a new car. Although I'd had the Olds for more than 15 years, there was only one spot of rust on the fender.

If you live where it snows frequently in the winter, as I do, you know that most cars start to rust well before they get to be 15 years old. The source of the problem, of course, is the road salt that highway departments spread during snowstorms. The salt rusts your car wherever it can get a foothold.

My advice for keeping your car rust-free is simple: don't drive it during a snowstorm. The concentration of salt on the roads is heaviest during a storm, when the road crews are spreading it. And the slush that spatters the salt all over your car only makes matters worse. I know it's not possible to follow this advice all the time, but if your errand or trip can be put off until the day after the storm, when the roads are cleaned up, you'll get very little salt on your car, and it will last longer.

And since the driving is likely to be safer then, maybe you'll last longer, too.

Preventing Salt Assault

❖ Minimize the rust-inducing effects of road salt on your car by storing the vehicle in a cool place during the winter. Rust and corrosion accelerate at warmer temperatures. Below freezing—when water is locked up as ice—it virtually stops. A car that is kept in a heated garage all winter is far more likely to rust than one that is left in an unheated garage or open carport, or simply parked in the driveway.

Give Your Car a Spring Cleaning

❖ Be sure to give your car a very thorough washing in the spring—including hosing off the wheel wells and undercarriage—so that salt deposits remaining from the winter don't cause accelerated corrosion during the warm months ahead.

❖ During winter thaws, spray salt off the undercarriage even if you aren't washing the body. (Make sure the temperature is above freezing when you do this, or you'll turn your driveway into a skating rink and risk freezing the car doors shut.)

Get to the Bottom of It

❖ It's easy to wash winter salt deposits from the exposed surfaces of a car, but how do you wash the underside? One way is to set up a hose and lawn sprinkler—or a perforated sprinkler hose—in the driveway. Straddling the hose with your tires, park over the sprinkler and turn on the water. Every few minutes, move either the car or the sprinkler back and forth so that the entire underbody receives a thorough rinsing.

A Real Blast

❖ If you drive often on dirt roads or on sandy paved roads, have your garage install a pair of mudguards just behind your car's front tires. Grit thrown up by the front tires can quickly sandblast the paint from the rocker panels, just to the rear of the doors, leaving them vulnerable to rust. (The problem usually appears first on the right side of the car, because roads are sandiest along the shoulder.) The mudguards will deflect sand and grit before they do any damage.

Help for Winter Drivers

❖ If you live in the snowbelt, keep a bag of kitty litter in your trunk. Whenever your vehicle gets stuck, sprinkle some of the litter under the wheels to provide quick traction. Some people keep a bag of salt for this purpose, but if that bag accidentally breaks open, it can rust the trunk from the inside before you notice the problem. If the bag of kitty litter breaks open, it may make a mess, but it won't do any real harm.

Let the Water Do the Work

❖ If your car is very dusty or has patches of dried mud on the paint, blast the material off with a jet of high-pressure water from the hose before you begin washing the vehicle. Rubbing muddy or dusty patches with a soapy sponge will cause the particles of dirt and grit to act as sandpaper and scratch the finish—opening the door for rust and corrosion to attack the underlying metal.

Scratch the Car Wash That Scratches Your Car

❖ If you take your car to a commercial car wash, choose one that uses soft cloths rather than revolving brushes, which may leave fine scratches in the finish.

❖ Avoid car washes that use recycled water, which may contain high concentrations of corrosive road salt.

Another Kind of Wax Job

❖ If you don't have any touch-up paint handy, you can repair fine scratches to a car's finish by coloring them in with a wax crayon. Follow up by buffing the affected area with a soft cloth.

Prevent Dashboard Fading

❖ You can protect your dashboard from sun damage and rejuvenate it if minor fading has already occurred. First wipe it clean with a damp sponge, then apply some high-protection-factor sunscreen to the vinyl, as you

---

BUY IT TO LAST

Protective Coloration

THE CHOICE OF your new car's color is more than just a cosmetic decision. A vehicle that is painted white or another light color will absorb much less heat from the sun than a dark-colored one. Besides increasing comfort, that will save fuel by reducing the load on the air conditioner and will allow the engine to run cooler in hot weather.

White paint also tends to last longer. To a large extent, the durability of automotive paint is determined by how much pigment it contains. Highly pigmented paints, including white, will last longest. Metallic paints—which contain relatively little pigment—are well-known for both premature fading and oxidizing, with silver paint having the worst reputation of all. It's something to keep in mind when shopping for a new car, especially if you plan to keep it for a long time.

would to your skin. Rub it in thoroughly and wipe off any excess. Wait a few hours, then apply a commercial vinyl protectant, available from auto parts stores. The ultraviolet light–absorbing chemicals in the sunscreen will help prevent the dashboard surface from cracking and fading.

Avoid Undercover Details

❖ Don't bother with car covers. They may seem like a good idea, but in most cases they do more harm than good because they prevent the vehicle from drying out after a

The Wagon Was a Woody

EARL remembers...

THE FIRST CAR I EVER HAD to maintain was the "beach wagon" my father used in his contracting business in the late 1930s. It was a large car with a wooden body, something like today's Chevrolet Suburban.

I didn't do any mechanical work on the beach wagon, but the body needed a lot of attention. Since it was made of wood, the joints had to be tightened regularly. And unless you kept it well varnished, the oak would turn black from exposure to moisture. All in all, I put in many an hour preserving that vehicle. We had it for about seven years. The guy we sold it to had it for a few more, before it burned up. He had it loaded pretty heavily, and I think the engine caught fire as he was going up a steep hill.

Caring for that car, I learned how important it is to keep ahead of the elements when maintaining a car. But it turned out that the more specific skills I developed while working on the beach wagon weren't all that useful in later years, when I had my own (metal-bodied) cars to take care of. They just don't make them like that anymore—thank heaven!

rain. If you keep your car's finish clean and waxed, further protection is unnecessary.

Take It to the Top

❖ Use vinyl penetrant to restore a faded vinyl roof cover. First wash and dry the top thoroughly, then apply the penetrant as directed by the manufacturer.

Seat Cover-Up

❖ Fitted fabric seat covers can improve the appearance of a car's interior, but to get maximum bang for the buck, don't install them until the original upholstery has begun to look well worn. The original seats will still wear, even under the covering, so if you install the covers when the car is new, you'll wear out the expensive new covers and the original seats at the same time, rather than one after the other.

ROOF RACKS

Thwart Rack Attack

❖ Rust is all too likely to form at the point where the mounting screws on your car's built-in roof rack penetrate the sheet metal of the roof. To prevent that problem, try this: Remove a screw, squirt a bit of clear silicone caulk into the hole and replace and retighten the screw. Move on to the next screw and repeat until the entire rack has been sealed.

Rack Up Another Tip

❖ If you use a roof rack only occasionally, make a habit of removing it when it is not needed. The aerodynamic drag of an empty rack decreases fuel mileage by several miles per gallon, besides unnecessarily exposing the rack to the effects of wear and weather.

Repair Work: Never on a Monday

WHEN YOU'RE NOT dealing with an emergency situation, put a little thought into scheduling your visits to the repair shop. Mondays are usually busiest, as vehicles that have developed problems over the weekend are brought in, along with those that amateur mechanics have tried—and failed—to repair during their days off. Fridays also are busy, because many motorists want to have repairs completed in time for the weekend. A midweek appointment increases the likelihood that your car will receive careful attention.

TRAILER HITCHES

Happy Trailering to You

❖ On any vehicle equipped with a trailer hitch, the trailer ball has a tendency to work loose over time and may eventually fall off. Try this preventive measure: screw the ball as tight as possible without stripping the threads, then use a hammer and a screw punch or a small-diameter nail set (the blunt-tipped steel tool used to set nail heads beneath a wooden surface) to dimple the first thread below the nut in a half dozen places. That will prevent the nut from working loose but still enable you to remove it (with a little extra force) should you ever need to replace the ball.

Bearing Up under Pressure

❖ To extend the life of the wheel bearings on small utility trailers, equip them with a set of inexpensive bearing protectors, available at auto parts or department stores. To install the protectors, simply pull off the existing bearing covers with pliers and press the new ones into place. They will keep the bearing grease under slight pressure for maximum lubricating efficiency and help keep moisture out—an especially important consideration for boat trailers, whose wheels are frequently submerged in water. The wheel bearings on any small trailer take tremendous punishment, because the small diameter of the wheels forces them to revolve much faster than the larger wheels on the tow vehicle.

It Pays to Have Good Connections

❖ To prevent many annoying problems with your trailer's lighting system, methodically spray all electrical sockets and connectors with a penetrating lubricant such as WD-40 from time to time—especially after a rainstorm or after the trailer has been submerged in water, but at least every

---

PUZZLER

TRAVELING BY HORSE-DRAWN carriage was a messy business, especially in mud season. In an era when skirts were long and dry cleaners nonexistent, this quickly removable wicker thingamajig helped keep ladies tidy.

ANSWER: Buggy wheel cover, slipped over muddy wheels when ladies were entering or leaving a carriage.

---

other month. That will drive out moisture that may cause short circuits and will prevent corrosion from forming.

Good-Bye, Old Salt

❖ If you use a boat trailer in salt water, give it a thorough freshwater rinse immediately after returning home. That will prevent salt-induced corrosion and dramatically extend its useful life.

❖ If you use a trailer—such as a snowmobile trailer—on salty winter roads, be sure to wash it thoroughly each spring.

SNOWMOBILES

Choose the Right Oil

❖ To make your snowmobile's engine last longer, use the brand of oil marketed by the manufacturer of your particular machine. Any high-quality two-cycle oil can be used in a snowmobile engine, but different oils are manufactured to slightly different specifications, and the one made precisely for your machine will make it hold up longer.

Let It Shine

❖ To protect the fiberglass body of your snowmobile, wash it with a liquid cleaning product designed specifically for boat hulls and other fiberglass surfaces. A snow machine's body is tough and impact resistant, but abrasive cleaning products will scratch and permanently dull the finish.

❖ Once a year or so, after cleaning the machine, apply a good coat of paste wax to help protect the surface from minor scratches.

Don't Give Yourself the Slip

❖ To clean your snowmobile's vinyl seat, dip a damp cloth in baking soda, wipe it over the seat and then wash with a mild solution of dishwashing liquid and water. Rinse thoroughly and dry with a soft cloth. Steer clear of spray-on vinyl cleaners or protectants, which may leave the seat dangerously slippery.

Stay on the Right Track

❖ Make a habit of checking the plastic lube strips on the outer edges of the snowmobile's track for wear after every few days' use, especially when the snow cover has been poor. Many snowmobile owners neglect these strips, which slide in matching grooves on the frame rails to keep the track in position. The strips themselves are easily and inexpensively replaced, but if they become too worn, the frame rails and the track itself will wear out, resulting in a much more costly repair.

To Bar Wear, Watch Those Wear Bars

❖ Every month or so—depending on how much you ride—check the replaceable steel wear bars on the bottoms of the snowmobile's skis. Ordinarily one-half inch thick when new, the bars protect the skis, which receive a lot of wear when crossing roads or other abrasive surfaces. When they have worn down to a thickness of one-eighth inch or so, replace them promptly before you begin damaging the skis themselves.

Prepare for Summer Hibernation

❖ Disconnect the starting battery of your snowmobile and remove it from the machine to prevent it from going flat over the summer. Clean the battery case and terminals with a damp rag dipped in baking soda, then store the battery in a cool place.

❖ If you want to keep dust and dirt from accumulating on your snow machine over the summer, use a fabric cover, such as a painter's drop cloth. Avoid plastic covers, which may trap moisture.

Give It a Lift

❖ Store your snowmobile in a cool, dry place when it's not in use. If you must leave it on a dirt or concrete floor—either of which will attract moisture—raise it off the surface on wooden blocks or pallets.

Index

NOTE: <u>Underscored</u> page references indicate boxed text. **Boldface** references indicate illustrations.

Bearings, wheel *(continued)*
  on utility trailers, protect-
    ing, 372
Beater, rug, **112**
Beaver hat stretcher, **69**
Beds
  recycling toddlers', <u>103</u>
  rope, <u>96</u>
Bedspreads, chenille, fluffing,
    89
Beer stains, 81
Beetles, in vegetable gardens,
    207-8, 209
Beets, storing, 10
Bellows, bee, **292**
Belts, automotive drive, <u>87</u>,
    <u>355</u>
  emergency replacements
    for, <u>87</u>, 351
  inspecting, 350
  noises indicating problems
    with, <u>355</u>
  preserving, 351
  replacing, 351
Belts, leather garment
  reconditioning, 65
  storing, 60
Belts, sanding, 334-35
  buying, 334
  cleaning, 334-35
  storing, **334**
Belts on power tools, rein-
    stalling, 331-32
Berry stains, 80
Bibs, cleaning burner, 46
Bicycle(s), 274-76
  chains on, 274
  cleaning, 275
  flat tires on, 275-76
  storing, 275
Bicycles, exercise, maintain-
    ing, 293-94
Bill hook, **39**
Billiard cues, storing, 265-66
Bindings, book
  grease on cloth, 230
  restoring brittle leather,
    229-30
Bindings, ski, 292-93
Bins, compost, building inex-
    pensive, <u>212</u>
Biocides, to remove moss
    from roofs, 168
Bird, sewing, **227**
Birdcages, precautions with
    knock-down models,
    297

Birds, nesting in tile roofs,
    171
Bird stop, **171**
Bits, drill, 335-36
  maintaining, 335-36
  storing, **319**
  substitutions for, 336
Bits, router, storing, **319**
Blades, saw
  cleaning, 329, 334
  recycling, 330
  storing, 333-34, **333**
  transporting, **333**
Blankets
  electric, 51
  recycling, 53
Blenders, electric, 30-32
  cleaning, 31-32
  safety and, 31
  use of, 30-31
Blight, potato and tomato,
    209
Blisters
  paint, 146, 149, 157-58
  in veneered furniture, 102
Blocked joints, **99**
Blocking sweaters, 68-69
Bloodstains, 79
Blouses
  ironing, 75-76
  soil lines on collars, 84
Board, stocking, **85**
Boards
  knots loose in, 127
  for subfloors, 124-25
  warping, 124
Boards, cutting, odors in, 16
Boards, ironing, padding for,
    53
Boats, canoes and kayaks,
    270-74. *See also* Oars
    and paddles
  cleaning, 270, 273
  leaks in, 273-74
  protecting, 272-73, <u>275</u>
  repairing, 272
  storing, 270-71, 274
  temporary sail for, 279
  trailers for, 372-73
  trim on, 272
Boilers, 311-12, <u>311</u>
Bolts, frozen, 326
Bone, yellowing in knife han-
    dles, 22
Book(s), 229-32
  bindings
    grease on cloth, 230

restoring brittle leather,
    229-30
  bookmarks in, 231
  effects of light on, <u>221</u>
  mildew on, 231
  placement on bookshelves,
    232
Book carrier, **118**
Bookcases
  placement of, 229
  sagging shelves in, **102**
Boot dryer, 81
Boots
  children's
    recycling, <u>79</u>
    removing, 60
  cleaning, 73
  fishing waders, **285**
  Maine Hunting Shoes, <u>286</u>
  salt stains on, 84
  water repellent, 61, <u>63</u>, 65
Boot tree, **285**
Bottle opener, milk, 6
Bottles, recycling plastic, <u>48</u>,
    <u>198</u>
Bowed window frames, 139
Bowling balls, 264-65
  cleaning, 264, 265
  scratches in, 264
Bowls, sticky wooden, 16
Bows, archer's, storing, 264
Boxes, litter, 297
Brackets, angle, for hanging
    paintings, **219**
Brakes, car, 360-62
  breaking in, 360
  time to replace, 361
  using, 362
Branches, removing tree, **200**
Brass
  cleaning
    kitchenware, 28
    musical instruments,
      244
  polishing, 28-29
    doorknobs, 131
    musical instruments,
      244
Bread
  freezing, 12
  reviving stale, 12
Brick(s)
  chimney, sealing and pro-
    tecting, 311
  patios, laying, 162
Briefcases, restoring leather,
    65

NOTE: <u>Underscored</u> page references indicate boxed text. **Boldface** references indicate illustrations.

NOTE: Underscored page references indicate boxed text. **Boldface** references indicate illustrations.

NOTE: <u>Underscored</u> page references indicate boxed text. **Boldface** references indicate illustrations.

NOTE: <u>Underscored</u> page references indicate boxed text. **Boldface** references indicate illustrations.

NOTE: Underscored page references indicate boxed text. **Boldface** references indicate illustrations.

NOTE: <u>Underscored</u> page references indicate boxed text. **Boldface** references indicate illustrations.

NOTE: <u>Underscored</u> page references indicate boxed text. **Boldface** references indicate illustrations.

NOTE: Underscored page references indicate boxed text. **Boldface** references indicate illustrations.

NOTE: Underscored page references indicate boxed text. **Boldface** references indicate illustrations.

NOTE: <u>Underscored</u> page references indicate boxed text. **Boldface** references indicate illustrations.

NOTE: <u>Underscored</u> page references indicate boxed text. **Boldface** references indicate illustrations.

NOTE: Underscored page references indicate boxed text. **Boldface** references indicate illustrations.

NOTE: Underscored page references indicate boxed text. **Boldface** references indicate illustrations.

Scarecrow, panty hose as
part of, 87
Scorp, **97**
Scrapers, paint
sharpening, 145, 337
substitution for, 136
Screen doors. *See* Door(s),
screen
Screening
on gutters, 176
recycling, **142**, 321-22
as substitution for sandpaper, 321-22
types of, 134
Screwdrivers, 324-26
matching size to screw,
324-26
storing, **319**
uses for old, 324
Screws, 324
eyeglass, 242
fence, 216
frozen, 325-26
loose, 102
Scrubber, from old screening,
142
Scuba gear, 266-67
Scythes, 197-98
Sealing
chimney bricks, 311
driveways, 180-81, 181
grout on tiled walls, 122
rope ends, 342
seams in camping equip-
ment, 277-78
seams in outdoor clothing,
62-63
walls before papering, 121
window casings before
painting, 137-38
Seam Grip, 277-78
Seasoning, firewood, 308-9
Seasoning, kitchen
equipment
cast iron, 15
waffle irons, 39, 40
Seat covers
for cars, 371
for dining chairs, 111
Seeder, **188**
Seeds, saving plant, 210-12
Septic tanks
driving over, 307
garbage disposals and, 306
Sewing bird, **227**
Sewing machines, 55
Shakes vs. shingles, 168

Sharpener, knife, **18**
Sharpening
items needing
garden tools, 196-97
hammer claws, 322
hatchets, 337
ice skates, 287-88
knives, 196-97, **197**
lawn mower blades,
187-88
metal-cutting tools, 327
paint scrapers, 145, 337
planes, 327
scythes, 197
wood-cutting tools, 327
tools used for, 336-37
Sheds
heating, 215
rusty latches and padlocks
on, 216
termiteproofing, 216
water damage to, 216
Sheet music, storing, 235
Sheets, elastic in fitted, 58
Shelves, sagging, **102**
Shingle rippers, 166-67, **167**,
170
Shingles
asphalt roof, 172, 173
vs. shakes, 168
wooden roof
moss and fungi on, 163,
165-66, **165**, 167-68
replacing, 166-67, **166**,
167
wooden siding
cupping in, 154
installing, 155
matching weathered,
153-54
Shirts. *See also* Collars, shirt
cleaning, 57, 69
ironing, 75-76
Shoehorns, 64
Shoes
buying, 65, 70
cleaning, 73
heel repairs, **88**
odors in, 73
polishing, 65, 87
preserving, 60
salt stains on, 84
storing, 64
types of old
chestnut-hulling, **40**
drag, **362**
sod, **266**

Shoe trees, **64**
Shoulder pads, securing, 62
Shovel(s)
maintaining, 195
potato, **215**
recycling handles from, 198
sharpening garden, 197
Showerheads
clogged, 299
low-flow, 299
Showers, cleaning, 122
Shrinking
sweaters, 68
testing for, 70
Shrubs. *See* Trees and shrubs
Shutters, window, 142-43
cleaning, 142-43
loose joints in, **143**
sagging, 143
Siding, 150-57
aluminum
paint and, 155, 156-57
protecting while work-
ing on, **156**
nails for, 155
vinyl
buckling, 157
mildew or chalking on,
157
paint and, 155, 157
protecting while work-
ing on, **156**
sanding, 157
wooden lap, 151-53
caulking, 153
drying before installing,
151
flat-sawn vs. radially
sawn clapboards, **152**
graduated exposure of
clapboards in, 151
rust on nail heads in,
153
ventilation through, 153
water damage to, 150-
51
watertight joints for, 152
wooden shingles, 153-55
aging, 153-54
cupping, 154
installing, 155
Silk
cleaning, 67-68
ironing, 74-75
neckties, water marks on,
84
Sills, lumber for, 124

Note: Underscored page references indicate boxed text. **Boldface** references indicate illustrations.

NOTE: <u>Underscored</u> page references indicate boxed text. **Boldface** references indicate illustrations.

NOTE: <u>Underscored</u> page references indicate boxed text. **Boldface** references indicate illustrations.

NOTE: Underscored page references indicate boxed text. **Boldface** references indicate illustrations.

NOTE: <u>Underscored</u> page references indicate boxed text. **Boldface** references indicate illustrations.

NOTE: <u>Underscored</u> page references indicate boxed text. **Boldface** references indicate illustrations.